1 7 JUL 2019

THE EMERALD ISLE

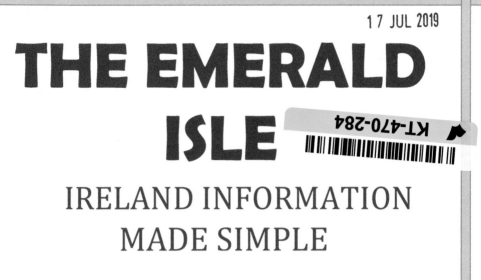

IRELAND INFORMATION MADE SIMPLE

**A ONE STOP ACCESS
FOR INFORMATION ABOUT IRELAND**

GEOGRAPHY- POLITICS -HISTORY- RELIGION -BUSINESS -PEOPLE -
CULTURE

FOREWORD WRITTEN BY

TAOISEACH LEO VARADKAR

RESEARCHED, COMPILED AND EDITED BY
CAROL AZAMS

**SKYLINE
PUBLISHERS**
www.skylineBureau.com

PUBLISHED BY SKYLINE PUBLISHERS
(Republic of Ireland 2019)
www.skylineBureau.com/Publishing

British Library Cataloguing in Publication Data
A catalogue record for this book is available from the British Library and
the National Library of Ireland.

ISBN: 978-0-9955-34995

TABLE OF CONTENT

SECTION ONE: Fast Facts: (Part 1)   16

1.1 Official Name

1.2 Location

1.3 Land Area

1.4 Population

1.5 Capital City

1.6 Province & Counties

1.7 Official Language

1.8 National Day

1.9 Driving Mode

2.0 GDP PER Capita

2.1 Monitary Unit

2.2 Minimum Wage

2.3 Unemployment rate

2.4 Literacy Percent

2.5 Religion

2.6 Life Expectancy

2.7 Birth Rate

2.8 Infant Mortality

2.9 Country Code

3.0 Internet Code

3.1 Time Zone: GMT

3.2 Proclaimation

3.3 Independence Day

3.4 Government

3.5 President

3.6 Taoiseach

3.7 Tánaiste

3.8 Police Force

3.9 Climate

4.0 Motto

Acknowledgements

Putting this book together was culminated from the many people I spoke to both locals and foreign, the countless online resources that I consulted for my research and I'm particularly thankful to the people who put up these websites on the Internet to share very useful information about Ireland including contents in the public. Many thanks also to the kind-hearted individuals who willingly donated photos to be included in the book.

My utmost gratitude goes to the Taoiseach, Leo Varadkar, T.D (Prime Minister of the Republic of Ireland), who took time off from his busy schedules to write the foreword for this book. Thank you for believing in my ability to produce an information book that may very well be useful to other people with interests in Ireland—despite being a stranger myself. Huge thank you to Staff of the Prime Minister, who made sure that my request for the Taoiseach's foreword was put through.

Many thanks to my family back home in Nigeria whom I love & miss very much. To my husband, we've been together for 30+ years, it's not been easy, and I thank you for standing by me. To our five children, I thank you for the joy that you bring to me everyday. (for the tireless help in meeting with my demands for countless cups of tea and coffee throughout my time of compiling this book.) To our two eldest who now live independently, loving you from afar is not the easiest, but it is the prayer of every parent for their young to grow up & succeed in life—so, continue to soar! I love you all so dearly— the light of my world!

Lastly, many thanks to the people of Ireland for giving my family and I the opportunity to belong and be part of you. To my friends in Ireland & elsewhere, thank you all and wishing you God's many blessings!

Author's Note

The culture of the Irish and Ireland itself as a country has been widely written about. But as with every story, there is always a fresh angle to it, and this is the angle from where this book has been developed—on a migrant's perspective after living and experiencing the country. I love being a part of a country that is so unique and famous for its hospitality throughout the world. Having lived here for more than 15 or so years not just as a legal resident but having become a naturalised citizen, I'm always looking for ways and opportunities to give back to Irish society and I can proudly say that I have been doing my humble bits through community participation and volunteerism. Ireland has been a blessing for me and my immediate family in so many ways. It has also motivated me personally to self-develop my innate creative talents more than I ordinarily would have. I have in no doubts, gone far from being a full-time stay at home mum of five kids, to now a very skilful, strong-willed and feisty middle-aged woman who is very much involved in activism and community service.

My Inspiration for this book comes not only from the fact that Ireland, as a country is endowed with a lot of tourist opportunities and beautiful attractions. I believe that I have lived here long enough to create a unique voice to be heard across the country and being a writer has also helped me to do just that, so crafting the idea for the compilation of such a book like this one has come quite naturally. It can be a challenge for anyone to indulge in writing about a country like Ireland for many reasons, and more so for someone not ordinally born here. But as we become new citizens, it is really important that we share not only in the opportunities that are presented to us, but we also inherit the Irish history in order for us to fully understand where we fit in, so this is one challenge that I was happy to take on. A few years back I published a cultural book about my native country (Nigeria: Beyond the Perceptions) which is in the same style and context as this one. Nigeria has a widespread public image of corruption and issues of security which unfortunately is an ugly reality. Nonetheless, there is the beauty sides to Nigeria such as the cultures, the people, our entangled histories with the British Empire, the different ethnic groups and myriads of languages that exists but don't make the headlines often enough because they have now been over-shadowed by these other issues. From all indications, I can say that my sense of personal relationship with Ireland runs much deeper than I can ordinarily express and have always tried to express that in some of the projects that indulged in, including a desire to replicate an Ireland version of my Nigerian book. So, armed with that desire and to also challenge my own level of understanding about the cultures of the people, my understanding of how the system work in this country, to find out a bit of their complicated past, in addition to the unpredictable weather and the countless attractions surrounding the country. So, I set out to search, and have researched every paper I could lay my hands on in local libraries and consulted hundreds of webpages on the internet, including verbal conversations with natives, to bring about this compilation; a centralised source of information in book form that will serve as a valuable tool and a handy guide not only to tourists but to those interested in knowing more about the Republic of Ireland, particularly foreign students, and new settlers. I am not oblivious to the fact that there is so much information about Ireland that could be easily found scattered across the internet and what I have done is collate this information from the various sources covering a wide variety of topics, to being in one place to make it easier for people when they need it.

Finally, this book is not an attempt in trying to override other such publications but to celebrate the beauty and rich cultural heritage of Ireland through the people, top tourist attractions and other vital statistics, from a different perspective and at the same time discusses products and opportunities that abound in the country. What I have done may be a mere scratch on the surface but it took a good deal of time to dig into the very complex Irish history, to observe and assemble these facts together, and I must say that it has been a rewarding and stimulating journey, opening my eyes to many things I hadn't realised about Ireland until this point, and I now hope that this publication serves the general purpose for which it is intended; to inform, educate, inspire, and to give a general overview of the land fondly referred to as the 'Emerald Isle!'

Carol Azams - Author & Publisher

(Proudly Irish)

carolazams

FOREWORD BY An TAOISEACH, LEO VARADKAR T.D.

Ireland in the 21st Century is a changing and ever evolving place. It can sometimes be difficult to get a basic understanding of our history, our politics, our culture and our society. So, I would like to thank Carol for her work in going through various credited resources, for example, Government department websites, to produce a book which aims to provide important information simply.

This book is a labour of love and is dedicated to the Irish around the world and I look forward to reading what Carol has selected for us, the reader.

Today one in six of us were not born in Ireland, and the truth is that Ireland has always been a nation of migrants over the centuries. Each brought a new infusion of knowledge, culture and wealth to Ireland enriching us before becoming more Irish than the Irish themselves. In more recent years, migrants have come from all over the world have infused our country with new knowledge, new ideas, new cuisine, words, art and music. Migration brings with it challenges but I have always been convinced its benefits outweigh these many times over.

The Ireland of today is a free, more tolerant, inclusive, open and diverse country than the leaders of the 1916 Rising could ever have hoped one hundred years ago, and we have all benefited as a result.

This book, I hope, is an opportunity to think about some of the elements that make up this great country of ours and allow us to reflect on what we have to do next.

Dedicated to

All Irish Around the World

For the Love of Ireland

Éirinn go Brách! - Ireland Forever!

SECTION ONE

KEY FACTS (Parts 1 & 2)

Part 1– Quick Facts:

Official Name:	Republic of Ireland / Éire (Irish)
Location:	Europe
Area :	70, 273 (SQ KM)
Population:	4,761,865 (2016 April: CSO Estimate)
Capital City:	Dublin
Provinces:	4
Counties:	32 (26 in the Republic & 6 in Northern Ireland)
Official Languages:	(English & Irish)
National Day:	17th March
Driving Mode:	Left Side of Road/ Right-hand Steering
GDP Per Capita:	$76,787 (2018 estimate)
Monetary Unit:	Euro (€)
Minimum Wage:	€9.80 per hr
Unemployment:	5.4% (March 2019)
Literacy:	99% (2008-2014 est.)

Religion:	Christianity
Life Expectancy:	Male: 78.2 / Female: 83.6
Birth Rate:	16.8 per 1000 Inhabitants. (highest in the EU)
Infant Mortality:	3.4 per 1,000 live births (CSO 2015)
Country Code:	+353
Area Code:	Eircode. ISO Code: IRE
Internet:	IE
Time Zone:	GMT/WET (UTC). Summer (DST) IST/WEST (UTC
Proclamation:	24 April 1916
Independence:	21 January 1919
Government:	Parliamentary Democracy
President:	Michael D. Higgins
Taoiseach: (Prime Minister)	Leo Varadkar
Tánaiste: (Deputy Prime Minister)	Simon Coveney
Police Force:	Garda Siochana
Climate:	Mild Temperature
Motto :	The Irish United for God, King, and Country

SECTION ONE (Part 2– Summary)

Ireland - A Brief Introduction

The Republic of Ireland is an Independent island country that is distinctively different from the United Kingdom. The country is divided into four geographical regions known as Provinces; which has 26 Counties within the provinces from what it originally used to be 32 Counties altogether. Six Counties were carved out for Britain as part of a deal to restore peace for the two countries.

The six counties are therefore part of the United Kingdom, which is known as Northern Ireland and otherwise referred to as, 'the north' by both the British people and the Irish people in Ireland. This parcel of the island holds the only land border between Britain and the Republic of Ireland and is currently embroiled in the main topic of the Brexit negotiations between the United Kingdom and European Union. This can be confusing to many strangers who still assume that Ireland is a section that belongs to Britain–this assumption is incorrect. There is significant resemblance though, for example the English language is the official business language in the Republic of Ireland while it has its own dialect. But because it was the British that colonised Ireland and for that, the country has been strongly influenced by British lifestyle–but it does not mean that Ireland belongs to the United Kingdom.

There are equally significant differences between the two countries which must be considered when discussing either of the two including the two sections of the island of Ireland—which are 'The Republic of Ireland and Northern Ireland.' Both once existed as one unified country before the invasion of Britain, but it is important to understand that the Republic is an autonomous country which runs its own independent government and goes by their own laws.

For many people when they talk about Ireland, their knowledge is usually limited to the stories they've heard or read about which is that of the famine and mass emigration. These incidents are facts about Ireland; the Republic emerged from a country that was for centuries fought many battles and were invaded by others, including Vikings so many times, and for a long period of time engaged in complicated fights with Britain, although both countries settled their issues and currently share a friendly relationship, but those incidents also helped to shape the ways of the Irish people as they are now. But more importantly, Ireland is a changing nation, it not only survived those periods of troubles, it is now a country of prosperity that boasts of many achievements and attracts people from other lands. It has worked so hard to shape the future of generations of their own people and as well created a huge difference in the lives of many foreigners that arrived in the country and it continues to do so.

Location, Size & Border

The island of Ireland is located in the North-Western Continent of Europe, off the coast of England and Wales and measuring a total area of around 84,421 square kilometres (32,595 square miles with a total coastline of 3,172 kilometres, slightly larger than the state of West Virginia in the USA.

The Republic occupies five-sixths of the entire Island measuring up to 70,273 sq.km, while Northern Ireland which is part of the United Kingdom covers the rest of it at 14,148 square kilometres (5463 square miles). It is a small island known to be the second largest in the British Isles after Great Britain, the third largest in all of Europe after Great Britain and Iceland. It is also placed at as the twentieth-largest island on planet earth. A glance of the map of Ireland shows a unique shape that has been likened to be the shape of a sitting teddy bear, the head being Northern Ireland. It is otherwise surrounded by the Atlantic Ocean, with the Celtic Sea to the South, Saint George's Channel to the South-East, and the Irish Sea to the East. Great Britain and Ireland, along with the group of nearby islands collectively make up the British Isles. The 'Island of Ireland' is a geographical term for the whole island comprising of Northern Ireland and the Republic of Ireland. The only border between the Republic of Ireland and the United Kingdom is located in Northern Ireland which is a part of the UK. However, both countries are parts of the European Single Market and they share a

Common Travel Area (CTA) comprising the Republic, the Channel Islands, Isle of Man, the United Kingdom of Great Britain and Northern Ireland. The only land border between Ireland and the UK which is in Northern Ireland is basically open, allowing free passage of people since 1923, and goods since 1993. The border is linked with 200 border crossing points and around 177,000 lorries, 200,000 vans, and at least a 1000's cars cross the border each month, including an estimate of around 30,000 people who make their way to cross the border to and from on a daily basis.

So far, the future of the border seems uncertain now since the United Kingdom voted to leave the European Union as it remains one of the key points in the UK Brexit withdrawal negotiations with the EU. Their withdrawal agreement could effectively change the status of the border and make it an external EU boundary post-Brexit. The Irish and UK governments as well as EU representatives have said that they do not wish for a hard border between the North and South of Ireland, considering the sensitivities surrounding the histories of the island. They vow to protect an open border between the Republic and Northern Ireland and the retention of the Common Travel Area. Whatever the outcomes and how Brexit impacts on the future of the Irish border remain to be seen, as negotiations is still ongoing at this time.

Offical Name

Ireland is known officially as the Republic of Ireland. There have been other names for the country in the past. For example, in 1922 when the State was first created it was named then as the 'Irish Free State.' But it adopted a new constitution in 1937 and in its Article 4 of the Constitution, it claimed all Ireland as its territory, and it became known Ireland in

Photo: Map of Ireland

English and Éire in Irish. Then in 1949 it declared itself a Republic and adopted the term Republic of Ireland or 'Poblacht na hÉireann' in Irish as its official description, hence the Irish State has two official names– which are Éire in Irish, and Ireland in English, as the constitutional names of the country.

When Ireland joined the European Economic Community (now known as the European Union) in 1973, its accession treaty was drawn up in all the EU's official treaty languages then (including English and Irish) and as such, the Irish State joined the EU under both of its names - Éire and Ireland. To this extent, the Irish government always uses the names

Ireland for all official documents written in English, and Éire for all documents written in the Irish language. Also, whenever the State is being discussed in diplomatic relations with other foreign countries or at meetings of the United Nations, European Union, Council of Europe, Organisation for Economic Co-operation and other such organisations, the terms Republic of Ireland (ROI) or the South are used to distinguish it from Northern Ireland (NI or the North) which now belongs to Britain and is a part of the United Kingdom. This also implies that when Ireland attend official meetings of foreign nations, nameplates for the Irish State always displays as 'Éire – Ireland.'

Ireland is fondly nicknamed the 'Emerald Isle' because of its lush landscape of gentle green hills, Castles and Ancient sites

Population

Ireland has a population of 4,761,865 according to figures released by the Central Statistics Office (CSO) in April of 2016. The vast majority of people in Ireland live in the capital city and around other urban areas while the rest of country remains sparsely populated with fewer dwellers including farmers who still live off their farms in the rural areas. The figures of the Irish population have ever been changing from period to period due to the facts that Irish people tend to migrate quite a lot due to the fact that the population is young compared to other EU countries, and like young people everywhere, Irish youth or the millennials tend to migrate a lot.

In the mid-1840s, the population of Ireland was said to have risen to about 6.5 million then it started to decline. In 2014, the population was estimated to be around 4,609,600, and 4,635,400 according to CSO Statistical released in 2015, a sharp rise in numbers from previous years since the 19th Century. At the turn of the twentieth century the population started to show real growth in figures and has continued to grow steadily especially during the Celtic Tiger period which was such a time that attracted foreigners in their thousands from countries all over the world to Ireland, believed to have been due to the free movement arrangements by the European Union (EU) and economic factors. Not only that, but the economic boom also attracted many Irish who have already been living overseas to return to the country. Meanwhile, the total population of Ireland is only a small fraction of Irish descendants living abroad. Ireland has a massive and flourishing Diaspora communities scattered around the world. There are an estimated 70 million Irish people in the Diaspora, with countries like the United States, Canada, England, Australia having the highest Diaspora Irish figures.

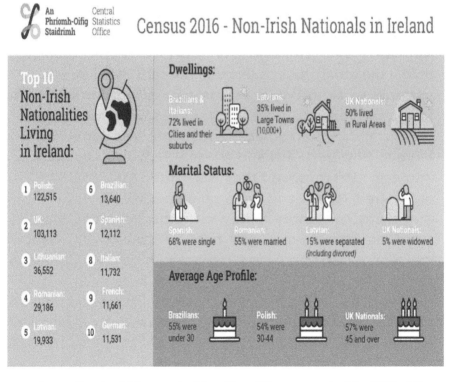

An Phríomh-Oifig Staidrimh — Central Statistics Office

Census 2016 - Non-Irish Nationals in Ireland

Top 10 Non-Irish Nationalities Living in Ireland:

1. Polish: 122,515
2. UK: 103,113
3. Lithuanian: 36,552
4. Romanian: 29,186
5. Latvian: 19,933
6. Brazilian: 13,640
7. Spanish: 12,112
8. Italian: 11,732
9. French: 11,661
10. German: 11,531

Dwellings:

Brazilians & Italians: 72% lived in Cities and their suburbs

Latvians: 35% lived in Large Towns (10,000+)

UK Nationals: 50% lived in Rural Areas

Marital Status:

Spanish: 68% were single

Romanian: 55% were married

Latvian: 15% were separated (including divorced)

UK Nationals: 5% were widowed

Average Age Profile:

Brazilians: 55% were under 30

Polish: 54% were 30-44

UK Nationals: 57% were 45 and over

According to CSO reports, 10 nationalities accounted for 70% of the general population of non-nationals in Ireland.

Ethnic Groups

History shows that Irish people are descendants of a Celtic tribe, and it is the native ethnic group of the Irish people. That is because in the past, Ireland was said to be made up of different clans and as a result, there has been an indigenous mix of ethnic groups comprised of Gaelic, Norse, Anglo-Norman, French and British ancestry. All have combined to define the ethnic groups through the centuries in Ireland. For example, when the Vikings came, they founded many coastal towns and took charge, and after the several generations of co-existence, intermarriages and interbreeds between them, a group of mixed Irish and Norse ethnic background came into new existence, and they were often called Norse-Gaels or Hiberno-Norse, and were characterised by their shared Irish ancestry, identity history, customs, traditions which are some of what formed the base of the main ethnic or indigenous Irish population. However, there are other factors to the cultural landscape of modern Ireland that can be described as 'new cultures' as the State is now composed of people from different tribes who have recently arrived from foreign countries and now settled in almost every corner of Ireland. There is also the 'Irish Travellers' who are a distinct group that can be categorized as a 'national minority group' and one that has been, historically an important aspect of Ireland and contributes to the cultural mix even as they are often portrayed in popular culture as being beneath the accepted social class system. Thankfully, Ireland has evolved since it witnessed a large influx of foreign people in the last two decades of the 20th century, which has led to a gradual change in ideologies.

Ethnicity and racial diversity are major key elements that go with increased immigration to any countries with many new settlers, and Ireland is no exception. The new settlers have now mixed with the existing native Irish and as a result, Ireland can no longer be a monoculture, it has instead, transformed into a country of multiple ethnicities because the many nationalities have now given birth to varied ethnic groups in Ireland. On the contrary, the population is still predominantly White, even though there are a wider variety of 'Whites' including many who can easily be identified as 'White' but still do not belong in the traditional Irish bracket. This group are often referred to as 'Other White' (usually on government forms). The overall majority identified with this group are either from Britain, America, and other EU member States, including Irish Travelers communities which only until recently gained official recognition of self-identify as an indigenous minority ethnic group in Ireland. While the remaining are people from the old Commonwealth countries like Australia and New Zealand.

Ireland has also a high number of foreign-born residents with non-white backgrounds who are normally residents in all parts of the country, this group comes from the countries of birth within the 'Rest of the World' bracket and are a large mixed-race such as the Africans, South Americans, Asian,

Arabs, Caribbean, etc. All have their own native lifestyles which they have brought with them and use it to make the Republic increasingly multi-ethnic and racially diverse nation, which together with the rest of the populace as well as the Irish communities have created the new variant ethnic groups that the modern day Republic of Ireland truly deserve.

Ireland is now a country of mixed cultures & diverse ethnic groups. Dublin has the largest non-white population, and these are mostly evidenced in the Fingal County area as having the greatest proportion of multi-ethnics living there. Fingal County is the second largest of the four Dublin Local Authorities.

THE CAPITAL CITY
Dublin

Dublin City is the Capital of the Republic of Ireland, it is otherwise known as 'Baile Átha Cliath' in ancient Irish. Dublin is located within County Dublin in the Leinster Province on the East-Coast region of the country. It takes approximately 30 minutes by car from the main airport to get to the city centre. As the capital, Dublin is also the largest city in Ireland, with a population of around 1.2 million people out of the country's total of 4.7 million inhabitants in the country. Outside of Dublin, the next largest cities are Cork City with approximately 205,000 people, followed by Limerick which is the third largest city in the country, with a population of slightly less than 100,000. Dublin is the only single city in Ireland with a population that that reaches more than one million.

The Capital was originally founded by Vikings who invaded the country, it was the first point where the Vikings entered and settled. They first berthed and anchored their boat at the mouth of the equally famous Liffey River which flows through the town. The Vikings made Dublin City their principal base and main servicing point during their eras of raids in Ireland and named it 'Dubh-linn' (pronounced duvlin), meaning dark pool or black pool. The name 'Dublin'as we know it now is the anglicised version from the original that was given by the Vikings. Modern-day Dublin, however, is a vibrant and diverse city bustling city with a very contemporary feel.

Dublin is a city that is steep in ancient history, not only of the Vikings, but of Kings, and of Stone Castles and all the enchanting stories of old—spanning a thousand years. Culturally, it is a city that is distinctive in so many ways, it is where most of Ireland's national treasures can still be found and governments have worked so hard to preserve the past that is physically evidenced in architectures and famous landmarks throughout the capital. Dublin is quite compact now, giving the fact that it is the most populous city in the country. But it is best known for its many tourist's attractions such as Trinity College, which is the oldest University in Ireland, Dublin Castle that was the admin headquarters during when British ruled the country, Chester Beatty Library, St Patrick's Cathedral, Christ Church Cathedral also first founded by the Vikings, the General Post Office on O'Connell Street (famous for the main point during 1916 Uprising, Temple Bar which is Dublin's most popular nightlife and culture district), etc. These are just a few among many famed historical sights and visitor centres found in and around the capital city of Dublin that is home of the world's lovable Guinness Stout, the birthplace of some of Ireland's notable personalities, and not to mention the sprawling grounds of Phoenix Park that is home the President of Ireland.

Historically, the city's geographical position has helped it to establish its economic stance which appeals to commercial business sector both within and outside the country especially as thriving trade is now evident in all areas of the city. Unquestionably the cultural and educational capital in the country and offers some great shopping experience in the heart of the city centre. It is also the seat of the Irish Government and Political Administrative Headquarters and Principal Financial and Economic nerve centre of the country with very impressive comprehensive commercial activities, practically with all kinds of trade being carried on daily.

Dublin is fast developing into one of Europe's number one multicultural city and it continues to expand in population, development and infrastructures and as a result, foreigners and people from rural Ireland flock in daily, all hoping to benefit from its growing economy after recovering from the last recession not so long ago. The city remains the most popular destination for most first-time visitors to the country, as it is filled with so much more to do and places to visit.

Official Language

The Republic of Ireland has two official languages; English language and Irish language. English is the main language that is widely spoken by the majority of the population and the language in which businesses are conducted.

The indigenous Irish language is defined as Gaelige and is heavily influenced by the language spoken by the Celts during the Celtic period in Ireland. This is "National Language" and the 'First Official' language of Ireland, recognised by the Constitution of Ireland. In Ireland, all official documents of Ireland, including the Constitution and Public Service documents are written and made available in both the Irish language and in English. The same goes for Public Notices in places such as the Post Office, Libraries, as well on public transportation systems, including messages left on official telephone answering machines all have Irish interpretations. The Road Signs for motorists and Road Markings are conspicuously visible in both English and Irish. The Irish language is used mostly around official government circles and other sensitive departments where the native language may be viewed as compulsory or as part of a workplace requirement. For example, to be eligible to join An Garda Síochána (Irish Police) a candidate must have proven proficiency in one of the two languages (Irish or English).

Learning a new language can be a relatively new challenge for many people as they move to settle in a foreign country and can't speak the official language like everybody else, even if it's for a short period visit. Irish is considered by many as very difficult to learn, but unlike in those other countries where visitors or new settlers may have to devote extra time into learning a language prior to their arrival, or at least do so while they are living there in order to help them integrate and find work, or in some cases just enough to get by and socialize with their neighbours. It is not so in Ireland as the state is officially bilingual. Only a small proportion of the population can use Irish in their everyday conversations and so, there are no such hurdles to scale by to communicate with others if at least you already have some English.

Newcomers with little or no English can avail of a government program known as 'Failte Isteach' it is a free service group organised by local authorities all over the country to teach basic English to non-speakers.

Likewise, visitors can immerse themselves in the native Irish language by visiting a Gaeltacht community in the rural areas of Ireland. These are the Irish-speaking region of the country where Irish traditional culture thrives and where Irish-speaking Irish is the community language and dedicatedly spoken as a first language. The people in these regions are fluent Irish speakers, they conduct their daily activities in Irish only and they are known collectively as the Gaeltacht (pronounced Girltact). For those arriving in the country with no English at all, this can work out as a separate option if they want to settle down first and then learn English or go straight to the Gaeltacht areas to settle and learn Irish once and for all.

IRISH LANGUAGE IN SCHOOLS

The Irish language became diluted at some point in the past and the government was concerned about it and it took conscious actions to revive it. Now it is a compulsory part of the school curriculum and a taught subject in all schools across the country. Although exemptions are made for students on grounds of learning difficulties, e.g. if a student is diagnosed with dyslexia, also on the basis that a student is new in the country. It is otherwise a taught subject from Senior Infant class (kindergarten) until the end of secondary school. There are also dedicated schools where Irish is the main method used in teaching throughout. The Irish-speaking schools are known as (Gaelscoil), these exist around the country within and outside the Gaeltacht Irish-speaking regions. But Irish language then becomes optional at University level, but some colleges still require Irish as an entry qualification regardless of other language choices.

That said, Irish has become an official working language of the European Union since 2007, and foreign students with an intent to work within the EU after they graduate can use their knowledge of the language to their own advantage. Other than the two official languages (Irish and English), many different languages are also being spoken in today's Ireland, including the Irish Sign Language and other different native dialects due to the presence of foreign nationals who make up the general Irish populace. Reports show that 1.76 million people (39.8%) can speak Irish. The 2016 Census revealed that 612,018 residents spoke a language other than Irish or English at home, an increase of 19.1% since 2011. Of these, 363,715 were non-Irish nationals, and the top languages spoken were Polish (113,225), Lithuanian (30,502) Romanian (26,645) and Portuguese (16,737). Polish is now regarded as the second most spoken language in Ireland after English, therefore placing native Irish somewhere in third most spoken language in the Republic.

There is mush effort by government to promote the use of the Irish language and to keep it alive, as it is an integral part of the country's identity. The Irish language became an official working language of the European Union on the 1st of January 2007.

Religion in Ireland

Christianity is the dominant religion in the Republic of Ireland and for the most of its recorded history, it has been primarily Catholicism. Roman Catholic is the largest religious group in the majority across the country and has a percentage of around 84.2%. Nonetheless, the religious landscape is fast changing in Ireland and which has clearly affected the Catholic church as there have been reports of a decline in the Catholic faith altogether. As Ireland becomes multicultural the people have learnt to be more tolerant towards the faith of other people, and in recent years Ireland has seen many of its own people as not belonging to the Catholic church anymore and others who refuse to acknowledge belonging to any religion at all. All of which has resulted in a decline in church attendance in congregations on worship Sundays or Mass. But just like other new traditions that are been experienced in the country, the story of religion in Ireland has also started to take a completely different turn now, because the rivers of faith are truly flowing through the country and some are finding other ways through a landscape that is relatively new for them. Ireland had no real experience of other types of faith in the past until the increases in immigration of foreigners and the new arrivals from all over the world who are now part and parcel of a new multi-cultural Ireland; meaning one really cannot tell the story of a new Irish society and publicly acknowledge it for being multicultural without also having to accept the fact that it is now multi-religious also. The new immigration has brought with it different religious sects into the country and Ireland's Christian beliefs are changing, especially with those who were already struggling with their faith, as they encounter new neighbours of other faiths are also changing as they are learning to work together in many public places including religious spheres. Although, new religious communities on the other hand also feel some challenges, sometimes more acutely because a few of them find the need to change their faith from the one they practised originally from home before coming to Ireland and they are now Catholics. Deep down it doesn't really go to prove abandonment of one's original faith that they belonged before arriving in Ireland because for many of them it was merely a matter of convenience and a desire to fit in and belong in their new community. There may not necessarily be a physical line-up of Orthodox and Pentecostal church buildings, and mosques, or the Hindu or Buddhist temples right across every streets from one another to drive home the point that in every part of Ireland today, there are religious groups other than the Catholic church or the Church of Ireland or any of which presumably are some of the more well-known churches that have always existed right from ancient times. New religious traditions are beginning to form and flourish in Ireland. So, Christianity today in Ireland is more diverse than ever before as a result of churches which largely caters for these new communities, such as the Asians, a growing Hispanic Baptist congregation, a mega Pentecostal church that has over twenty-five branches around the country and mostly dominated by the Africans, and others that are multi-denominational in their outlook and which are a huge part of a spirited Pentecostal revival ministries. Most charismatic churches also have worships taken place from inside buildings in industrial estates and in community centres and even school premises at weekends. The invisible architectural evidence of Ireland's new religious diversity is unmistakable still but if for anything else - it straightens the faith of some believers even further because religion is far more than the physical structures that give its identification to such centres. The irony is that they all play vital roles in their various ways in trying to build a better future for the new Irish society and Irish Christiandom. In all, Ireland stands to expand peace strategies between the various religious communities in order to accommodate every faith as it grows because the story is not going to change otherwise; Ireland is officially multi-denominational and multi-religion as well as multi-cultural as long as the population continues to increase in size every year.

"One thing is certain, that all of these religious traditions will continue to change in the new context of multi-religious Ireland as these changes are taking place today right before our very eyes."

Public Holidays

There are many official holidays in Ireland, These Public Holidays are called 'Bank Holidays', and are observed accordingly. During Bank Holidays all schools and official businesses are closed, and employees are entitled to take time off work. If a public holiday falls on a Saturday or a Sunday or possibly coincides with another national holiday, it is generally observed on the next available weekday.

Apart from the usual holidays which are observed in other countries of the world such as Christmas Day, New Year's Day or the first day in May commonly known as Workers Day, etc, in Ireland the first Monday in June first Monday in August, and last Monday in October are confirmed Bank holidays in Ireland. Boxing Day is known as St. Stephen's Day in Ireland, which normally is the day after Christmas and most people spend visiting friends and family or shopping or just to rest. But there is much more attached to it than just a day off here in Ireland. Saint Stephen's Day is a Christian Saint's day to commemorate Saint Stephen, the first Christian Marty and is celebrated on 26 December. The Easter Monday in Ireland also holds a slightly different meaning than just the day after Easter Sunday which is a Christian holiday celebrating the resurrection of Jesus as He arose from His death at Calvary. Easter Monday in Ireland – also coincides with the commemoration of the Easter Uprising, known also as the Easter Rebellion, which took place during Easter week of 1916. Then, there is the world-renowned St. Patrick's Day, or the Feast of Saint Patrick. The day is observed as the national day. It commemorates Saint Patrick, the foremost Patron Saint of Ireland and the arrival of Christianity in Ireland, it also celebrates the cultural heritage of the Irish people in general. Saint Patrick's Day is a public holiday which is also observed in Northern Ireland, the Canadian province of Newfoundland and Labrador (for provincial government employees), and the British Overseas Territory of the Caribbean Island of Montserrat. (More on St. Patrick's Day celebrations in the Festival section).

 Below are listed 9 official Public Holiday Months as earmarked to be observed in the Republic of Ireland.

New Year's Day	January
Saint Patrick's Day	March
Easter Monday	April
Workers' Day (May Day)	May
June Bank Holiday	June
August Bank Holiday	August
October Bank Holiday	October
Christmas Day (Birth of Jesus Christ)	December
St. Stephen's Day (Boxing Day)	December

Weather & Climate

Ireland's climate is defined as a temperate oceanic climate with mild average temperatures of around 50 - 60°F. It is considerably warm compared to other areas at a similar latitude, due mainly to its proximity to the Atlantic Ocean and the influence of the warm Gulf Stream all year. Generally, Ireland does not have extreme temperatures, rather it receives warm summers and mild winters and abundant rainfalls mostly during the month of August with an average of 80mm of rain. The weather itself is very unpredictable and changes so often regardless of which time of the year. The country normally gets about 1600 hours of sunshine on the average each year, with the sunniest months in May and June when sunshine lasts between 5 and 6.5 hours per day across the country. Meanwhile, the hottest month is July with an average temperature of around 16°C (60°F) and the coldest is January at 5°C (41°F). The wettest month besides August is December, the most festive period in the country and also the dullest with cold and dark days with average daily sunshine of just about 1 to 2 hours.

Changeable Weathers

Ireland weather is famed to be one of the most unpredictable as it can go from a rather dull and damp start in the morning to a dry and breezy afternoon with sunny spells breaking in intermittently to brighten the mood, and then suddenly develop into occasional showers of rain. Depending on what's happening at a given period, but temperatures always adapt to the right amount. While during winter, it can be all the above in addition to hail-stones and snow.

Extreme Weathers

Ireland weather is mainly mild, but the country has also suffered extreme repercussions caused by severe weather conditions. There may not be rampant occurrences of earthquakes, twisters, tornadoes, Ireland has experienced severe damage to properties and lives have been lost from weather-related natural disasters such as flooding and hurricanes at various scales on numerous occasions.

Topography

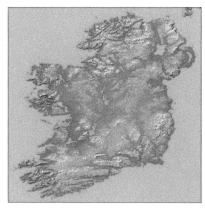

Ireland's topography features a hilly, central lowland composed of limestone surrounded by a broken border of coastal mountains and ridges. The eastern part of the county is part of the Golden Vale, which is an area of rolling pastureland in the province of Munster, covering parts of counties, Limerick, Tipperary and Cork, best land known for dairy farming.

Flora & Fauna

As a small country, Ireland boasts a relatively small flora compared to countries which are larger in size and more varied geologically. However, Ireland flora and fauna are remarkably rich and diverse and comprises all the plants, flowers and crops that are native to the country and animal species inhabiting the island and its surrounding waters with species of mammals, birds, insects and a wide variety of fish, amphibians and reptiles.

Flora

There are around 900 native plant species from the various species of orchids, cherry, shrubs and berries etc., that can be spotted across fields or found in bogs and marshes all over the country at different times of the year. The Burren in County Clare alone for instance, has more than 70% of the 900 plant species, while County Armagh is famous with the white and pink apple blossom, and the pink/purple heather is very popular in the hills of County Wicklow from around mid-June to September.

The National Botanic Gardens situated in Glasnevin area of Dublin contain more than 20,000 different plants.

Mammals

There are around only 26 land mammal species that are native to Ireland, such as the red fox, European hedgehog, stoat, otter, pygmy shrew, and badger are common, whereas, others like the Irish hare, red deer, and pine marten are less common and generally seen only in certain national parks and nature reserves around the island, and also some introduced species that have become naturalised, like the European rabbit, grey squirrel, and brown rat. In addition, ten species of bat are also found in Ireland.

Fish

Ireland has 375 fish species in its coastal waters and rivers and lakes, including many aquatic mammals too, such as bottlenose dolphins, killer whales, the basking shark, and harbour porpoises. Other fish species in Irish waters are mussel, crayfish, slug, sea turtles and around 24 species of cetaceans and giant squid that are seen on occasions.

Crops & Vegetables

Vegetables and crops that are native to Ireland include Carrots, Parsnips, Celery, Turnip, Roots, Berries, Cabbage, Potatoes, Onion etc.

The followings are examples of crops which are introduced into Ireland –

Mango Wheat, Watermelon, Tobacco, Mustard, Cashew, Coffee, Papaya, Pomegranate, etc.

Insects

There are an estimated 11,500 species of insect recorded in Ireland and they are made of well-known groups of moths, cricket, bell spider, dragonflies/damselflies and butterfly.

Reptiles

Ireland fauna also includes the only one land reptile native to the country, which is the viviparous lizard and commonly found in national parks, particularly in the Wicklow Mountains. Slow-worms are common in parts of The Burren area in County Clare, but they are not a native species.

Amphibians

Three amphibians are found in Ireland, the common European brown frog, the smooth newt, and the natterjack toad found in a few localised sites in County Kerry and western part of County Cork.

Birds

Birdlife in Ireland is quite colourful. Aabout 400 bird species have been recorded in Ireland and most species are migratory birds, they include the swallow, which comes from Africa in the summer to breed. Other common birds are the wren, robin, pigeons, blackbird, rook, starling, among those commonly seen, including seabird colonies usually dotted around its Coastline on the Saltee Islands off the southern coast of County Wexford and the north side of Wexford Harbour, home to around 10,000 Greenland white-fronted geese present each winter.

Highest Mountains

Ireland's mountain ranges are mostly in the coastal counties. These also includes landforms that are usually known as hills. In Ireland Mountains, are commonly defined as any summit at least 2,000 feet (or 610 metres).

There are over 250 mountains being of at least 600 m (2,000 ft) in height with a prominence of at least 15 m (50 ft), in addition to more than 400 measuring at least 500 m (1,600 ft) in height with a prominence of at least 30 m (100 ft.

List of Ireland's Highest Peaks by Province:

Leinster	Munster	Connacht
Luqnaquilla, Co Wicklow – 925m Mullaghcleevaun, Co Wicklow – 849m Tonelagee, Co Wicklow – 817m Cloghernagh, Co Wicklow – 800m Mt Leinster, Co Wexford – 796m	Carrauntoohil, County Kerry – 1,038 m BinnChaorach/Benkeeragh, Co Kerry – 1,008m Caher, Co Kerry – 1001m Cnoc na Péiste, Co Kerry – 988m Caher West Top, Co Kerry – 975m	Mweelrea, Co Mayo – 814m Nephin, Co Mayo – 806m Barrclashcame, Co Mayo – 772 m Croagh Patrick, Co Mayo – 764 m Benbaun, Co Galway – 729m

Ulster	
	• Slieve Donard, Co Down – 852 m • Slieve Commedagh, – 767m • Slieve Binnian, Co Down – 747m • Slieve Bearnagh, Co Down – 727m • Slieve Meelbeg, Co Down – 708m

Source: Mountainviews.ie

THE EMERALD ISLE: IRELAND INFORMATION MADE SIMPLE

Main Rivers

There are numerous rivers and lakes in Ireland. The largest is **River Shannon**, measured at 360.5 kilometres (224.0 mi), and develops into three separate lakes along its course. They are known ae the Lough Allen, Lough Ree and Lough Derg situated in between County Tipperary on the east, and counties Clare and Galway on the west. The Lough Derg is the largest of these three lakes. The **Shannon River** runs through over ten counties and enters into the Atlantic Ocean at the Estuary, with some tributaries within the River Basin, such as the Owenmore River in County Cavan-and the Boyle River with its source in County Mayo.

In the Capital, Dublin, the **Liffey River** flows through its centre and from the Wicklow Mountains into the Irish Sea. The Liffey is also known as the Anna Liffey, from an anglicisation of the Irish phrase 'Abhainn na Life' which translates into English as "River Liffey". It is the most popular River in Ireland and is understood to be the eight longest rivers in the country, it supplies much of Dublin's water.

Shown below are other main Rivers in Ireland

• River Suir	• River Lee
• River Bann	• River Slaney
• River Erne	• River Lagan
• River Foyle	• River Moy
• River Nore	• River Swilly
• River Boyne	River Blackwater
• River Barrow (The Three Sisters)	

Irish Police & the Military

The Irish Police:

The Police Force in the Republic of Ireland is called Garda Síochána na hÉireann, meaning Guardians of the Peace of Ireland.They are more commonly referred to as An Garda Síochána or just simply as the 'Gardaí' (pronounced gardi) for short. A single Policeman or Policewoman is referred called Garda, collectively they are referred to as the Gardai and they are responsible for all aspects of policing the entire country both in terms of territory, infrastructure including overseeing the safety and security of the people. The Gardai is usually headed by a Garda Commissioner who is normally appointed by Government. The Irish Garda operates in civilian style policing, because of that its uniformed members do not carry firearms with them even while on patrol because by law they are not authorised to use them. However, the absence of an armed police force does not mean there is a lack of security in the country.

The Garda Síochána (Police) have the primary responsibility for law and order in the country and they respond to crime-calls and other incidents requiring their attention swiftly. They carry other typical police devices like handcuffs and such other gadgets to help them perform their duties effectively. Within the Gardai, there are also special divisions that are assigned to counter-terrorism or emergency responses and such units are issued with firearms and can use them whenever necessary.

The Irish Military: The Military in Ireland incorporates the Army, Air Corps, Naval Service and the Reserve Defence Forces. Altogether, they make up the Military of the Republic of Ireland. It is the land component of the Defence Forces of Ireland and its known in Irish language as 'Fórsaí Cosanta' or Óglaigh na hÉireann. The President of the country is usually the Supreme Commander of the Irish Defence Forces, from whom all Defence Forces officers hold their commission and the Minister for Defence routinely acts on behalf of the President and reports to the Government of Ireland. The Irish Army, on the other hand, has its primary responsibilities to defend the Irish State and internal security within the country. It also holds a history of continuous presence in peacekeeping missions in many different countries around the world since it was founded in 1958. The Forces also participates in the European Union Battlegroups. According to reports, there are approximately 9,000 men and women currently serving in the Irish Army.

Irish Neutrality: Ireland is neutral in terms of wars, it remained neutral during World War II, at a period described as the Emergency. But despite that, during World War II, Ireland had more than 50,000 participants in the war through enlistment in the British armed forces. During the Cold War, Irish Military policy, while supposedly neutral, was said to have been biased towards NATO in that during the Cuban Missile Crisis, Ireland's then Taoiseach, Seán Lemmas authorised the search of Cuban and Czechoslovak aircraft passing through Shannon and took the

information to the CIA. In 2003, Ireland's air facilities were used by the United States military for the delivery of military personnel involved in the invasion of Iraq through the Shannon Airport and previously used also for the invasion of Afghanistan in 2001, as well as the First Gulf War. The Irish government has followed its policy of neutrality through non-alignment since immediately prior to World War II and the country is therefore not a member of NATO, although since 1999, the country has been a member of NATO's Partnership for Peace (PfP) program and NATO's Euro-Atlantic Partnership Council (EAPC), which is aimed at creating trust between NATO and other States in Europe and the former Soviet Union. EU leaders have endorsed moves for more co-operation in the fight against terrorism, putting increased pressure on internet providers to actively fight the use of networks to distribute hate material and the leaders also agreed for the first time to allow the EU States to increase Defense co-operation under limited conditions. While Ireland's position on neutrality is unchanged, they believe it should not be totally cut off from the developments in terms of fighting crime and threats on terrorism in the world today.

COMMENT

"The threats that we face in the world are less about wars between countries, and more about threats created by terrorism, by extremism, and by cyberattacks for example. Those areas are not areas in which we should be neutral. We should be very much involved in working with European partners to prevent cyberattacks to manage migration and to stand against terrorism." - ***Taoiseach, Leo Varadkar***

SECTION TWO

HISTORY

A BRIEF HISTORY OF IRELAND
(An Overview)

*I*reland has very complicated history that is much deeper than c ould ever be possibly imagined; not with the strings and series of the many battles it has been involved in the past, or the many struggles by various tribes and empires for dominance for the area. Some of which have caused a great suffering for the people through its losses of lands and properties to the so-called invaders and all kinds of heroic sacrifices by the people of Ireland, which included sectarian brutality, and forgetting to mention the period of the great famine that wiped out a large chunk of the nation's population and forced millions of Irish people to flee their country in the 1840s. Irish history consists of some of the most fascinating and yet very complex of world histories which are far beyond the scope of this book and my own basic understanding to deal with in more detail. However, it is quite easy to see that Irish history is full of captivating stories, not only for being a country that had always found itself to be the subject of power-hungry invaders from neighbouring countries who threatened to take them over, but it has come to be known as a land of beauty with big rolling green hills – as it is often described by the general public.   Not only that, Irish legends tell a far more picturesque story of the people's origin and how the country came to be. That is however is the truth, because no matter how complicated the story becomes, in all its complexities, if looked at it from a positive light, the history of Ireland as told has all the trimmings of aspiration, of revival and of hope, and one which can only be characterised as a continuous process of re-discovering itself and in that process forged the country into what it is now . Many past events had also influenced the present state as we see it today and which will continue to be so in the great future.

In Search of the Past

*E*arly Medieval history of Ireland often called Early Christian Ireland, spans the 5th centuries from the gradual emergence out of the Primitive period to the beginning of the Viking Age. The period notably includes that which marked the arrival of Saint Patrick and other Christian Missionaries in the mid-5th Century when Christianity replaced indigenous pagan worship around 600 AD. Archaeological evidence also suggests that Ireland had emerged from a mysterious decline at the start of the Irish Dark Age around c. 100 BCE to c. 300 CE. due to the standards of living at that period which was entirely rural and known to have a population of just around 40,000 to 50,000. The prehistory accounts had been pieced together from archaeologists and genetic evidence; beginning with the first evidence of the humans who settled in the country after 8000 BC and finishes with the start of the historical record around 400 AD. The prehistoric period covers the Mesolithic, Neolithic, Bronze Age and Iron Age societies which occurred in Ireland at different stages. For much of Europe, the historical record began when the Romans invaded and conquered most of the continent; but Ireland was never invaded by the Romans, so its historical record started only later with the coming of Christianity.

According to records, the first settlement was found at Mount Sandel in Derry County. The first inhabitants in the country were said to have arrived from Scandinavia and Scotland around 6000 B.C. They were Mesolithic (Stone-Age) hunter-gatherers who spent most of their time hunting wild animals and collecting grains. The Mesolithic or hunter-gathering society was later replaced by Neolithic settlers who brought the technology of farming to Ireland from Britain. As a more settled farming society, the Neolithic people also known as New Stone Age no longer had to spend all their time hunting for the wild to make food. They brought with them domestic animals such as sheep, goats and cows and they grew crops such as Cereal, Barley and Oats being the most important crops. They also made various intricate items out of stone that were useful to their livelihood. For example, they made axes, digging tools with which to cut down trees and clear farming areas for tilling the soil and growing their crops for foods.

Later, settlers from France also arrived in Ireland around 2000 BC and they introduced the knowledge of Bronze working to the existing inhabitants whose cultures gradually merged and both formed the Irish Bronze-Age. The people during the Bronze Age period were good at making ornamental objects for warfare like daggers, swords and shields and other ornamental objects. They were believed to have lived in circular houses constructed from timber beams with thatched roofing. The Bronze Age in Ireland however ended following the arrival of the Celts around 500-BC in Britain and Ireland from mainland Europe. They brought with them in their period, a new cultural influence onto Ireland and within a few centuries of settling, the culture of the Irish Bronze Age all disappeared – fully ushering in the Celtic tradition and Ireland's Iron Age.

The Celt people, having come from warring tribes with a culture based around conflicts and warfare, they were understood to be Warriors who fought other powerful groups such as the Romans and at other times were violent towards each other as well. Celtic period Ireland was divided into small kingdoms and what was known as Tuaths with up to 200 of them and each was ruled by a King. In each Kingdom or Tuath, they built huge Stone Forts on the top of a hill and surrounded by a stone wall. These Forts were used either as the King's permanent residence and assembly point in times of conflicts. But the best of their history was that the Celt people were also blessed with skills of making tools and other objects out of iron, and with their skills they made several objects such as the Celtic Brooches, and they carved the stone High Crosses and other stronger and more superior weapons that was used in fighting their wars.

The Celts had a strong foothold and huge influence on the island as they continued to dominate the land they had settled in for centuries. Nonetheless, it was aid that there had been periods of prolonged peace in between, although at these times, however, they managed to get in at war with each other. They also left lasting legacies, one of which is strongly evidenced in today's Ireland is in the first official language, which is traditional the Irish/Gaeilge having its origin from the Celtic language. Others include many old traditions that are said to have been passed down from that period, for example the Irish cultures and love of storytelling.

(Source: Country Study Handbook).

• Viking Eras in a Nutshell

The first recorded Viking raid in Irish history occurred in AD 795 by the early Vikings who were a group of people who originated in the Scandinavian territories of the modern-day Denmark, Norway and associated. They were said to be the younger sons of noble men, who were not in the position to inherit nothing of their fathers, and they believed that they had nothing to lose after all, should anything happens to them, so they gathered themselves together in groups of warriors and devised a means of securing their livelihood and started raiding and looting various settlements, with Britain and France included.

They finally arrived in Ireland for the first time in 795 AD and carried out their various escapades and for several decades, the Vikings continued terrorising settlements with more raids and other committing other barbaric acts which did not stop at only looting and carting of goods and burning down prominent Monasteries alone; the Vikings also kidnapped individuals whom they held as prisoners and later on sold off as slaves. They were said to be the first influx of new people to arrive on the Island since the Celts during the Iron Age.

The Vikings would normally return to their camps after their carnage and when they were not attacking, life went on as normal for people in Ireland. Not that the Irish did noting and just fold their arms in wait for the next attacks of the Vikings on their coasts. A few times the Vikings were caught in battles with rival Irish Kings who were defeated unfortunately, but a few times they too had succeeded in defeating the Vikings. The Kingdom of Ulster (Ulaid) were said have defeated a gang of raiders in 811, and as well another group that was also defeated in Connaught in 812 and one more in the Munster region around the same time.

Nonetheless, Vikings activities continued in Ireland and more so as they soon improved their tactics and intensified their pillaging of the island. At a point they were no longer satisfied with landing just a few boats, raiding and then returning to Scandinavia. Their next move was that they went back and recruited more Viking Warriors and brought with them around one hundred more boats full of them and they set up camp permanently, from where they carried out more massive attacks into the surrounding country-sides— looting farms, monasteries, and churches for several months in one stretch of time and spending a whole year pillaging the coasts on Lough Neagh and around the monastery of Armagh to the point that Scholars and Monks of Louth Monastery were captured and sold into slavery. It was said to be the most intense period of Viking activities at the time and Irish Kings seemed to be able to do very little to prevent the large-scale destruction of their Provinces, until it finally got a point when it seemed almost certain the Vikings was set to conquer Ireland once and for all, but then the attacks suddenly died down, with the last major raid taking place in 851. It marked the end to a phase, as the Vikings seemed to have turned their attention to somewhere else.

• Vikings Second Coming

After a long absence, there was a 'Second Coming' of the Vikings to Ireland around 914, this time around they arrived with a large fleet of Viking ships at the Waterford Harbour and promptly re-captured their settlement from which the Irish had expelled the first set of Vikings. They reinforced by a second fleet which also arrived the following year, and the Vikings re-launched a series of offensives deep into the Provinces of where they met very little Irish resistance as they freely pillaged both monasteries and ordinary settlements.

In 917, they moved to re-capture Dubhlinn [Dublin] which the Irish had taken back in 902, they continued to raid inland from the towns of Cork and Waterford for many decades. In a turn of event, some Irish Kings and Lords joined forces with the Vikings to attack other Irish lords and they engaged in bitter battles. Vikings influence however, declined decades later as they eventually stopped raiding, and settled down in the lands they had conquered. By 952, Dubhlinn (Dublin) now had its own dynasty of Viking Kings and the city was by now well known as a trading and slaving centre of the Nordic world.

Brian Boru Scupture outside Chapel Royal, Dublin Castle (Source: Wikipedia.org)

• Brian Boru

Brian Boru was an Irish war legend and a fierce Warrior of wars in Irish history and is still regarded as a hero in present day Ireland

Brian Boru is hailed as the downfall of the Vikings and a hero who sacrificed his life to secure Irish victory from Viking oppression.

In 999AD, Brian Boru was said to have gone to war with the Vikings in the famous 'Battle of Clontaff' where he not only defeated the Vikings; Brian conquered them and that brought Viking rule in Ireland to an end. He then became the High King over the whole of Ireland in 1002AD and he used his position to at that to unify the country because, the ultimate end to Viking activities meant that Ireland returned to peace for some decades although there were still some of in-fightings between several clans. Nonetheless, this was a period which allowed the people to re-develop society. However, the unfortunate happened on a Good Friday of 1014AD. Brian Boru, aged 70 at the time, was caught in a similar 'Battle of Clontarf' in the north side of Dublin, involving both Irishmen and Vikings in what was described as a violent struggle, and he was killed along with others.

Following Brian Boru's death, the political situation in Ireland became volatile once more and even more complex than it was before, because the country was not only in troubled again—this time it was not from external powers, but rivalry for the High Kingship, from several dynasties and clans each wanting sectional dominion. Brian's descendants had failed to maintain a unified throne, and the in-fighting over territory led indirectly to the invasion of the Normans in 1169 under Richard de Clare 2nd Earl of Pembroke of Britain, who was soon nicknamed Strongbow!

British Rule

The 11th Century brought about Normal Rule for Ireland and was the beginning of yet another troubled Century. Following Brian Boru's death at the Battle of Clontarf in 1014 and the political instability in the country due as a result of Brian's descendants failing to maintain a unified throne after ending Viking rule, the regional rancour over territories continued and eventually led the invasion of the Anglo-Normans armies in 1169 whose arrival of marked the beginning of more than seven centuries of Norman and English rule at various stages in Ireland. They were believed to being sponsored by the King of England who at that time were more than prepared to dispossess native Irish Kings and take over dominion of their land. On first arrival to Ireland, the Normans carried out Fierce and Ferocious activities and did not hesitate to crush anyone who stood in their way. In due cause, they conquered Ireland and eventually ruled over it for many many decades. At first, Richard de Clare (Strongbow) had been invited to Ireland by a Gaelic lord Dermot MacMurrough, who was also the king of Leinster. He had been driven out of his kingship by a rival Irish king due to his neferious activities, and needed external help to win it back, so he invited Strongbow who brought with him an army of Welsh archers to help the King.

Dermot MacMurrough had also promised his seventeen years old daughter, Aoife's hands in marriage to Strongbow as part of his compensation to him. The marriage, which took place in Waterford in August of 1170. However, King Dermont died in 1171, and Strongbow became the new king of Leinster, meaning that the Normans had taken over much of the east of Ireland at this time. Strongbow died on 20 April in 1176 aged around 46 years, and buried at Christ Church Cathedral, Dublin.

• King Henry II of England

The coming of King Henry II of England began with the invasion in the Winter of 1171, arriving on October 17th, 1171 near Waterford at the head of a vast army in a fleet of 400 ships carrying around 500 armed knights and 4000 archers with large quantities of weapons, and ready to fight and take over the dominion of the Irish territory. He had been authorised by a Papal - the English Pope Adrian IV, in the guise of bringing the Irish into the Catholic fold and to correct the behaviour of the Irish people which they, in England viewed mostly as Savages. King Henry II was ready to conquer not only the Kings of Ireland but the Normans who were previously sponsored by his Kingship as well, and who by this time had already settled and ruled Ireland for over half a Century submitted to the King of England and promised to remain loyal to him. Eager to show their allegiance, they handed over the land they already gained from their previous invasions. Irish Sub-Kings and the High King of Ireland were under the impression that the King of England would protect their territory from further invasions from outsiders and they paid homage to him and agreed to take an oath to be loyal and to pay tax to him. Though not all the Irish Kings were pleased with this arrangement, but that not notwithstanding, King Henry II succeeded to carry out his plans especially with the backing of Adrian IV who granted him Lordship of Ireland. His eventual reign flourished, and his legacy in Ireland went on to last for another 700 years or so but with dire consequences to the Irish people who through the Centuries at various intervals witnessed diverse changes of English Rulership of their land.

Crown of Ireland Act 1542

From the 13th Century onwards the Hiberno-Norman occupation in Ireland started to wane gradually as they had increasingly assimilated into Irish culture and formed alliances with independent Gaelic Lords. They had settled in Ireland for so long after the Conquest and by now and had developed similarities between the Irish Chieftains and the Anglo-Irish lords, and also because they were the last of the invaders who had in Ireland, they had some Irish blood through intermarriage and were now Norman-Irish. However, in the 14th Century, Henry VIII declared the Kingdom of Ireland and embarked on the Tudor Conquest of Ireland. He overruled earlier court decisions, recognised the privileges of the Gaelic lords and thereby expanding the Crown's authority and in return for recognising the crown's authority under the new Kingdom of Ireland. The Gaelic-Anglo-Irish lords had their positions legalised and were entitled to attend the Irish Parliament as equals under the policy of surrender and regrant. The 14th and 15th Centuries saw continuous shrinking numbers of those loyal to the British Crown because of the growing power of landed families, and a growing "Gaelic resurgence" that was political as well as cultural. Eventually, the Crown's power shrank to a small enclave of only a few areas around Dublin known as the Pale. The Parliament that was created around the 13th century which had initial one representation from each county thereafter became essentially the forum for the Pale community until the 16th Century, it brought a series of events which led to the Church of England to brake away from the authority of the Pope and the Roman Catholic Church. This was in part associated with the wider process of the European Protestant Reformation, a religious and political movement that affected the practice of Christianity across the whole of Western and Central Europe.

Other factors surrounding the Reformation contributed to the introduction of a series of (Penal Laws), imposed to force Irish Roman Catholics and Protestant dissenters to accept the reformed denomination, as defined by the English State established Anglican Church and practised by members of the Irish State established Church of Ireland. The introduction of Penal Laws led to hostility between Irish Catholics and Protestants, it led to the discrimination of all

Catholics in Ireland. For example, Irish Catholics were forbidden to practice their faith in their own land. The laws also prohibited them from speaking their native Irish language. They were banned from intermarrying and forced to give up ownership of their lands. All Catholic education was deemed to be illegal, in addition to being politically marginalized, including ridding of their voting rights and excluded from holding any public office. By 1703, Catholics in the country owned less properties, about 10 per cent as the Protestants were more favoured. This bias was evidenced by an unequal allocation of Council Houses to Protestant families. But by 1778 another law was passed allowing Catholics to buy property, England still held all political power over Ireland even then, but the Penal Laws which preserved the position of the Protestant Domination began to be dismantled through the 1780s and 1790s. Irish Parliament had little significance and the government of Ireland remained in English hands still. Most of the country's population remained Catholic, but its Protestant minority remained socially, politically, and economically dominant. Nonetheless, all Penal Laws were finally repealed by the United Kingdom of Great Britain and Ireland by the Government of Ireland Act 1920.

Hunger for Home Rule Leads to Counter Rebellions

The hunger for Home Rule was always real for the Irish people, it was a vision that led to counter-rebellions. In October 1791, a Pro-Catholic campaigner named Theobald Wolfe Tone and a group of men set out and formed the  **Society of United Irishmen**, it was an organisation that embraced both Catholics, Protestants and Dissenters in its aim to remove English control from Irish affairs. They had been inspired by the example of 'The French Revolution' that took place in 1789 and successfully overthrew the ruling powers in France because it conveyed a powerful message that the will of the people was enough to effect change. This new group of Irishmen started a bloody rebellion in 1798 and it was unsuccessful, however it resulted in the '1801 Act of Union' which brought Ireland under tighter British control and led the British government to seek the Union of Ireland with Great Britain; this also in effect resulted in the formation of the United Kingdom of Great Britain and Ireland. In 1801, the Irish Parliament was abolished, and Ireland became part of the United Kingdom of Great Britain and Ireland' formally becoming a constituency of the United Kingdom on the 1st of January 1801 and remained until 6th December 1922 and for the most of this period, Ireland was governed by the UK Parliament in London through its Dublin Castle administration office in Ireland. Over the course of the next two Centuries on a number of occasions, the Irish tried to challenge English rule but were often not successful in their attempts to gain back control of their country.

Rebellions were launched in 1803, 1848, 1867, and 1916 to try and end British rule over Ireland.

The Home Rule Vision

Home Rule was a visionary crusade that was driven by aspirations and hope for the future of Irish Self-Government that would ultimately end the intimidation on Irish people by Britain. In the 1830-1840s there was a campaign to repeal the Act of Union of the United Kingdom of Great Britain and Ireland. From the 1870s onwards Irish Nationalists who favoured Home Rule therefore made several attempts to pass a Home Rule Bill. Accordingly, the people were optimistic about the future of Ireland under Home Rule and hopefully anticipated the roles they would play in a self-governing Ireland should they realise their dream. However, the first attempt to legislate Home Rule was officially made in 1886 and it was defeated, a second attempt followed in 1893, that as well was not successful and only about nineteen years after that, a third Irish Home Rule Bill was finally passed under the UK Parliament Act to establish self-government for Ireland. However, Home Rule did not happen because it was suspended due to the outbreak of World War One in 1914 and the 1916 Easter Uprising in Dublin.

Easter Rising

The Easter Rising was a Rebellion against British Rule in Ireland. It was organised by a group of armed Socialist Trade Union men and women from the Supreme Council of the Irish Republican Brotherhood (IRB), members of the Irish Volunteer Force, the Irish Citizen Army and women of Cumann na mBan came together to join forces and staged an Uprising during Easter week of 1916. It lasted for six days.

The Uprising, led by the activist Patrick Pearse began after they seized key locations in Dublin City centre including St. Stephen's Green, the Four Courts, and the Irish General Post Office (GPO) in Sackville Street (known now as O'Connell Street in the city centre of Dublin). The Rebels made the GPO their headquarters, from where James Connolly, who was the overall Military Commander, together with the other members of the Military Council were. On 24th Easter Monday the Volunteers hoisted two Republican flags and read out the Proclamation of the Irish Republic at the General Post Office by Patrick Pearse, he was named the President of the Provisional Republic. However, fighting broke out between the insurgents and the British army. It was said that, although the British Army were totally unprepared and taken unawares, but they called for reinforcements from England which arrived in their thousands, and the rebels were subdued, especially as they failed to capture some key places like Trinity College and most so Dublin Castle which at the time was the main centre of British Rule in Ireland.

Ultimately, the Rising was not successful, and the Irish Forces eventually surrendered. Thousands of Irish people were killed in the week-long fighting, followed by extensive lootings in the aftermath in the city centre, especially around the O'Connell Street area resulting in the arrest of hundreds of people for looting. Dublin city centre was ultimately left in ruins. Human casualties included British rebels, men of the Irish Forces, hundreds of civilians, including children who lost their lives, and thousands more were wounded even though the fighting had not to spread beyond Dublin.

Following the failure of the Rebellion, the British executed a total of 16 men, including most of the leaders and the seven men who signed the Proclamation of the Irish Republic all within 12 days.

Many Irish people were said to have condemned the actions of the insurgents initially. It was until the execution of the leaders took place, that public support grew among the people. The execution of James Connolly, one of the leaders and Head of the Irish Citizen Army was said to have particularly infuriated Irish people the most. He was wounded during the fight and had to be evacuated from the GPO on a stretcher after the surrender and was sentenced to death by firing squad. But on the appointed day of execution, he still could not stand by himself, but the British had to carry him out to the firing squad regardless as he still laid on a stretcher. They propped him up in a chair to allow the firing to take place. He was also the last one to be shot. This act of inhumanity was said to angered Irish people further and that gave rise to an even greater desire for the Independence of

Ireland. The executecuted 16 of the Rising's most prominent leaders became Ireland's National Heroes, most especially the 7 signatories to the proclamation that were all killed by firing squad, at Kilmainham Gaol between 3rd and 12th of May 1916. Today, no document in Irish history is more important than the Proclamation of the Irish Republic, that was read out at the General Post Office in Dublin on that faithful Easter Monday by Patrick Pearse, President of the Provisional Republic.

Read profiles of the 7 signatories under the section heading

'Founding Fathers of Ireland'.

POBLACHT NA H EIREANN.

THE PROVISIONAL GOVERNMENT
OF THE
IRISH REPUBLIC
TO THE PEOPLE OF IRELAND.

IRISHMEN AND IRISHWOMEN : In the name of God and of the dead generations from which she receives her old tradition of nationhood, Ireland, through us, summons her children to her flag and strikes for her freedom.

Having organised and trained her manhood through her secret revolutionary organisation, the Irish Republican Brotherhood, and through her open military organisations, the Irish Volunteers and the Irish Citizen Army, having patiently perfected her discipline, having resolutely waited for the right moment to reveal itself, she now seizes that moment, and, supported by her exiled children in America and by gallant allies in Europe, but relying in the first on her own strength, she strikes in full confidence of victory.

We declare the right of the people of Ireland to the ownership of Ireland, and to the unfettered control of Irish destinies, to be sovereign and indefeasible. The long usurpation of that right by a foreign people and government has not extinguished the right, nor can it ever be extinguished except by the destruction of the Irish people. In every generation the Irish people have asserted their right to national freedom and sovereignty ; six times during the past three hundred years they have asserted it in arms. Standing on that fundamental right and again asserting it in arms in the face of the world, we hereby proclaim the Irish Republic as a Sovereign Independent State, and we pledge our lives and the lives of our comrades-in-arms to the cause of its freedom, of its welfare, and of its exaltation among the nations.

The Irish Republic is entitled to, and hereby claims, the allegiance of every Irishman and Irishwoman. The Republic guarantees religious and civil liberty, equal rights and equal opportunities to all its citizens, and declares its resolve to pursue the happiness and prosperity of the whole nation and of all its parts, cherishing all the children of the nation equally, and oblivious of the differences carefully fostered by an alien government, which have divided a minority from the majority in the past.

Until our arms have brought the opportune moment for the establishment of a permanent National Government, representative of the whole people of Ireland and elected by the suffrages of all her men and women, the Provisional Government, hereby constituted, will administer the civil and military affairs of the Republic in trust for the people.

We place the cause of the Irish Republic under the protection of the Most High God, Whose blessing we invoke upon our arms, and we pray that no one who serves that cause will dishonour it by cowardice, inhumanity, or rapine. In this supreme hour the Irish nation must, by its valour and discipline and by the readiness of its children to sacrifice themselves for the common good, prove itself worthy of the august destiny to which it is called.

Signed on Behalf of the Provisional Government,

THOMAS J. CLARKE.

SEAN Mac DIARMADA.	THOMAS MacDONAGH.
P. H. PEARSE.	EAMONN CEANNT,
JAMES CONNOLLY.	JOSEPH PLUNKETT

War of Independence

The War of Independence also known as Anglo-Irish war began in 1919 and continued until 1921. In 1918 a general election saw an overwhelming majority vote in favour of Irish Independence. A group of elected leaders made up of 73 out of Ireland's 106 Members of Parliament (MPs) were Sinn Féin members who refused to take up their seats in the British House of Commons. But they went ahead to set up an Irish Parliament (Dáil Éireann) in January 1919 and Declared Irish Independence and proclaimed the Irish Republic, upholding the first declaration of the 1916 Proclamation with the additional provision that Ireland was no longer a part of the United Kingdom. Britain rejected it and the new Irish Republic was recognised internationally only by the Russian Soviet Republic. Britain's refusal to acknowledge the Irish Republic a second time ultimately led to the Irish War of Independence which started in 1919 and ended in a ceasefire on July 11th of 1921. Subsequent negotiations between the major party, Sinn Fein and the UK government ensued; it led to the signing of the Anglo-Irish Treaty, which eventually resulted in (26 counties) five-sixths of Ireland break away from the United Kingdom in 1922. Under the terms of 'The Treaty', the whole Island of Ireland was granted Dominion status as the Irish Free State with an opt-out clause for the Northern Ireland region, which resulted in its decision to remain part of the UK.

A CASE FOR NORTHERN IRELAND

The Irish Treaty signed on the 6th of December 1922 in London between the British and an Irish delegation the end for the Irish War of Independence.

In accordance with the Treaty that was signd, the entire island of Ireland became a self-governing dominion called the Irish Free State which was a Constitutional Monarchy sharing with the United Kingdom and other Dominions of the British Commonwealth. However, under the Constitution of the Irish Free State, the Parliament of Northern Ireland had the option to leave the Irish Free State and return to the United Kingdom if they desired. During the intervening period, Northern Ireland exercised its right under Article 12 of the Treaty to leave the new dominion and rejoined the United Kingdom on the 8th of December 1922, having written to notify the King of their intentions on December 7, 1922 (only a day after the establishment of the Irish Free State), and to which the King replied to them in the affirmative on the 8th of

December through then Prime Minister. Northern Ireland established its own Parliament at Stormont in Belfast. But the Irish Republican Army (IRA) had a United Ireland as its goal during the conflict with British Security Forces and loyalist paramilitaries which continued from the 1960s to the 1990s known as The Troubles. Both British and Irish governments started to seek a peaceful resolution to the violent conflict, with the Good Friday Agreement signed in 1998, ending the conflict and at the same time acknowledged the legitimacy of the desire for a united Ireland, while maintaining that it must be achieved and exercised with the agreement and consent of a majority of the people of Northern Ireland, which presently upholds the wish of a majority of the people of Northern Ireland, to maintain the Union of Northern Ireland's status as part of the United Kingdom. Meanwhile, Some people in Northern Ireland and the Republic still believe strongly in the idea of a United Ireland and expect to see an Irish reunification for the whole of the island of Ireland as a single Sovereign state someday, even as Britain continues to retain Northern Ireland's current Constitutional position as part of the United Kingdom.

Recent Histories

The status of the Dominion of **Irish Free State** that was created as a result of the Anglo-Irish Treaty was upheld until 1937 when a new constitution was adopted in which the state was named "Ireland" and effectively became a Republic, with an elected non-executive President as Head of State. It was officially declared a Republic in 1949, following the Republic of Ireland Act 1948. Ireland became a member of the United Nations in December 1955, after previously being denied membership because of its neutral stance during the Second World War and not supporting the Allied cause. At the time, joining the UN involved a commitment to using force to deter aggression by one state against another if the UN thought it was necessary.

The country applied for membership of the European Economic Community (EEC) now known as the European Union (EU) in July 1961, due to the substantial economic linkages with the United Kingdom, but the founding EEC members were skeptical regarding Ireland's economic capacity and neutrality policy, and the prospect of EEC membership became doubtful in 1963. It was after much negotiations and a referendum in 1972 that Ireland finally joined the EEC in January 1973 along with the United Kingdom and Denmark.

Ireland is also a founding member of the Council of Europe and the Organisation For Economic Co-operation and Development (OECD). The Irish government has followed a policy of military neutrality through non-alignment since immediately prior to World War II and the country is consequently not a member of NATO, although it is a member of Partnership for Peace. Ireland in recent years, has been through economic crisis at different times and been through many policy changes with economic reforms, tax cuts, welfare reform, an increase in competition, and a ban on borrowing to fund current spending by the various governments since the start of Independence onwards. In the 1980s the Irish economy was in recession and large numbers of people emigrated to countries like Australia, the United Kingdom, and the USA mainly due to economic reasons. Then by the late 1990s it experienced the boom and became one of the world's fastest-growing economies in what was known as the Celtic Tiger period, lasting until the global Financial crisis leading to a recession in 2007-08. However, Ireland has recovered from the recession since and has continued to experience strong economic growth.

IRELAND'S TIMELINE

HISTORICAL EVENTS & KEY DATES

- **Circa 6,000 B.C. - 432 A.D.--Prehistoric Period**

- **6,000 B.C. - 600 B.C. -- Pre-Celtic period (Stone Age, Bronze Age)**

- **Approx. 600 B.C. - 150 B.C.** -- Arrival of Celtic peoples and establishment of Celtic culture (Iron Age)

- **Approx. 150 B.C. - 432 A.D.** - Celtic, pagan culture.
- 431 AD Palladius went as Bishop to 'the Irish who believed in Christ'.
- 432 - 1170 - Christian Celtic Culture
- 432 - 793 -- Arrival of writing, St. Patrick, and Christianity.
- St Patrick arrived to slowly convert the kings. Gaelic-Christian golden age follows.
- 500s - Christianity matured slowly in a stable society.

- 600s - The concept of a kingship of Ireland first appeared and the Uí Neíll claimed kingship over all Ireland.

- 793 - 1014 Scandinavian invasions and settlement.

- 795 - The first Vikings arrived in Ireland, pirates led by aristocrats

- 800s - Viking traders brought slaves into Ireland from now until the 1000s.

- 802 - Burning of Iona.

- 806 - Another massacre at Iona, in which 68 monks died More attacks followed. The Irish had some successes in striking back.
- 840 - Vikings began setting up defended bases and their attacks became so intense that it seemed the country was about to be conquered.
- 842 - -First Viking-Irish alliance .
- Mid 9thC - Dublin became the most important Viking city
- 860s - The Vikings turned to England
- 914-930s: - Second Viking period. After beating the Uí Neílls, the Dublin Vikings were powerful for a while. No great but monasteries were ever destroyed, even in Dublin.
- 928 - Viking massacre at Dunmore Cave, Kilkenny.
- 940s – 960s: Dublin boomed as a great European trading city.
- 956 – 980: Domnall ua Néill was King of Tara, High King of Ireland.
- 976 - Brian Boru became king of the Dal Cais, becoming a serious rival to the Uí Neílls. Supported by the Ostmen, he conquered Dublin and Leinster, then the whole country.
- 1002- Boru demanded that Mael Sechnaill recognise him as King of Ireland.
- 1005 - Brian Boru was declared Emperor of the Irish at Armagh.
- 1014 - Brian Boru defeated the Vikings at the Battle of Clontarf. The army he fought contained both Norsemen from Dublin and Leinster Irishmen. Boru was not supported by the other great kings, and he was killed by a Danish king.
- 1014 – 1170 -- Amalgamation of Scandinavian and Celtic
- 1170 "Strongbow" lands in Ireland.
- 1170 – 1922 English conquest and control of Ireland

- 1170 - 1602-09 Loose, sporadic control, mainly confined to "the Pale"

- 1186 - De Lacy was assassinated, and Meath was then passed to administrators.

- 1176 - Rebellions took place against Strongbow he died, transferring Leinster to Henry. By then he had a greater financial stake in the conquest.

- 1177 - Henry gave his rights as Lord of Ireland to his son, John.
- 1210 - King John intervened to take back lands from his nobles, and twenty Irish kings did homage to him. He expanded his King's Council in Ireland, which evolved into parliamentary sessions.

- 1216 - King John was succeeded by his young son Henry III.

- 1217 - First Treasurer of Ireland promoted. The government in England issued an order that no Irishman should be promoted to high ecclesiastical office.

- 1248 - King's Bench in Dublin instituted (today contained within the Four Courts).The liberties were gradually phased out and an elaborate system of government came in.

- 1254 - Edward I, was granted lordship of Ireland.

- 1260 - Brian O'Neill, who declared himself king of Ireland, was killed in battle by colonists. There was a series of revolts which has been seen as the beginning of a Gaelic recovery, but the colony was still expanding.

- 1277 - First salaried barons of the exchequer. A separate royal seal for Ireland was made under Henry

III. King John had also instituted sheriffs, shires, county courts and itinerant justices.

- **Late 13th C:**- English peasantry were not introduced to the west; the tenants were almost all Irish, governed by native rulers who answered to the English.

- **1303** - The Armagh succession passed to a series of Anglo-Irish prelates.

- **1315-18:**-Edward and Robert Bruce attempted to gain Irish support for the Scottish war, but alienated the colonists.

- Their three year campaign devastated much of the land, while the population were also affected by the famine sweeping Europe. There were rebellions. Edward was killed in 1318.

- **1327** - The agricultural boom in Europe was levelling off and the barons had become more interested in their more profitable English holdings.

- **1348/49** - The Black Death struck Europe during this time. This and bad harvests led to the migration of colonists of all classes back to England.

- **14th Century:**- By the beginning of this century, all native rulers were legally subject to some Anglo-Norman Baron or Earl, or the English King.

- **1459** - Richard, Duke of York, was convicted of treason against King Henry VI and lost his title of Lieutenant of Ireland. Even so, the Anglo-Irish parliament confirmed him as leader and declared Ireland independent of English law.

- **1494** - The Tudors reinstated English royal dominance. An attempt was made to dismiss the Great Earl of

Kildare from his title of Lord Deputy, but he was reinstated after raids by his Irish allies.

- **15th C:-** The Anglo-Irish magnates were more successful during this period than the Irish or the Crown, whose control shrank to four counties including Dublin.

- **1515:** Sixty counties were 'inhabited by the King's Irish enemies'. There were 60 Irish chieftains who gave themselves various titles and 30 English doing the same, all warring against one another without input from the King.

- **1534** -- Henry VIII breaks with Roman Catholic Church

- **1541** - English monarchs were styled kings of Ireland.

- **1562** - Elizabethan wars took place in Ireland.

- **1570** - Excommunication of Queen Elizabeth I

- **1602-09** - Battle of Kinsale, Flight of the Earls, beginning of Ulster Plantation.

- **1609 - 1782** : Growing English control, Cromwellian Settlement, Penal Laws.

- **1641-49** : English Civil War and Irish rebellion.

- **1649-50** : Cromwell's invasion, massacre of Drogheda
- 1685 : James II (Catholic) crowned King of England

- **1688** - William of Orange (Protestant) invades England; James II flees

- **1689** - James II lands in Ireland; seige of Derry
- **1690** - Battle of the Boyne

- **1690** - William of Orange landed in Ireland and defeated James II at the Boyne on July 1st. The Battle of the Boyne is now marked by Protestants on July 12th every year.

- **1695 -1727:-** Period of the most severe Penal Laws

- **1700:** Dublin had a population of 50,000. It boasted two ancient cathedrals and various learned societies. The country was being integrated into a single coherent unit with interrelated local economies and a common law. There was also a chain of garrison towns for maintaining a standing army. The principle landed families frequently intermarried.

- **1782 - 1800:** Grattan's Parliament
- **1789:** French Revolution begins

- **1791:** Founding of the Society of United Irishmen

- **1793:** Catholic Relief Act -- allows Catholics to vote for Parliament, but not to serve in Parliament.

- **1798** – 'The Year of the French'; United Irish uprisings and French invasion defeated.

- **1800** -- Act of Union reincorporates Irish Parliament into English Parliament -- Ireland becomes part of the "United Kingdom"

- **1801** (1st Jan). The two kingdoms were united 'forever'. The Act of Union abolished the Irish parliament, which had met at the grand Parliament House at College Green - still a potent image of Irish achievements. However, its powers were always uncertain.

- **1803** (July 23rd) - Robert Emmet's Rising. His plan had been to seize Dublin Castle to encourage the rest of the country to rebel. His followers murdered the Chief Justice, Lord

Kilwarden, and Emmet fled. He is famous for his speech in the dock after his capture, in which he said his epitaph should not be written until Ireland was a free nation. He was executed on September 20th.

- **1817:** A severe famine took place.

- **1829:** Catholic Emancipation passed. Catholics were allowed to sit in parliament and hold most high offices.

- **1831 – 1836:** Violent resistance to the collection of church tithes
- **1829** -- Catholic Emancipation Bill passed by English Parliament.

- **1830s:-** The Orange Society was banned over a political plot to put the Duke of Cumberland on the throne. Respectable Irish opinion towards the Orangemen was ambivalent. The Young Ireland movement of this decade was led by Protestant nationalists who were often anti-English.

- **1845-50** -- The Famine or Great Hunger (An Gorta Mor)

- **1879-82** -- The "Land War" -- Parnell dissolves Ladies Land League in 1882

- **1886** -- Gladstone's Home Rule bill defeated
- **1891** -- Death of Parnell

- **1893** - A 'Gaelic League' was founded to encourage every aspect of Gaelic culture that would distinguish Irishness from Englishness.
- **1894** - Irish Trades Union Congress formed.

- **1898** - The franchise was widened, making possible nationalist control of local government The United Irish League was formed.

- 1900: Queen Victoria visited Ireland and was greeted with enthusiasm by the crowds, although nationalists such as Maud Gonne were infuriated.

- 1903: Land Purchase Act (Wyndham's Act) became law, aimed at forcing landlords to sell land and allow tenants to buy it at low prices. Security of tenure prevented the consolidation of uneconomic farms, increased indebtedness and discouraged innovation.

- 1904: Sinn Féin was formed by Arthur Griffith
- 1905: Ulster Unionist Council was formed.
- 1907: Sinn Féin League inaugurated.

- 1909: The Irish Transport and General Workers' Union was formed, led by Jim Larkin and James Connolly.

- 1912: (28th Sept). Nearly half a million Protestants signed the Ulster Covenant in opposition to the Home Rule Bill. They accepted they couldn't block Home Rule for most of Ireland, but they wanted to retain Ulster within the Union. The minimum demand included the exclusion of six counties.

- 1913: Dublin Lock-out (labour dispute); Founding of Irish Citizen Army and Irish Volunteers.

- 1913: (4th Oct) The Irish Transport Union launched a six-month strike which ended without gain for the workers. At this time, the slums in Dublin were the worst in Europe. The slum owners and the major employer, William Martin Murphy, were supporters of Home Rule, which implied that this Home Rule was insufficient for the workers.

- 1914: (Aug 4th) Outbreak of World War One - most of the Irish supported Britain. (Sept). With the outbreak of war. Home Rule was postponed. An Amending Bill was to be introduced for Ulster.

- 1915: The founder of the Gaelic League Douglas Hyde was forced out by Fenians. Fenians also controlled the GAA.

- 1916 -- The Easter Rising

- 1918 -- Sinn Féin wins general election
- 1919 -- Formation of Dáil Eireann (Irish Parliament); beginning of war of independence.

- 1921 - Truce between IRA and English forces; Anglo-Irish Treaty
- 1922 - 1948 -- Irish Free State. Dominion status, gradual loosening of ties with England.

- 1922 - 23 -- Irish civil war began. The fighting lasted eight days on O'Connell Street, but elsewhere, particularly in the south and west, the anti-Treaty IRA were strong. They held Cork. Aided by the British, both in guns and soldiers. Collins pressed into action against his former comrades. The anti-Treaty IRA could no longer rely on popular support. (Aug). Cork was retaken. A week later, Arthur Griffith died of a heart attack on 12th. After attending his funeral, Collins went to Cork to tour the newly won positions.

- 1922: (Aug 22nd). Death of Michael Collins in an ambush. Some nationalists who had supported him fervently the year before now rejoiced at his death.

- 1922 - Free State leadership passed to William Cosgrave, a Veteran of 1916. His cabinet were all committed nationalists. An Emergency Powers Bill was introduced which would allow the shooting of any republicans taken in arms. 27 people were executed during the next 7 months.

- (24th Nov)Republican Erskine-Childers was shot for possessing a small revolver Collins had given him. The anti-Treaty Republican Command decreed that any Dail member who had voted for the Emergency Powers Bill could be shot on sight. Four of their leaders were then shot without trial.

- 1923: (Jan). Thirty-four more Republicans were executed. The bodies of those executed were not admitted to any churches, and wakes had to take place in theatres.

- 1926 - De Valera founded Fianna Fáil ('warriors of Ireland') from the ashes of Sinn Féin. The Republicans had split into violent and non-violent factions. De Valera believed their purposes could be achieved through democracy.

- 1927 - Fianna Fáil won almost as many seats as Cosgrave's party but refused to sit in the Dáil; this lost them votes. De Valera went to the Dáil but refused to take the oath; rejected, he went out and gave a speech to the crowd.

- 1932 - A new Parliament was built at Stormont.

- 1938 - Britain gave up rights to Treaty ports and ended the 'economic war' The loss of these ports made south-west Britain more vulnerable during the Second World War and seriously affected the Battle of the Atlantic.

- 1939: (Sept.3rd). Britain declared war on Nazi Germany. The Republic of Ireland, remaining neutral, declared an Emergency. During this year, an IRA bombing campaign hit Britain. Bombs were put in letter boxes and public lavatories, and one in a Coventry street on the 25th of August killed five people.

- 1939 --- Irish Free State declares neutrality in World War II

- 1948 - Present -- Republic of Ireland Act

- **1949** -- Éire formally declared a Republic on April 18, making the Republic of Ireland become official. Britain accepted it but guaranteed support for Northern Ireland until the Northern Irish parliament decided differently.

- **1950;** May 12˸ - Nationalists in the North of Ireland asked the government of the Republic to give Northern-elected representatives seats in the Dáil and Seanad.

- **1951˸** June 13˙ Eamon de Valera became Taoiseach with one of the smallest majorities on record˸ 74 - 69. (July 18th) The Abbey Theatre in Dublin was burned to the ground.

- **1952˸** (Jan 10th) An Aer Lingus aircraft crashed in Wales killing twenty passengers and crew.

- **1953** Jan 31st. The Princess Victoria ferry sank on its journey from Scotland to Larne in Northern Ireland, with the loss of 133 lives. (Aug 29th) Kilmainham Gaol became a national monument.

- **1954** (Jan 11th) The Irish Council of the European Movement was formed in Dublin (April 20th) Michael Manning, aged 25, was executed at Mountjoy Prison, becoming the last person to be judicially executed by the state. (Sept 5th) 27 people died when KLM Flight 633 crashed two minutes after leaving Shannon Airport.

- **1955˸** (Dec 12th) Cork Opera House at Emmet Palace was destroyed by fire. (Dec 14th) Ireland was admitted into the United Nations.

- **1956˸** (May 21st) First Cork International Film Festival opened by President Seán T O'Kelly.

- **1957** (July 22nd) The Gough Monument in Phoenix Park was wrecked by an explosion so violent it was heard all over Dublin. (Aug 7th) A 20-foot high war memorial, commemorating Limerick men who had died in World War One, was blown up.

- 1958 - (Sept 8th) Pan Am's Boeing 707 became the first Transatlantic jetliner to land in Ireland at Shannon Airport. Oct 29th - The government announced that proportional representation would be put to referendum. (Nov 4th) De Valera attended the coronation of Pope John XXIII.

- 1962: (July 6th) First airing of the Late Late Show, compered by Gay Byrne. July 13th) U Thant, Secretary General of the United Nations, arrived in Dublin. (Aug 21st) Former US President Dwight D. Eisenhower arrived in Belfast.

- 1963: (June) President John F. Kennedy visited his ancestral home at New Ross, County Wexford. He was to speak at the Oireachtas the following day.

- 1966 -- UVF (Ulster Volunteer Force) founded

- 1967 -- Formation of Northern Ireland Civil Rights Association (NICRA)

- 1968 -- Civil Rights marches begin; People's Democracy movement formed

- 1969 -- General election held, Jack Lynch declared winner.

- 1970: (21st August) The Social Democratic and Labour Party formed by Gerry Fitt. (3rdOct). Richard Nixon visited Jack Lynch in Dublin. His presence in Ireland was greeted by protests over the Vietnam war

- 1971 (3rd April). Eurovision Song Contest held in Dublin. (22nd May). Members of the Irish Women's Liberation movement took a train from Belfast to Dublin bringing back contraceptives that were banned from import into the Republic.

- **1972** -- Bloody Sunday (January 20)-British troops kill 13 civilians during peaceful march; Stormont government abolished; British embassy in Dublin burned. (22nd Jan). Taoiseach Jack Lynch and the Minister for External Affairs, Patrick Hillery, signed the Treaty of Accession to the European Communities.

- **1973:** (1st Jan). Ireland joined the European Community alongside Britain and Denmark. (6th Jan). Patrick Hillery was appointed Social Affairs Commissioner in the European Economic Community (28th Feb). The National Coalition of Fine Gael and the Labour Party won a general election in the Republic, ending sixteen years of Fianna Fáil government.

- (24th June). De Valera retired from office at the age of ninety. He was to spend his retirement at Talbot Lodge in Blackrock. Childers was inaugurated as the fourth President of Ireland.

- **1974:** (17th May) Dublin and Monaghan were attacked by loyalist Paramilitaries in the Republic in one day, killing 33 people .

- **1974:** (1st Sept). Transition Year was introduced on a pilot basis in three schools. (17th Nov). Sudden death of President Childers aged 69. (10th Dec).
- Seán MacBride, former Minister for External Affairs, was presented with the Nobel Prize for Peace. (19th Dec). Cearbhall Ó Dálaigh sworn in as the fifth President of Ireland.

- **1975:** 29th Aug). Éamon de Valera died at the age of 92. His wife had passed away on Jan 7th 1975.

- **1976:** (29th June). The highest temperature record for the twentieth century was set in Boora at 32.5C. (21st July). Christopher Ewart-Biggs, the UK ambassador, and a civil servant, Judith Cooke, were killed by an IRA landmine at Sandford, County Dublin. (22nd Oct). The President resigned after being called a 'thundering disgrace' by the Minister for Defence Paddy Donegan. (3rd Dec). Dr Patrick Hillery was inaugurated as the sixth President of Ireland.

- **1977:** (5th July). The 21st Dáil elected Jack Lynch as Taoiseach. (10th Oct). The founders of the peace movement, Mairéad Corrigan and Betty Williams, won the Nobel Peace Prize.

- **1978:** (19th Aug). Over 5,000 people took part in a rally against a nuclear power station at Carnsore Point, County Wexford. (1st Sept). The Dublin Institute of Technology was created on an ad-hoc basis by the City of Dublin VEC. (2nd Nov). Ireland's second national television channel, RTÉ 2, opened.

- **1979:** (29th Sept). Pope John Paul II arrived in Ireland for a three day visit. On the first day he appealed to the IRA for peace. (29th Nov). The Taoiseach Jack Lynch greeted European Economic Community heads of government who had come to Dublin Castle for a summit meeting. On the 5th December he announced his resignation as Taoiseach, and was succeeded by Charles Haughey on Dec 11th. (Nov).

- **1979** - Family Planning Act came into operation.

- **1980:** (April). Ireland won the Eurovision Song Contest. Mella Carroll became the Republic of Ireland's first female high court judge.

- **1981-2 --** Hunger strikes in Long Kesh Prison ("The Maze"); ten die, including Bobby Sands.

- **1982** (Feb). Corporal punishment was banned in Irish Schools. (May). The Republic of Ireland affirmed its neutrality in the Falklands Conflict and opposed European sanctions against Argentina.

- **1983:** A referendum in the Republic led to the Eighth Amendment of the Constitution, concerning abortion. This was to prevent abortion, which was already illegal, from being legalised.

- **1984** (Jan). A 15-year-old girl, Ann Lovett, died after giving birth in a religious grotto. (March). Gerry Adams shot and wounded in Belfast. (June). A visit to Ireland by US President Ronald Reagan was met by protests in Dublin.

- **1985:** (July). Ballinspittle became a place of pilgrimage after two women claim to have seen a statue of the Virgin Mary move.

- **1986:** June). Referendum on removing the prohibition on divorce returned a no vote.

- **1987:** (March). Irish National Lottery launched. (26th May). A referendum approved the Single European Act.

- **1998 --** Good Friday Agreement, signed April 10th. (19th March). Major anti-Apartheid demonstration in Dublin. Nelson Mandela was awarded the freedom of Dublin in July.
- **1989:** (March). Three Irish soldiers with the United Nations were killed in South Lebanon.
- **1990:** (3rd Dec.) - Mary Robinson became the first woman president of Ireland. (July 1st) ANC Leader Nelson Mandela and his wife Winnie arrived Dublin for a two-day visit.

- **1991** - Ireland signed the Treaty on European Union at Maastricht. It received a guarantee that its strict abortion law would not be affected.

- **1992** (5th Feb) - In the Republic, Irish voters approved a loosening of the abortion law. Access to information was guaranteed and travel abroad to have an abortion was permitted.

- **1993:** (15th Dec). The Downing Street Declaration began a peace process to end in a political settlement. John Major signed for Britain and Albert Reynolds for the Republic. Reynolds was Taoiseach of a Coalition dominated by Fianna Fáil.

- **1994:** (31st Aug). IRA ceasefire. It was met with enthusiasm in republican areas of NI, but the Unionists had reservations because it looked like the republicans had achieved something. (Dec). Martin McGuinness headed a Sinn Féin delegation at Stormont. This was ground-breaking contact between Sinn Féin and the British government.

- **1995 :** (Nov). - Bill Clinton met Gerry Adams and shook hands with him. His involvement was partly down to personal conviction and partly due to the fact that there were forty million Americans of Irish descent.

- 1996 - **(Oct).** Mary McAleese became President of Ireland.

- **1998 :** (1st April) - Disagreements dragged on between the British and Irish governments over the North/South body that was to associate NI with the Republic of Ireland.

- **1999:** (17th Dec). Inaugural summit meeting of the British-Irish Intergovernmental Conference.

- **2000:** (Sept). Bertie Ahern came under pressure to cut taxes in order to combat inflation. (Dec 12th). Bill Clinton came to Dublin as part of his peace mission for Northern Ireland.

- **2001:** (March 8th). Tony Blair and Bertie Ahern met for talks with the major political parties in Belfast. (June 7th). Irish voters rejected the Nice Treaty in a referendum.

- **2002** (Jan). The Euro replaced the punt in the Republic of Ireland. (9th Jan). Mikhail Gorbachev received the Freedom of Dublin. (March) An attempt by the Irish government to tighten already strict anti-abortion laws was defeated by a small majority in a constitutional referendum in the Republic.

- **2002** (21st July). On the 30th anniversary of Bloody Friday, the IRA offered its 'sincere apologies and condolences' to victims who had been 'non-combatants'.

- **2003:** (21st Jan). The Spire of Dublin on O'Connell Street was officially completed. (7th (April). US President George W Bush arrived in Northern Ireland for discussions with Tony Blair, and also met Taoiseach Bertie Ahern. (10th April). The British and Irish governments suspended a blueprint for devolution in Northern Ireland at the last minute. (1st May) Ireland, as holder of the EU presidency, hosted ceremonies to welcome the EU's ten new member states. (25th June).

- US President George W Bush arrived at Shannon Airport for a n EU-US summit. (30th June). French President Jacques Chirac said that Ireland's presidency of the EU was 'the best presidency ever'.

- **2004** (1st Oct). Mary McAleese was elected unopposed for a second term as President of Ireland. She was inaugurated on Nov 11th. (16th Oct). Taoiseach Bertie Ahern held talks with United Nations Secretary General Kofi Annan in Dublin.

- **2005** (7th Feb). Irish Taoiseach Bertie Ahern laid the foundation stone of a new town in the Republic, Adamstown. (13th June). The Irish language was officially recognised as a working language by the European Union. (June). Death of former Taoiseach Charles J Haughey. He was given a state funeral.

- **2006**: (22nd May). Belfast City airport was renamed the George Best Belfast City Airport on what would have been George Best's 60th birthday. Best, an internationally famous footballer from Belfast, had died the previous year.

- **2008**: (April 2) Taoiseach Bertie Ahern announced his resignation. (May 6th) Bertie Ahern stepped down as Taoiseach. (May 7th) Brian Cowen was confirmed as the new Taoiseach. (Sept). Ireland officially declared it was in a recession.

- **2009**: (Feb 27th). The largest bank robbery in the Republic of Ireland's history targetted the Bank of Ireland in Dublin. Seven suspects were arrested and €4 million was recovered the next day. (March 17th).

- Taoiseach Brian Cowen and Northern Irish leaders met US President Barack Obama in the White House.

- (March 21st). Ireland won the Grand Slam for the first time in 61 years. (April 7th). A severe budget was announced in the

Republic. (June 25th). The International Monetary Fund said Ireland was suffering the worst recession of any advanced economy.

- **2010:** Feb 15th-16th). The Pope met Irish Bishops and condemned child abuse. (March 30th). It was announced that the Irish government was to provide the Anglo Irish Bank with a bailout of €8.3bn. Next day, the Anglo Irish reported a €12.7bn loss. (Nov) - Government agrees 85bn euro rescue package with EU and IMF, in bid to tackle huge hole in public finances. Government drafts austerity programme entailing four years of tax rises and spending cuts.

- **2011:** Jan 18th). Taoiseach Brian Cowen survived a Fianna Fáil confidence vote. However, on the 22nd he announced he would be stepping down as leader of Fianna Fáil, but would continue running the government until the next election.

- (Jan- 26th) Micheál Martin was elected leader of Fianna Fáil. May (17th - 20th). British Queen Elizabeth began a four-day visit to the Republic of Ireland, the first visit by a reigning British monarch in a century. One of the Queen's first acts was to lay a wreath at the Garden of Remembrance. (May 23rd).

- US President Barack Obama visited the Republic at the start of a week-long tour of Europe. (Oct 29th). Michael D. Higgins emerged as the next President of Ireland. (Dec 15th). The International Monetary Fund released €3.9 billion in loans to Ireland.

- **2012:** (March 24th). Former Taoiseach Bertie Ahern announced that he would resign from Fianna Fáil in the wake of the Mahon Tribunal's final report. The tribunal found that he had failed to account 'truthfully' for a number of financial transactions, but it did not accuse him of corruption.

- **2013:** (Jan 1st). Ireland took on a six-month Presidency of the EU. (May 7th). Irish soldiers who had fought for the Allies during World War Two and had subsequently been accused of desertion were granted an official amnesty and apology. (June). The G8 summit was held in Enniskillen amid massive security. A large protest was held on June 17th, but the summit passed off without serious incident. (August 30th). Nobel prize winning poet and playwright Seamus Heaney died. (Sept). The Church of Ireland appointed its first female bishop.

- **2014:** Jan 31st. Two Irish students died in a fire at a hall of residence in Belgium. Feb 1st). People were evacuated in Limerick following flooding. (Aug 21st). Death of former Taoiseach Albert Reynolds. (Sept 12th). Death of former DUP leader and First Minister Ian Paisley. (April) - President Michael D Higgins makes official visit to Britain, the first ever by an Irish head of state.

- 2015: (May 22nd). A referendum was held on same-sex marriage in the Republic. A majority voted in favour. (July 6th). The oldest Irish-born woman, Kathleen Snavely, died aged 113 in New York. (Dec 17th). Arlene Foster became the first woman to lead the Democratic Unionist Party.

- **2016:** (March) Events commemorating the Centenary of the Easter Rising took place. (Aug). - European Commission orders Ireland to recover up to 13bn euros (£11bn) from the technology giant Apple in back taxes, after ruling that the firm was granted undue benefits amounting to illegal state aid. The government says it will appeal against the ruling, on the grounds that it implies that Ireland is a tax haven and will harm job creation and investment.

- **2017**: (March 1st) - Irish travellers were granted recognition as an ethnic minority. (March 21st). Death of Sinn Féin's Martin McGuinness from a rare heart condition.

- (June 14th) Leo Varadkar of Fine Gael became Taoiseach. He was the youngest person ever to do so, and also the first gay and ethnic minority person to take the role of Taoiseach in the Republic (Nov. 18th) Sinn Fein's Gerry Adams announces hie intention to step aside as party leader in 2018. (Oct. 16th). Storm Ophelia struck Ireland, resulting in three deaths. (Nov. 2017) Ireland's deputy Prime Minister Frances Fitzgerald agreed to resigned over handling of a police whistleblowing scandal, to avoid a snap election.

- **2018**: (Feb 6th) 100 years since women in Ireland got the right to vote for the first time. (Feb 10th) Mary Lou McDonald was named as Gerry Adam's replacement as the leader of Sinn Féin.

- (May 25th) Ireland voted decisively in a referendum to reform the country's strict abortion laws, which had effectively banned all terminations. It was Ireland's sixth referendum on the issue, and the country's younger voters led it in a two-thirds landslide in favour of ending the ban.

- (August 25th) Pope Francis visited Ireland as part of the World Meeting of Families.

- **2019** – Government Officials gathered in the Mansion House to mark the centenary of Dáil Éireann's formation. (100 years of the Irish Parliarment).

SECTION THREE

NATIONAL SYMBOLS

National Symbols of any country are the pride of that country as they represent the varied customary beliefs and heritage of the country, and Ireland has quite a few which ideally represents the country's rich cultural heritage. Among the official symbols of Ireland is the 'Coat of Arms' featuring the Harp or even the harp itself. Then there is the National Flag, National Flower, National Colours, the Irish National Anthem, National Bird and Motto, although there controversies as to whether Ireland has a national motto or not. There are some other symbols directly associated with Ireland that are not neccesarilly national symbols, but they are considered very important in Irish culture. For example, the Irish Celtic Cross, the traditional Irish Ring that is otherwise called the Claddagh Ring; it is_believed to symbolise love & friendship. There is the Irish Potato also, or the mythical leprechaun, even the famous Guinness Beer, etc. Most of the natiional symbols are used by State institutions as well as private bodies throughout the Republic of Ireland and by the Irish abroad, especially images that are related to the Celtic Harp and St. Patrick's Shamrock. They can be seen on many souvenirs and traditional costumes of the locals too because they are unique and very much valued by the people of Irish origin and other citizens of the country at home and abroad.

THE COAT OF ARMS

The Irish 'Coat of Arms' is the Official National Emblem of the Republic of Ireland. It is comprised of a Celtic Harp with silver strings on a field azure on deep blue background. There has been Earlier versions too, such as the Coat of Arms of the former lordship of Ireland, the Ancient Arms of the Province of Meath, and the Shield of Arms of Ireland.

THE HARP:

The Harp, although a musical instrument, it's the symbol of the Ireland. The Harp symbol is used extensively by the State to mark official documents, such as on the Seal of the President of Ireland, Seal of the Taoiseach, Tanaiste and Government Ministers. The Harp is also the image used on the cover of the Irish Passport and on the back of Irish coins that are minted in Ireland. Some business corporations wishing to display their 'Irish-ness' use it too. For example, Arthur Guinness—makers of Guinness Beer have the 'Harp' as their logo. It is also used as part of the logo of popular Irish budget airline, Ryanair.

The popular National Symbol is also the Personal Arms of the President of Ireland and flown as the Presidential Standard whilst he or she is in office. The Harp was adopted as the emblem of the Irish Free State when it separated from the United Kingdom in 1922 and were formally registered as the Arms of Ireland with the Chief Herald of Ireland in November 1945. The symbolic significance of 'Coat of Arms' particularly the importance of the 'Irish Harp' (also known as the Celtic-Harp or Gaelic-Harp) represents nationalism and the historical splendour of Ireland.

OVERVIEW:

According to ancient history, Ireland Arms have been in use as the heraldic emblem dating as far back as the 12th century, and there have been several variants of the arms since then, from the Lordship of Ireland, the medieval realm of Ireland that existed under the English crown are all said to have had separate arms. When the crowns of England, Scotland and Ireland were united in 1603, they were integrated into the unified royal coat of arms of kingdoms of England, Scotland and Ireland. Before then, the arms were adopted by Henry VIII of England when he ended the period of Lordship of Ireland declared Ireland to be a kingdom in 1541. As the King of the new Kingdom of Ireland, King Henry VIII declared the arms as the official national symbol of Ireland and stamped it onto the currency of his new dominion.

National Flag of Ireland

The Republic of Ireland's National Flag is made up of three colours (Green – White - Orange) and divided into three rectangular sections of equal size and twice as long in length. The flag is known in Irish as Bratach na hÉireann, translated as the 'Irish Tricolour' due to its vertical three colours of the Green, White and Orange which is also used by many as the nation's favourite colours. But the National Colour of Ireland is Green.

The Green section of the flag is said to represent Irish Roman Catholics, the Orange represents the minority Protestants, and the middle White section stands for peace and hope for a United Ireland. The flag symbolises the rich cultural heritage of Ireland and has been a fundamental part of Irish identity. It is expressed in the Constitution as the entitlement of every person born in Ireland to be part of the

Independent Irish nation, regardless of religion, ethnic origin, or political affiliation.

BRIEF HISORY OF THE IRISH FLAG:

"The flag was said to be presented as a gift in 1848 to an Irish man named Thomas Francis Meagher by a small group of French women who were sympathetic to the Irish cause – it was intended to symbolise the inclusion and hoped-for union between the Roman Catholics and Protestants. The significance of the colours outlined by Meagher himself was – "The white in the centre signifies a lasting truce between Orange and Green and I trust that beneath its folds the hands of Irish Protestants and Irish Catholics may be clasped in generous and heroic brotherhood." The tricolour came to be regarded as the national flag after it was raised above Dublin's General Post Office during the Easter Rising of 1916, and thereafter adopted by the Irish Republic during the Irish War of Independence. It was not until later before the tricolour was given constitutional status under the 1937 Constitution of Ireland.

In 2016 in the lead up to mark the centenary anniversary of the 1916 Easter Rising, every school in Ireland received tricolour flag, presented by a member of Ireland's Defence Forces, who educated the students on the history behind the flag and its meaning.

An Earlier Flag (The O'Neill Flag)

The O'Neill Flag was the national flag and was used as early

as 1642, by the leader of the O'Neill Dynasty, Owen Roe O'Neill. It was considered the Primary Flag of Ireland. Then, the flag was a simple green with a harp in the middle. It was used until the Easter Rising of 1916.

The Irish National Flag has similarities to the Flags of other countries, and it is importance to note the differences. See the followings: -

The Irish Flag and Italian Flag — *Both country's flags are a vertical tricolour and have the Green colour at the hoist. This can be a cause for be mistaken the flags for each country. The clear difference is that the third band Irish flag is orange while that of the Italian flag is flame red.*

Irish Flag (Green-White-Orange) & Italian Flag (Green-White-Red)

The Irish Flag and Ivory Coast Flag – *Both the Irish flag and that of Côte d'Ivoire (Ivory Coast) flag are vertical tricolour flags with the same three colours. Green, White, Orange colours. The only difference is that while the Ireland Flag place the green first (at the hoist), the Cote d' Ivoire (Ivory Coast) place their Orange colour first instead.*

Irish Flag (Green-White-Orange) & Ivory Coast Flag (Orange- White-Green)

The Irish Flag and Indian Flag — *Both country's flags have the Green, White, Orange colours. The clear difference is that the Irish flag is placed vertically, that of the Italian flag placed horizontally, with the Ashoka Chakra, wheel, in navy* **blue** *at its centre.*

Guidelines for the Care of the Irish National Flag

- The National Flag of Ireland should **never** be defaced by placing slogans, logos, lettering or pictures of any kind on it, draped on cars, trains, boats or other modes of transport and should always be carried aloft and free, except when used to drape a coffin; on such an occasion, the green should be at the head of the coffin.

- Care should always be taken to ensure that the National Flag does not touch the ground, trail in water or become entangled in trees or other obstacles.

- When displaying the flag, no flag should fly higher than the National Flag and it should be placed on the right of any formation, that is to the observers left.

- When being flown with the EU flag, the EU flag should go immediately bedside the Irish flag.

Flag of Ireland & the EU Flag

The National Flower of Ireland

Shamrock is The National Flower of Ireland

SHAMROCK LEAF

The word Shamrock is derived from the Irish word 'Seamrog' meaning 'little plant' or 'young plant.'

The Shamrock is a small green three-leafed plant that grows in Ireland. It holds much meaning to Irish people and probably the most loved symbols of Ireland. It is said to represent the green landscape of the Irish nation. As a National Symbol, the three leaf Shamrock is adopted by Ireland's National Airline, Aer Lingus as their official Logo. The Irish National Rugby Union team also has a clover on their T-shirts. However, shamrock is most associated with Saint Patrick, Ireland's Patron Saint. It is said that the Saint had found the three-leaf clover to be an extraordinary plant and used it as a symbol to illustrate the doctrine of the Holy Trinity of the 'Father, Son and Holy Spirit. It is now a common sight and on displays everywhere across Ireland and around the world during St. Patrick's Day Festival celebrations in March every year.

As a symbol of good relationship between Ireland and USA, the Taoiseach presents US President with a bowl of shamrock at the White House on 17th March each year.

The plant also has a four-leafed variation of the three-leafed and its often referred to as the 'lucky clover' is but they are quite rare and considered a symbol of good luck in Irish culture because its rarity.

The followings are a few more myths behind the four-leaf clover or Shamrock.

- That it drives away bad omen and protects against evil.
- Gives fortune to those who finds it.
- If you give a four-leaf clover to someone else, your luck will double. It is also an old age belief that if someone carried a four-leaf clover, they would have the ability to see fairies.

Because of its rarity, it is estimated that the chances of finding a four-leaf clover is one to 10,000.

NATIONAL BIRD OF IRELAND

Credit: John Holden

The Republic of Ireland has no known official National Bird but the Northern Lapwing, also known as the Peewit or Pewit was declared the Republic of Ireland's National Bird in 1990 by a committee of the Irish Wildlife Conservancy. Other than that, the 'Rook' (Corvus frugilegus) has also been considered Ireland's national bird by some groups. In 2016 Niall Hatch of Birdwatch Ireland listed 10 more possible birds to be considered the national bird. These includes European Robin, Peregrine Falcon, Common House Martin, Eurasian Curlew, Roseate Tern, Barn owl, common Swift, Bohemian Waxwing, Eurasian Blackcap, Northern Pintail. While many people favour the Wren, which is one of Ireland's smallest birds. stocky in nature and constantly moving or twitching.

National Bird

The Lapwing

National Songs

The National Anthem of Ireland

The Irish National Anthem is the national song of the Republic of Ireland. It is called 'A Soldier's Song' (Amhrán na  bhFiann in Irish). It serves as a call to unify the country and bring an era of prosperity and peace upon the people. It has two versions to it – The English version and the Irish language version.

Brief History: The words of the Anthem were written by someone named Peadar Kearney in 1907. He was said to collaborate with another person called Patrick Heeney who was mainly responsible for producing the melodic tune. It was then published by an Irish Freedom Newspaper titled Bulmer Hobson in 1912 and translated the Irish-language version in 1923 by a third person by the name Liam Ó Rinn. The Anthem was not popular until it was sung by the Easter Rising Rebels in front of the Irish General Post Office (GPO) during the Rising in 1916. The chorus of the song was officially adopted as the National Anthem of the Republic of Ireland in 1926, and henceforth sung at all national functions at official level and in schools.

The first two lines are played together to form the Presidential Salute, and this is normally played whenever the President of Ireland attends an official event. Prior to the adoption of the new Anthem (A Soldier's Song), a different one known as Amhran na bhFiann "God Save Ireland" was used from the 1870s until Independence in 1922.

THE NATIONAL ANTHEM IN ENGLISH

A Soldier's Song

Soldiers are we
whose lives are pledged to Ireland;
Some have come
from a land beyond the wave.
Sworn to be free,
No more our ancient sire land
Shall shelter the despot or the slave.
Tonight we man the gap of danger
In Erin's cause, come woe or weal
'Mid cannons' roar and rifles peal,
We'll chant a soldier's song.

THE NATIONAL ANTHEM

IRISH VERSION

Amhrán na bhFiann

Sinne Fianna Fáil
A tá fé gheall ag Éirinn,
buion dár slua
Thar toinn do ráinig chugainn,
Fé mhóid bheith saor.
Sean tír ár sinsir feasta
Ní fhagfar fé'n tiorán ná fé'n tráil
Anocht a théam sa bhearna bhaoil,
Le gean ar Ghaeil chun báis nó saoil
Le guna screach fé lámhach na bpiléar
Seo libh canaídh Amhrán na bhFiann.

THE EMERALD ISLE: IRELAND INFORMATION MADE SIMPLE

SECTION FOUR

FOUNDING FATHERS OF IRELAND'S & THE HEROES OF 1916

Officially, the 7 Revolutionaries who signed the Declaration of the 1916 Easter Rising and were executed by the British Military, are considered the 'Founding Fathers' of Ireland and the people of Ireland continue to honour them as such. There are several monuments dedicated to them in Dublin and other parts of the country and major streets named in their memory. The Proclamation that they signed sets out their aspirations for freedom for Ireland away from British Rule and to create an Ireland where all people will be free to accomplish their potential regardless of their wealth, class or religion.

A SHORT PROFILE OF THE 7 SIGNATORIES AS FOLLOWS:

Éamonn Ceannt

Born in Galway in 1881, prior to the Rising, Ceannt was an employee of the Dublin Corporation. He was a co-founder of the Irish Volunteers. As the commander of the Fourth Battalion of Irish Volunteers during the Rising, he took possession of the South Dublin Union, precursor to the modern-day St. James's Hospital. He was executed on the 8th of May 1916.

James Connolly

Born in Edinburgh, Connolly emigrated to Dublin in 1896 where he founded the Irish Socialist Republican Party. He spent much of the first decade of the twentieth century in America, he returned to Ireland to campaign for workers' rights. In 1913, Connolly was one of the founders of the Irish Citizen Army. During the Easter Rising he was appointed Commandant-General of the Dublin forces, leading the group that occupied the General Post Office. Unable to stand to during his execution due to wounds received during the Rising, Connolly was executed while sitting down on 12 May 1916. He was the last of the leaders to be executed.

Séan MacDiarmada

Born in 1884 in Leitrim, MacDiarmada emigrated to Glasgow in 1900 and from there to Belfast in 1902. He joined the Irish Republican Brotherhood in 1906 while still in Belfast, later transferring to Dublin in 1908. MacDiarmada was appointed as a member of the provisional committee of Irish Volunteers from 1913, and was subsequently drafted onto the military committee of the I.R.B. in 1915. During the Rising MacDiarmada served in the GPO He was executed on 12 May 1916.

Joseph Mary Plunkett

Born 1887 in Dublin, Plunkett was initially educated in England, though he returned to Ireland and graduated from U.C.D. in 1909. He joined the Irish Volunteers in 1913, subsequently gaining membership of the I.R.B. in 1914. During the planning of the Rising, Plunkett was appointed Director of Military Operations, with overall responsibility for military strategy. Plunkett was one of those who were stationed in the GPO during the Rising. He married Grace Gifford while in Kilmainham Gaol following the surrender and was executed on 4 May 1916.

Patrick Pearse

Born in Dublin in 1879. He graduated from the Royal University in 1901 with a degree in Arts and Law. He was a keen believer in the value of education, and established two schools, Coláiste Éanna and Coláiste Íde, devoted to the education of Irish children through the Irish language. One of the founder members of the Irish Volunteers, and the author of the Proclamation of Independence, Pearse was present in the GPO during the Rising, and was Commander in Chief of the Irish forces. He was executed on 3 May 1916.

Thomas MacDonagh

A native of Tipperary, born in 1878, MacDonagh spent the early part of his career as a teacher. MacDonagh was well versed in literature, his enthusiasm and erudition earning him a position in the English department at University College Dublin. He was appointed director of training for the Irish Volunteers in 1914, later joining the I.R.B. MacDonagh was appointed to the I.R.B. military committee in 1916. He was commander of the Second Battalion of Volunteers that occupied Jacob's biscuit factory and surrounding houses during the Rising. He was executed on 3 May 1916.

Thomas James Clarke

Thomas James Clarke Born on the Isle of Wight in 1857, Clarke's

father was a soldier in the British army. He served fifteen years imprisonment for his role in a bombing campaign in London, 1883-1898. He held the post of Treasurer to the Irish Republican Brotherhood and was a member of the Supreme Council from 1915. The first signatory of the Proclamation of Independence through deference to his seniority, Clarke was with the group that occupied the General Post Office (GPO) He was executed on 3rd of May 1916.

THE FOLLOWING PAGES
FEATURE IRELAND'S HEROIC
(1916) WOMEN

A SHORT PROFILE:

Elizabeth Farrell

Elizabeth O'Farrell was born on the 5th of November 1884. She was an Irish nurse and member of Cumann na mBan, (pronounced – Cumann na man), and best known for delivering the Surrender during the Easter Rising of 1916.

She acted as a dispatcher delivering bulletins and instructions to the rebel outposts around Dublin. She was one of three women, including Winifred Carney, who remained in the General Post Office in Dublin until the end of the Rising. Along with her friend and fellow nurse, Julia Grenan, she cared for the wounded including James Connolly.

O'Farrell was handed a Red Cross insignia and a white flag and asked to deliver the surrender to the British military. She emerged into heavy fire on Moore Street, which abated when her white flag was recognised. Accompanied by a priest and three soldiers she brought the order of surrender to the insurgent positions throughout the city. Despite assurances that she would not be taken prisoner, O'Farrell was held overnight at Ship Street Barracks after the surrender, but was later released and apologised to. She remained active in Republican politics until her death in Fatima House in Bray, County Wicklow on 25 June 1957. She was buried in the Republican Plot in Glasnevin Cemetery alongside Julia Grenan.

Margaret Skinnider

Margaret Skinnider was born in 1893 to Irish parents in the Lanarkshire town of Coatbridge in Scotland. She trained as a mathematics teacher and joined Cumann na mBan in Glasgow, she was also involved in the women's suffrage movement in Glasgow. During her trips to Ireland Skinnider came under the influence of Constance Markievicz and became active in smuggling detonators and bomb-making equipment into Dublin (in her hat) in preparation for the 1916 Easter Rising. She, along with Madeleine Ffrench-Mullen spent time in the hills around Dublin testing dynamites.

She was told of the plans for the Rising and came to Ireland on Holy Thursday, 1916. Countess de Markievicz had a uniform made for her. Margaret joined the Irish Citizen Army as a dispatch rider and was a scout for the St Stephen's Green garrison. She was mentioned three times for bravery in the dispatches sent to the GPO. On the Wednesday she was wounded and hospitalised for several weeks. The doctors decided she was too ill to be imprisoned and she evaded arrest on her release from hospital. In 1917 she went to the US where she lectured on the Rising, she also wrote her story there, and published it in New York in 'as Doing my bit for Ireland'. Skinnider later returned to Ireland and took up a teaching post in Dublin in 1917. During the War of Independence, she was arrested and imprisoned. In the civil war she became Paymaster General of the Irish Republican Army until she was arrested in 1923 and held at North Dublin Union. There she became Director of

Training for the prisoners. After her release from prison she worked as a teacher in the Sisters of Charity primary school in Kings Inn Street, a position that she retained until her retirement in 1961. She was a member of the National Teacher's Organisation, INTO, and later became its President in 1956. During her tenure as President she represented Ireland at the World Conference of the Organisation of the Teaching Professions in Manila, Philippines. She fought in particular for the rights of women - this agitation resulted in the introduction of common incremental salary sales for women and single men in 1949. She lived her last years in Glenageary, County Dublin. She died on 10 October 1971 and was buried in the Republican plot in Glasnevin Cemetery.

Kathleen Florence Lynn

Kathleen Florence Lynn was an Irish Sinn Féin politician, activist and medical doctor. She was born in County Mayo, on 28 January 1874 to a Dublin Church of Ireland family and educated in England and Germany before graduating as a doctor in 1899 from the Royal University of Ireland. During the Easter Rising Dr Kathleen Lynn was ordered to join the City Hall Garrison. When arrested, she described herself as a 'Red Cross' doctor but also belonged to the Irish Citizen Army. After the Rising she was held under house arrest until August 1916. Dr Lynn remained active in politics after the Rising, joined Sinn Féin and took part in the War of Independence.

She also opposed the Treaty of 1921 and, although elected to the Dáil, she did not take her seat. By 1926 she withdrew from national politics but continued with her involvement in local politics. Her main preoccupation for the remainder of her life was St Ultan's Hospital, the first infant hospital in Dublin which she had founded in 1919 with the assistance of her friend Madeleine ffrench Mullen. Dr Kathleen Lynn died in Ballsbridge on September 14, 1955.

Constance Georgine Markievicz

 Georgine Markievicz was an Irish Sinn Féin and Fianna Fáil politician, and revolutionary nationalist. She was born Constance Gore-Booth on 4 February 1868 in United Kingdom. She became the wife of a Polish Count and was officially known as Countess de Markievicz. She was also an artist and an actress. Countess de Markievicz came to the national, social and labour causes in her forties when she joined a number of organisations including the Daughters of Ireland, (Inghinidhe na hEireann) and the Irish Citizen Army and became an active member of the organisation. She took part during Easter Week as a member of the Irish Citizen Army, her rank was Staff Lieutenant and she became Second-in-Command in the garrison. As a leader of the Rising, Countess de Markievicz was sentenced to death. This was commuted to penal servitude for life because she was a woman and was imprisoned until 1917. In the 1918 General Election she became the first female that was elected to the British House of Commons. She too refused to take her seat as she supported the

Sinn Féin policy of abstentionism. Along with the other Sinn Féin TDs, they formed the first Dáil Éireann and she was appointed Minister of Labour in the First Dáil, (1919-1922), but spent much of this period in jail. She died in Dublin on July 15, 1927.

Maria Winifred Carney

Maria Winifred Carney, also known as Winnie Carney, was a suffragist, trade unionist and Irish Independence activist. She was born on 4 December 1887 in Bangor, County Down. Carney joined Cumann na mBan, the women's auxiliary of the Irish in 1914. She was present with Connolly in the Dublin General Post Office during the Easter Rising in 1916. Carney was the only woman present during the initial occupation of the building, which she entered armed with a typewriter and a revolver. While not a combatant, she was given the rank of adjutant and was among the final group (including Connolly and Patrick Pearse) to leave the GPO. Carney, left the GPO with the rest of the rebels after their surrender and was held in Kilmainham Gaol and later moved to Mountjoy Prison. By August 1916 Carney was imprisoned in Aylesbury prison with two others. However, she was released two days before Christmas of 1916. After the Anglo-Irish Treaty and the formation of the Irish Free State, Carney sided with the Anti-Treaty forces and was arrested several times. Carney suffered years of ill health which meant that she was no longer active in politics in her later years. She died in November 1943.

Lucy Agnes Smyth

As a member of Cumann na mBan Lucy Agnes was heavily involved in the activities of the organisation, and on Easter Monday in 1916, Smyth, aged 34 years at the time, played a dangerous role of carrying the arms from a house prior to it being raided. The following day she was given the task of carrying vital messages to the GPO while also being a member of the First-Aid department. Lucy tended the wounded - including James Connolly at the GPO and the Hibernian Bank. She was also part of a group of 11 Cumann na Man nurses who escorted the wounded - under fire in the battlefield to Jervis Street Hospital at the time of the evacuation of the burning GPO. In the years following the Rising, Lucy was an integral member of the Irish National Aid Association and Volunteer Dependents' Fund. Considered as an 'ordinary' person who did extraordinary things, she was also awarded the 1916 Easter Rising medal, the Service (1917-1921) medal, the 1916 survivors medal and the Truce (1921) In 1938, she was given a military pension. Lucy Agnes Smyth died at the age of 90, in November 1972 and buried in Glasnevin cemetery in Dublin along with her husband Tom Byrne and son Myles Byrne.

Áine Ceannt

Áine Ceannt on the other hand, was wife to Eamonn Ceannt. Aine and she was vice-president of Cumann na mBan from 1917 to 1925, and as an anti-Treaty activist was jailed in Mountjoy for a year during the Civil War. She later became a founding member of the apolitical White Cross organisation, helping to provide sustenance, education and benefit to the dependents of those Volunteers killed or permanently disabled during the course of the Irish revolution. The night before her husband, Éamonn Ceannt' was executed, he wrote a heartbreaking letter in Kilmainham Gaol to his wife saying that, he was 'calmly awaiting the end.' Ceannt, like the other Easter Rising leaders, knew the firing squad was going to happen in the morning. **Aine Ceannt** is seen as a good example of the wives of all the men who fought and died in 1916 Easter Rising, including widows of the husbands who had not signed the Proclamation. One of the wives was said to be the only family member who had five children under the age of 13, and five months pregnant with her fifth child during the period of her husband's execution. For the 7 Signatories; Séan MacDiarmada was said to have a girlfriend but he didn't get to marry her before his execution.

2016 marked the 100 years (Centenary) anniversary of the 1916 Easter Rising, with commemorations around the country.

SECTION FIVE

IRISH SYSTEM OF GOVERNMENT

Houses of the
Oireachtas
Tithe an Oireachtais

(Official Logo of the Irish Parliament)

*I*reland is a Constitutional Republic with a Parliamentary System of Government with the President as the Head of State and the Prime Minister as Head of Government. The **National Parliament** is known as the Oireachtas in Irish, it consists of the President of Ireland and two Houses of legislature, which are the Houses of Representatives known as the Dáil Éireann (Lower House), and the Senate is known as (Seanad Éireann) which is the Upper House. The Houses of the Oireachtas sit in Leinster House, an eighteenth-century Ducal Palace situated in Kildare Street, Dublin 2.

The leading party in power at any time directly runs the government, which includes all departments, headed by elected officials such as the Ministers, and Junior Ministers that are appointed by the Head of government, who also directs the Cabinet Ministers. The current government is under the Fine Gael party that is led by Taoiseach Leo Varadkar, who is also the President of the party. It is in the

Irish Constitution that should the Government at any point fails to retain the support of the majority of the Members of Dáil Éireann, it should be dissolved, and a General Election called to form a new Government.

Legislative Arms

THE DAIL ÉIREANN: The *Dáil Éireann* or 'the Dáil' for short, is the Lower House of Representative and principal chamber of the Irish Parliament (Oireachtas). Members are known as *Teachta Dála*, which in English means "Deputy to the Dáil" and they are generally called "TDs" or "Deputies for short.

The Irish Constitution states that, there must be at least one TD for every 20,000 to 30,000 people. Currently, every Constituency in Ireland elects at least three and up to five TDs, depending on the size and population of an area, and there are one hundred and fifty-eight (158) TDs representing 40 Constituencies in the Dáil, including some who do not belong to a political party and are Independents. TDs are directly elected at least once every five years by the public – usually by local people in the constituencies they come from to represent their interests and concerns in the Dáil. And as the main legislative arm of government with responsibilities for making laws for the good governance of the country, their main functions demand that they bring forward matters of public interests to the House to be debated upon, propose new bills to be passed into law and also introduce amendments to existing policies. TDs also hold regular advice sessions (advice clinics) throughout their constituencies which enables constituents to continue to meet them personally to discuss matters of importance.

The Dáil acts as the government's 'Watch-dog' and make government accountable. Opposition Party Leaders engage the Head of Government and Ministers to Parliamentary questions sessions on set days and specific times set aside for Dáil members. They ask serious questions which demand direct answers. TDs also have an option to submit written questions which could not be put forward during the oral sessions and expect to receive written replies equally to their respective questions. The Ceann-Comhairle (pronounced Kian Ko-orla) is the Chairperson and Speaker in Dáil Éireann (Parliament). The person who holds this position is elected by members of the Dáil from among their numbers in the first session after each General Election. The Ceann Comhairle conducts the affairs and business of the House and ensures there is orderliness in the House especially during Leader's Questions. ministers is in charge of handling national issues concerning the area special committees are also established among the TDs to cover certain topical issues for example committee for housing I'll committee for the environment etc.

IN VIEW

By law, a General Election to Dáil Éireann must be held at least once every five years following the dissolution of a previous one. Membership of the Dáil is open to Irish citizens who are aged 21 and above.

THE SEANAD ÉIREANN:

*T*he Seanad Eireann (Senate Chambers) is the Upper

House of the Oireachtas (the Irish Parliament), It is commonly called the Seanad in Irish and Senate in English and its members Senators. The Seanad Eireann has powers like those of the Lower House, and is the dominant branch of the Oireachtas, and can pass any law it wishes, subject to the limits imposed by the Constitution of Ireland, however, the Dáil also has the power to over-ride the Seanad's rejection of a Bill.

It adopts its own standing orders and appoints its President that is usually called the Cathaoirleach (pronounced Car-her-lock and is the Chairperson of the House). It establishes its own Standing Committees and Select Committees; Senators participate along with TDs (members of the Dáil) in the case of Joint Committees of the Oireachtas. However, the Seanad share similar duties as Dail Eireann as well but with some added responsibilities. By and large, and by the powers vested in both Houses, the tasks of making and shaping the laws that govern the Republic rest on them.

Seanad Eireann is composed of 60 members and presided over by the Chairperson of the House (Cathaoirleach). The business of the day is governed by what is known as an Order Paper that must have been prepared by the House Leader and contains the motions and amendments that the distinguished Senators may deal with. However, Senators may also raise issues of national concern with the Cathaoirleach at the start of each day and to seek answers from Ministers about issues relevant to their Departments.

Unlike Dáil Éireann, members of Seanad Eireann are not directly elected by the public but consists of a mixture of members chosen by various methods. They are normally selected by Members of the incoming Dail, outgoing Seanad, County and City Councils. The makeup usually reflects the strength of the parties in Dail Eireann although the Seanad Eireann is designed not to recognise political parties as the main criteria in this case. But the set down directives has to be followed in electing Irish Senators to the Seanad.

The following below are methods in which the sixty (60) members of the Irish Senate are choosing:

- 43 Senators are elected by five panels representing vocational interests such as Culture and Education, Agriculture, Labour, Industry and Commerce and Public Administration. 6 Senators are elected by the graduates of two Universities: - three each by the National University of Ireland (NUI) and the University of Dublin (Trinity College). A total of 11 Senators are directly nominated by the Taoiseach.

Constitutionally, an Election to Seanad Éireann must be held within 90 days of the dissolution of Dáil Éireann.

Leader of the Opposition: (Ceannaire an Fhreasúra)

The Leader of the Opposition in Ireland is the Politician who leads the Parliamentary Opposition in the Lower House of the Irish Parliament (Dáil Éireann). When in the Dáil, the Leader of the Opposition sits on the right-hand side of the Ceann Comhairle (Speaker of the House) and directly opposite of the Taoiseach.

Michael Martin TD - Fiana Fail
Politician & Current Opposition Leader.

By agreement, the Leader of the Opposition is the leader of the largest party that is not in government, while the Second Leader of the Opposition is the person who leads of the second largest party that is not in government. Opposition Leaders leading a political party with five members or more have full speaking rights under Dáil Standing Orders, meaning that smaller parties and independent politicians are unable to speak as often.

The current Fine Gael led minority government is led by Leo Varadkar as Taoiseach and Simon Coveney as Tánaiste. It is held in place by a confidence and supply agreement with Fianna Fáil and supported by a number of Independents.

The Tánaiste

Simon Coveney is the current Tánaiste **(Deputy Prime Minister)**. In Ireland, the Prime Minister appoints his/her Second-in-Command and the person in this position is the most

 senior government official after the Taoiseach and their roles are to act on behalf of the Prime Minister in his or her absence either at home or overseas. The **Deputy Prime Minister** is always a member of the Government Cabinet.

Simon Coveney TD – Tánaiste
(Deputy Prime Minister) and Minister
for Foreign Affairs & Trade

Brief Introduction to the Irish Constitution

The Constitution of Ireland was voted in by the Irish people and passed in 1937. In the Irish language, it is known as 'Bunreacht na hÉireann' (Ponounced as 'Bunrocked-na-Herin') which means 'Basic Law of Ireland'. It is a detailed legal document which declares Ireland (*Éire*) as a Sovereign State and sets out to embody characteristics of a republic. The Constitution comprises of fifty Articles which are divided into two categories outlining the role of government and how it is organised, and defines the function of the President and their authority. It also establishes the court system and its powers.

• *Fundamental Rights of Citizens*

Personal Rights, The Family, Education, Private Property and Religion. The Constitution sets out that it is the right of the Irish people to govern themselves and establish their own laws. The law established by the Constitution cannot be changed unless a referendum was held, with a majority win.

OFFICE OF THE PRESIDENT

**Áras an Uachtaráin - situated in Phoenix Park in West Dublin:
The official residence and principal workplace of the President.**

The President of Ireland (Uachtarán na hÉireann) is the rightful Head of State of the Republic of Ireland and the Supreme Commander of the Irish Defence Forces.

The Presidency is largely a ceremonial office, but the President has the Constitutional powers that can be exercised in agreement with and advice of the Government and the Council of State. The President holds office for seven years and can be re-elected to a maximum of two terms either consecutive or otherwise. The President of Ireland is directly elected by the people and he or she acts as a representative of the Irish State and Guardian of the Constitution. Additionally, the President appoints the Taoiseach Prime Minister after Dáil approval by presenting the Seal of Office to the newly appointed Taoiseach. The office has absolute discretionary control in some other areas of functions as prescribed in the Irish Constitution.

The office of Vice President does not exist in Ireland, hence there is no person in that capacity. In the event of the absence, incapacity, death, resignation, removal from office or failure to perform functions by the President, the Constitution of Ireland provides for a Presidential Commission, consisting of the Chief Justice, the Ceann Comhairle (Speaker of the Dáil), and the Cathaoirleach (Chairperson) of the Seanad to exercise and perform the powers and functions of President, while they arrange for a successor to be elected within 60 days.

The Irish Constitution provides for a Council of State to aid and counsel the President on all matters on which the President may consult them. Members of the Council of State is made up of Ex-Officio, Former Office Holders and those directly appointed by the President, such as Past Taoisigh (Prime Ministers), Tánaiste (Deputy Prime Minister), Chief Justice, President of the Court of Appeal, President of the High Court, Ceann Comhairle (Chair of the lower house of parliament), Cathaoirleach (Chair of the upper house of parliament) etc.

Eligibility:

A person shall be eligible to vie for the office of President if he or she is an Irish Citizen and has obtained the age of at least 35 years old. He/she must also be a member of a political party and be sponsored by that party, or also be able to secure the nomination by at least 20 members of the Oireachtas or be nominated by at least four county or city councils out of the 31 Count Councils in Ireland. You can also nominate yourself if you are a former or retiring President. Where only one candidate is nominated, he or she is deemed elected without the need to go to the ballot.

The President has the powers entrusted by the Constitution and legislation, including those necessary to perform the functions of Head of State of the Republic of Ireland, including the followings:

❖ Summoning and dissolving the Dáil and convening the Oireachtas.
❖ Signing legislation into law and/or referring Bills to the Supreme Court.
❖ Representing the people of Ireland both at home and abroad.
❖ Appointment of the Taoiseach, members of the Government, judges and other officials
❖ Acting as Supreme Commander of the Defence Forces.

The first President of Ireland was Douglas Hyde. He took office in 1938 and became internationally recognised as Head of State in 1949, following the coming into force of the Republic of Ireland Act. The current president is Michael D. Higgins, who was first elected in October 2011. He was re-elected for a second term on 26 October 2018.

OFFICE OF THE TAOISEACH

Government Buildings - Dublin

The Taoiseach (Prime Minister) is Chief Executive and Head of Government of the Republic of Ireland. "Taoiseach" meaning Chieftain or Leader in English. The full pronunciation in Irish form, is '*An Taoiseach*' and 'The Taoiseach' is often used as the English version especially outside of the country. The title was adopted in the 1937 Constitution of Ireland as the official name for the "Head of Government." both English and Irish.

The position is the most powerful role in Irish politics. Under the Constitution, the executive power of the State is vested in the government, and since the Taoiseach is the Head of Government, he/she is the most powerful figure in the Irish Political System, and is duly assisted by a Deputy Prime Minister (Tánaiste), whose primary duties are to assist the Taoiseach run the country smoothly. Unlike the President, Irish voters do not go to ballot to vote for the Prime Minister (Taoiseach). He or she is however elected by members of Parliament (Dáil Éireann), and then appointed by the Irish President who presents the Seal of Office to him/her. The Taoiseach is usually the leader of the political party that gains the most seats in a national election, regardless to whether a government is formed by a coalition or a single-party government.

By Law, the Prime Minister appoints the other members of the government, like the Ministers and Junior Ministers who collectively work to initiate policies and programmes of the Government and ensures that they are properly implemented, including drafting new laws and other bills for the Seanad to ratify and pass into law and propose amendments to supersede existing laws they may find outdated and no longer fit for purpose.

The Cabinet

The government Cabinet or Executive Council of the government is constitutionally limited to fifteen members which consists the Taoiseach, *Tánaiste* (Deputy Prime Minister) and Minister for Finance, and a selection of other senior members of government from the Dáil and Seanad that is selected by the Prime Minister.

The position of an incumbent Taoiseach is retained by the continues support of a majority in the Dáil (Parliament). The country is yet to have a female Prime Minister.

A SHORT PROFILE OF IRISH PRESIDENTS & PRIME MINISTERS

(A chronological list of their periods in office.)

IRISH PRESIDENTS FROM 1938 TO PRESENT:

- ## Douglas Hyde 1938-1945

Douglas Hyde was an experienced academic and professor rather than a politician. His career was dominated by his desire

to preserve and promote the Gaelic language. Such was the impact of his work that he was supported by all the main parties in the election which made him the first president of Ireland. **Hyde** was Ireland's first President, he took office from June 25th 1938 to June 24th 1945. He was born on 17 January 1860 in Castlerea and grew up in Frenchpark, Co. Roscommon. He was Co-founder and First President of the Gaelic League (national movement for the revival of the Irish language) from 1893 to 1915. Before he became the President of Ireland in 1938, he previously held several positions including the followings:

- *Interim Professor of Modern Languages at the provincial University of New Brunswick, 1891.*
- *President of Irish National Literary Society, 1894-5.*
- *President Irish Texts Society; Assist. Editor, New Irish Library, 1897.*
- *Professor of Modern Irish, University College Dublin, 1909-32: Dean of Celtic Faculty.*
- *Member of the Senate N.U.I., 1909-19.*
- *Chairman of the Folklore Institute, 1930-34.*
- *Member of Seanad Éireann, 1925 & 38.*

He died on 12 July 1949

• Sean Thomas O'Kelly 1945-1959

Sean Thomas O'Kelly was was born on the 25th of August, 1882. He was a long-time politician and one of the founders of Sinn Féin party. He fought against the British in the Easter Rising, and worked in succeeding layers of government, including that of Eamon de Valeria, whom he succeeded. He was elected to Dáil Éireann and was the Speaker of the First Dáil Éireann between 1919-21. He also was the Vice President of the Executive Council (the Government) of the Irish Free State from 1932-38; Minister for Local Government and Public Health 1932-1939; Tánaiste (Deputy Head of Government) 1938-1945 and Minister for Finance 1939-1945.

He became the second President of Ireland and was elected for the maximum two terms before retiring on the 25th of June 1945. Sean T. O'Kelly died on 23rd of November 1966.

• Eámon de Valera 1959-1973

Eámon de Valera was born in New York on 14th of October 1882 and was brought to Ireland when he was two and a half years old. He was a teacher and University lecturer. He joined the Irish Volunteers when they were founded in 1913 and rose in ranks to s a Commandant and took part in the 1916 Uprising. Eamon was among those sentenced to death but his was commuted to penal servitude for life. He was released on General Amnesty in 1917 and was elected a Sinn Féin M.P. in the same year. He was President of the Executive Council of the Irish Free State and Minister for External Affairs. From 1932 – 1937. Eámon de Valera was president of Sinn Féin in 1917. He also founded the Fianna Fáil Party in 1926. Following enactment by the people of the Constitution, he became Taoiseach (Prime Minister) and Minister for External Affairs from 1937 – 1948.

He was Taoiseach again from 1951 – 1954 and 1957 – 1959, and finally became the 3rd President of Ireland on the 25th of June 1959. He was thought of as the most famous Irish politician of his era, and with good reasons.

Eámon de Valera died on the 29th of August 1975.

- ## Erskin Childers 1973-1974

Erskine Childers was born in London on the 11th of December 1905. His own father Robert Childers was an acclaimed writer and politician, he was executed in the struggle for Irish Independence.

After living in England and France, Erskine came to Dublin to become an Advertising Manager of an Irish newspaper in 1931. In 1936, he became Secretary of the Federation of Irish Manufacturers before he became a politician and was elected to Dáil Éireann in 1938 and subsequently served as a Junior Minister and held successive Ministerial appointments in a number of government departments. He also served as Tánaiste (Deputy Prime Minister) in 1969. He was eventually elected the 4th President of Ireland in 1973. **He died the following year.**

- ## Cearbhall O'Dalaigh 1974–1976

Cearbhall O'Dalaigh was born on 12th of February in 1911. He at first the was Attorney General of Ireland from 1946 – 48 and from 1951 – 53. In 1953 he was appointed a Judge of the Supreme Court. He served as Chief Justice and President of the Supreme Court from 1961 – 73 before being appointed a Judge of the Court of Justice of the European Communities in 1973.

He was the 5th President of Ireland on 19th of December 1974. He resigned from office on 22nd of October 1976, and died on two years later on the 21st of March, 1978.

- ## Patrick Hillery 1976 - 1990

Dr. Patrick Hillery qualified as a Medical Doctor before he transitioned into politics. In 1951, he was elected to Dáil Éireann for the constituency of Clare County and he received his first Government appointment as Minister for Education in 1959, and subsequently served in a

number of other Ministerial posts including Industry and Commerce, Labour and Foreign Affairs. Dr. Patrick was inaugurated as the 6th President of Ireland on the 3rd of December in 1976. Hillery was well noted to have bought stability to the Presidency after several years of upheaval promising to only serve one term but was asked back by the main parties to stand for a second.

He was born on 2nd of May 1923 in Miltown Malbay, County. Clare. He died in 1990.

• Mary Robinson 1990-1997

Mary Robinson was born in Ballina, County Mayo on 21st of May 1944. A Barrister by profession, Mary Robinson was appointed Reid Professor of Criminal Law in Trinity College, Dublin at the age of 25. She had a record of promoting Humans Rights when she was elected President. She was inaugurated on the 3rd of December 1990, as the first female President of the Republic of Ireland and seventh in the position. Before Mary Robinson was elected President, she was previously elected as a representative of the University of Dublin and was also a member of Seanad Éireann (Upper House of Parliament) where she was on various Parliamentary Committees, including Legal Affairs Committee and joint Committee on Marital Breakdown. When her seven years term in office was over, she moved into the role of United Nations High Commissioner for Human Rights and has continued campaigning on Human Rights issues.

• Mary McAleese 1997–2011

President McAleese was born on the 27th of June 1951 in Belfast and grew up in Northern Ireland through the violent times known as 'The Troubles'. She is the first President of Ireland to come from the North. Mary McAleese was another lawyer who transitioned into politics. She was called to the Northern Ireland Bar in 1974 and was appointed Reid Professor of Criminal Law, Criminology and Penology at Trinity College Dublin in 1985. In 1994, she became the first female Pro-Vice Chancellor of the Queen's University of Belfast. An experienced broadcaster, she also worked as a current affairs Journalist and Presenter in Radio and Television with RTE (National Broadcasting Service for Ireland). McAleese was inaugurated as the eighth President of the Republic of Ireland on 11th November 1997 and was re-elected on 1st October 2004 being the only nominated candidate. Due to her longstanding interest on issues concerned with Justice, Equality, Social Inclusion, Anti-Sectarianism and Reconciliation, the theme of her Presidency was 'Building Bridges'.

Michael D. Higgins 2011 to Present

President Michael D Higgins
(Incumbent: 2011–present)

Michael D. Higgins is currently the incumbent holder of the office of the President of the Republic of Ireland. Michael D. Higgins was first inaugurated on 11th of November 2011 as Ireland's ninth President. Before becoming the President of Ireland, D. Higgins has previously served at almost every level of public life in Ireland, including as Ireland's first Minister for Arts, Culture and the Gaeltacht.

Michael D Higgins was born on the 18th of April 1941 in Limerick city and was raised in County Clare. He was a factory worker and a clerk before becoming the first in his family to access higher education. He is best described as a passionate political voice, he is a Poet and Writer, Academic and Statesman, Human Rights Advocate, Promoter of Inclusive Citizenship and Champion of Creativity within Irish society.

In 2018, Michael D Higgins fought to retain his position as President of Ireland, he won with a landslide and was sworn in for a second term to serve the people of Ireland.

A SHORT PROFILE OF IRISH PRIME MINISTERS FROM 1938 - PRESENT

Below is a short Profile of all the people who have served in this position as Prime Minister/Taoiseach. You will note that some leaders in the past served more than one period, others just within their terms.

• William Thomas Cosgrave

William Thomas Cosgrave was born on the 6th of June 1880, he never officially held the office of Taoiseach but he was the first elected Head of Government in the Irish Free State and therefore recognised to have been the first Taoiseach. His son Liam Cosgrave, went on to serve fully as Taoiseach from 1973 to 1977.

W.T. Cosgrave was an active Irish Fine Gael politician and he held other official positions such as President of the Executive Council from 1922 to 1932, Leader of the Opposition from 1932 to 1944, Leader of Fine Gael from 1934 to 1944, Leader of Cumann na nGaedheal from 1923 to 1933, Chairman of the Provisional Government from August 1922 to December 1922, President of Dáil Éireann from September 1922 to December 1922, Minister for Finance from 1922 to 1923 and Minister for Local Government from 1919 to 1922. He served as a Teachta Dála (TD) from 1921 to 1944.

He was a Member of Parliament (MP) for the North Kilkenny constituency from 1918 to 1922. He died on 16 November 1965.

• Éamon de Valera

Éamon de Valera was a prominent Statesman and Political leader in 20th-century Ireland. His political career spanned over half a century, from 1917 to 1973 as he served several terms as the Head of Government and also Head of State. A Commandant in the 1916 Easter Rising, he also led the introduction of the Constitution of Ireland. Éamon de Valera was spared execution for his involvement in the 1916 Rising because he had American Citizenship.

De Valera was a political leader in the War of Independence and of the anti-Treaty opposition in the ensuing Irish Civil War (1922–1923). He founded Fianna Fáil Political Party. He served as Head of Government (President of the Executive Council, and later on became Taoiseach from 1932 to 1948, 1951 to 1954, and 1957 to 1959, when he resigned after being elected as the President of Ireland. **Eamon de Valera died in 1975 at the age of 92.**

• John Aloysius Costello

John Aloysius Costello was also a Fine Gael politician who served as Taoiseach from 1948 to 1951, again from 1954 to 1957. Before then he was Leader of the Opposition from 1951 to 1954 and 1957 to 1959, and he served as Attorney General of Ireland from 1926 to 1932. He was a Teachta Dála (TD) from 1933 to 1943 and from 1944 to 1969. It was under his government that Ireland became a member of the United Nations in 1955, and similarly a highly successful visit to the United States in 1956, during that visit began the tradition by which the Irish Taoiseach visits the USA White House every St. Patrick's Day to present the American President with a bowl of Shamrock.

Costello was presented with several awards during his career, especially from many Universities in the United States. He retired from politics in 1969, went on and practised at the Bar up until a short time before his death, in 1976. He was aged 84.

- ## Seán Francis Lemass

Seán Francis Lemass was an Irish politician who served as Taoiseach and Leader of Fianna Fáil from 1959 to 1966. He was Tánaiste (Deputy Prime Minister) from 1957 to 1959, 1951 to 1954 and 1945 to 1948, a Minister for Industry and Commerce from 1957 to 1959, 1951 to 1954, 1945 to 1949. He served as a Teachta Dála (TD) from 1927 to 1969.

Born John Francis Lemass, on 15th of July 1899, he was also a known Veteran of the 1916 Easter Rising, the War of Independence and the Civil War, Lemass was first elected as a Sinn Féin Teachta Dála(TD) for the Dublin South constituency in a by-election on 18 November 1924 and was returned at each election until the constituency was abolished in 1948, when he was re-elected for Dublin South-Central until his retirement in 1969. He was a founder-member of Fianna Fáil in 1926, and served as Minister for Industry and Commerce, Minister for Supplies and Tánaiste in successive Fianna Fáil governments. Lemass is widely regarded as the father of modern Ireland, primarily due to his efforts in facilitating industrial growth, bringing foreign direct investment into the country and forging permanent links between Ireland and the European Community. He died on the 11th of May 1971.

• John Mary Lynch

Popularly called Jack Lynch, he was born on 15 August 1917. He was a Fianna Fáil politician who served as Taoiseach from 1966 to 1973 and a second time from 1977 to 1979.

Jack Lynch was Leader of Fianna Fáil from 1966 to 1979, and Leader of the Opposition from 1973 to 1977. He also served as Minister for Finance from 1965 to 1966, Minister for Industry and Commerce from 1959 to 1965, Minister for Education 1957 to 1959, Minister for Gaeltacht Affairs from March 1957 to June 1957, Parliamentary Secretary to the Minister for Lands and Parliamentary Secretary to the Taoiseach from 1951 to 1954. He served as a Teachta Dála (TD) from 1948 to 1981.

Before politics, Lynch had a successful sporting career as a dual player of Gaelic games and once regarded as one of the greatest dual players of all-time by his locals.
He died on 20 October 1999.

• William Michael Cosgrave

William Michael Cosgrave was the son of W. T. Cosgrave, the first President of the Executive Council in the newly formed Irish Free State. He was born in Castleknock in West Dublin on the 13th of April 1920. William Cosgrave qualified as a Barrister before embarking on a political career.

He was elected to Dáil Éireann at the 1943 general election and sat in opposition alongside his father. The formation of the first inter-party government in 1948 saw Cosgrave become a Parliamentary Secretary to Taoiseach John A. Costello. He formally became a cabinet member in 1954 when he was appointed Minister for External Affairs and Government Chief Whip from 1948 to 1951. He lost the 1969 general election to the incumbent Jack Lynch but won the 1973 general election and became the Taoiseach in a Fine Gael-Labour Party government. He served as Taoiseach from 1973 to 1977.

William Michael Cosgrave was the longest-lived Taoiseach of Ireland, dying at the age of 97 years old on the 4th of October 2017.

• Charles James Haughey

Charles James Haughey was born on 16th of September 1925. An Irish Fianna Fáil politician, he was first elected to Dáil Éireann as a Teachta Dála (TD) in 1957 and was re-elected in every election until 1992, representing the Dublin North-East, Dublin Artane and Dublin North-Central constituencies.

He was also Minister for the Gaeltacht from 1987 to 1992, Leader of the Opposition from 1981 to 1982 and 1982 to 1987, Leader of Fianna Fáil from 1979 to 1992. He served on different Ministerial positions such as Minister for Social Welfare and Minister for Health from 1977 to 1979, Minister for Finance from 1966 to 1970, Minister for Agriculture from 1964 to 1966, Minister for Justice from 1961 to 1964.

Haughey served as Taoiseach on three different occasions, 1979 to 1981, March 1982 to December 1982 and 1987 to 1992. As Taoiseach, Haughey was generally regarded as the most dominant Irish politician of his generation and credited by some economists as starting the positive transformation of the economy in the late 1980s. He died of prostate cancer in 2006, aged 80 years old.

• Garret Desmond FitzGerald

Garret Desmond FitzGerald was the son of Desmond FitzGerald, the first Minister for External Affairs of the Irish Free State.

An Irish Fine Gael politician; he served as Taoiseach from 1981 to 1982 and 1982 to 1987, and was Leader of Fine Gael from 1977 to 1987. He was Leader of the Opposition from 1977 to 1981 and March 1982 to December 1982 and Minister for Foreign Affairs from 1973 to 1977. He was a Teachta Dála (TD) from 1969 to 1992. He was a Senator for the Industrial and Commercial Panel from 1965 to 1969.

FitzGerald was also the President of the Institute of International and European Affairs, he had a column in *The Irish Times* and made occasional appearances on television programmes. He was born on 9th of February 1926, and he died on the 19th of May 2011, aged 85.

• Albert Martin Reynolds

Albert Martin Reynolds served as Ireland's Taoiseach from 1992 to 1994, during which time he was Leader of the Fianna Fáil party. He was born on 3 November 1932.

Before he was Taoiseach, he served as Minister for Finance from 1988 to 1991, Minister for Industry and Commerce from 1987 to 1988. He was also Minister for Industry and Energy from March 1982 to December 1982, Minister for Transport from 1980 to 1981 and Minister for Posts and Telegraphs from 1979 to 1981.

Reynolds was first elected to Dáil Éireann as a TD for Longford-Westmeath in 1977 and was re-elected at each election (from 1992 serving as TD for the Longford-Roscommon area, until his retirement in 2002. During his first term as Taoiseach, he led a Fianna Fáil-Progressive Democrats coalition, and the second term as head of a Fianna Fáil-Labour Party coalition.

He died on the 21st of August 2014, aged 81.

• John Gerard Bruton

John Gerard Bruton was born on May 18th 1947. He joined the Fine Gael party in 1965, and was first elected to Dáil Éireann in 1969. He became the Leader of the Opposition from 1990 to 1994 and 1997 to 2001, and then Deputy Leader of Fine Gael from 1987 to 1990.

Like many before him, Bruton held various Ministerial roles before becoming Ireland's Taoiseach. In 1987, he was appointed Minister for Public Service. He was later made Minister for Finance and served from 1981 to 1982 and then 1986 to 1987, Minister for Industry, Trade, Commerce and Tourism from 1983 to 1986. He also served as Minister for Industry and Energy from 1982 to 1983, Parliamentary Secretary to the Minister for Education and Parliamentary Secretary to the Minister for Industry and Commerce from 1973 to 1977. He was a Teachta Dála (TD) from 1969 to 2004.

He eventually became Prime Minister (Taoiseach) in 1994 and served until 1997. He retired from political life in 2004, and was made the ambassador of the European Union to the United States from 2004 to 2009.

• Patrick Bartholomew Ahern

Popularly called Bertie Ahern, he was born on the 12th of September 1951 in Dublin. Ahern was first elected to Dáil Éireann in 1977 as a member of the Fianna Fáil party for a Constituency in Central Dublin. He later became Lord Mayor in 1986-87. An Assistant Whip (1980-81) in the first Government of Charles Haughey. He was also Leader of Fianna Fáil from 1994 to 2008, and previously Leader of the Opposition from 1994 to 1997 and then Tánaiste (Deputy Prime Minister) and Minister for Arts, Culture and the Gaeltacht from November 1994 to December 1994, Deputy Leader of his party (Fianna Fáil) from 1992 to 1994. Bertie held other Ministerial positions including Minister for Industry and Commerce in 1993, Minister for Finance from 1991 to 1994, Minister for Labour from 1987 to 1991 and Minister of State at the Department of Defence from March 1982 to December 1982.

Ahern became Ireland's Taoiseach in 1997, a position he held until his resignation on the 6th of May 2008. Bertie Ahern's term as Taoiseach is considered the second longest in the Republic.

• Brian Bernard Cowen

Brian Bernard Cowen was born on the 10th of January 1960. He served as Taoiseach from 2008 to 2011, following the resignation of his successor Taoiseach Bertie Ahern in May 2008. Before then, Brian Cowen was the Minister for Foreign Affairs, and Minister for Defence before becoming the Prime Minister.

Cowen also held other high profile Ministerial positions as Minister for Finance from 2004 to 2008, Minister for Health and Children, Minister for Transport, Energy and Communications from Minister for Energy, Minister for Labour, and was also Tánaiste (Deputy Prime Minister). However, Cowen's administration coincided with the period that Ireland was experiencing financial and banking crises which saw the government request for financial rescue from the European Union and the International Monetary Fund (IMF). Cowen's government was highly criticised for failing to arrest the crises situation.

In January 2011, Cowen resigned as leader of his party - Fianna Fáil, but stayed on as Taoiseach until the next election in that year during which he retired altogether from politics.

• Enda Patrick Kenny

Enda Kenny was born on the 24th of April 1951 in Countty Mayo.

Enda Kenny was first elected TD for Mayo West in a by-election in November 1975 following his father's untimely death. However, he would remain a Teachta Dála (TD) from 1975 until 1986, over 10 years after he was first elected before making a Ministerial role as a Junior Education Minister.

Enda Kenny was the longest-serving TD in Dáil Éireann, it earned him 'Father of the Dáil' nickname. Kenny went on to serve at various Ministerial positions including Minister for Defence from May 2014 to July 2014 and 2016 to 2017, Minister for Tourism and Trade from 1994 to 1997, and Minister of State for Youth Affairs from 1986 to 1987. He was Leader of the Opposition from 2002 and led his Fine Gael party to a historic victory at the 2011 General Election.

Enda Kenny was elected Taoiseach on the 9th of March 2011. He was the first Leader of his party to win a general election since 1982. He also became the first Fine Gael Taoiseach to be elected to a second consecutive term of office in May 2016 and was the longest-serving Fine Gael Taoiseach before he stepped down on June 13th of 2017.

• Leo Eric Varadkar

Taoiseach Leo Varadkar TD
(Current Prime Minister)

Leo Eric Varadkar is an Irish Fine Gael Politician and is currently the present Taoiseach (Prime Minister of Ireland. Born on the 18th of January 1979 to an Indian father and Irish mother. Having taken office at the age of 38, he is the youngest politician to occupy the office of Taoiseach in Irish history since the country gained independence from Britain. Varadkar was elected Leader of his party, Fine Gael on the 2nd of June 2017, after he won a leadership contest to replace former Toaiseach and Party Leader, Enda Kenny who had earlier step down from the position. Leo Varadkar took office on the 14th of June 2017. He was elected to succeed the former Taoiseach, Enda Kenny. Before veering into politics, Varadkar qualified as a Medical Doctor and spent several years as a non-consultant hospital doctor, before qualifying as a General Practitioner (GP). He started out in politics in his local constituency of Fingal County Council where he served as Deputy Mayor before being elected to Dáil Éireann in 2007. He was later promoted to the Front Bench as Spokesperson on Enterprise, Trade and Employment, a position he held until a 2010 reshuffle, when he became the Spokesperson on Communications, Energy and Natural Resources.

Leo Varadkar also served at various Ministerial positions before ascending to the highest office in the country as Taoiseach in 2017. He was Minister for Social Protection from 2016 to 2017, Minister for Health from 2014 to 2016 and Minister for Transport, Tourism and Sport from 2011 to 2014.

Taoiseach Leo Varadkar is from a minority ethnic background of Indian heritage, and the first openly gay Irish Government Official.

Departments in the Irish Government

There are 17 Government Ministries and Parastatals within the Irish Government, they're otherwise reffered to as 'Departments, and each department is aptly headed by a Minister and Junior Ministers who are appointed by the Taoiseach. The following table show each government department and what they are responsible for.

Department of the Taoiseach:	Department of Finance:
This Department provides administrative and support services to the Taoiseach and the	This Department is concerned with the economic and financial management of the State.

Government.	
Department of Public Expenditure & Reform: This Department advises the Government on the overall management and control of the public sector.	**Department of Rural and Community Development:** This Department is responsible for policy and supports in respect of community and rural development.
Department of Housing Planning and Local Government: This Department has functions relating to housing and it promotes development. It oversees the local authorities.	**Department of Health:** This Department is responsible for development of health policy and the planning of health services, provided by the Health Service Executive (HSE)
Department of Transport, Tourism and Sport: This Department is responsible for roads & traffic issues, including rail transport, aviation policy, and road safety. It is also responsible for the tourism and sports.	**Department of Justice and Equality:** This Department aims to protect the security of the State, to prevent and tackle crime and to protect individuals' rights and freedoms. It also deals with immigration.
Department of Foreign Affairs and Trade: This Department promotes and protects the interests of Ireland abroad. It pursues peace and reconciliation on the island of Ireland. It is also responsible for foreign trade and development.	**Department of Culture, Heritage and the Gaeltacht:** This Department promotes and protects Ireland's heritage and culture. It also advances the use of the Irish language, supports the sustainable development of the islands and develops cultural tourism.
Department of Education and Skills:	**Department of Employment Affairs & Social Protection:**

This Department This Department is responsible for providing public education at primary and post-primary levels. It also manages State subsidies for universities and third-level colleges. It also has responsibility for training and the work of the Expert Group on Future Skills Needs.	This Department provides income and other support services. It has responsibility for the provision of employment support, guidance and placement services as well as community services and the Rural Social Scheme.
Department of Communications, Climate Action and Environment: This Department has responsibility for the telecommunications and broadcasting sectors, with responsibilities for ensuring the security and reliability of energy supply. It also regulates, protects and develops the inland fisheries and natural resources of Ireland.	**Department of Children and Youth Affairs:** This Department is responsible for the development of policies and service delivery for children and young people through a range of sectors, including health, education, youth justice, sport, arts and culture.
Department of Business, Enterprise and Innovation: This Department is responsible for the promotion and development of enterprise, employment and for the regulation of businesses.	**Department of Defence:** This Department manages and controls the Defence Forces of Ireland. **Department of Agriculture, Food and the Marine:** This Department manages inland fisheries and natural resources of Ireland.

IRISH JUDICIARY SYSTEM

The Criminal Courts of Justice is the principal building for the criminal courts. It includes the Dublin Metropolitan District Court, Court of Criminal Appeal, Dublin Circuit Criminal Court and Central Criminal Court.

Souce: www.courts.ie

The Judiciary system in Ireland is comprised of the various Courts of Law: The **Supreme Court** which is the highest Court in the Republic, and is presided by the Attorney General who is effectively the Chief Justice of Ireland, also represents the government at the Supreme Court on an advising role on matters of technical constitutional laws and as well in a position to provide liaison between British and Irish legal issues. The Constitutional basis for the Irish Court system is found in Article. 34. 1 of the 1937 Constitution. All the Courts are obliged to apply the laws of the Republic of Ireland.

Courts in the Republic of Ireland

The Courts of Justice Act 1924 (built upon 1922 Constitution) made provision for the establishment and provided a description of the jurisdiction of the following courts:

- The Supreme Court
- The Court of Criminal Appeal
- The High Court
- The Circuit Court
- The District Court

There are three distinct sources of law in Ireland:

- ❖ Common Law System
- ❖ Statutory Law System
- ❖ Constitutional Law System

The Supreme Court being the highest court is usually the last option for legal appeal and includes the Chief Justice, the President of the High Court plus four other judges. They are normally responsible for dealing with constitutional matters, for example, the President of Ireland may refer bills passed by the Parliament and the Senate if she/he thinks they might affect the constitution.

The High Court, Court of Appeal and the Supreme Court have authority, by means of Judicial review to determine the compatibility of laws and activities of other institutions of the state with the constitution and the law. Unless in exceptional circumstances, court hearings in Ireland must occur in public.

Below is a diagram of the Irish Court Hierarch.

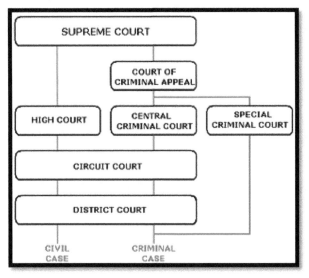

Source: https://lawinireland.wordpress.com/irish-legal-system

The District Courts are the lowest by hierarchy and may refer to the **Circuit Courts** but they are the essence of the judicial system because they perform important services over local and criminal jurisdictions.

Article 34.4 of the Irish Constitution states that the lower Courts follow the decisions of Higher Courts.

SECTION SIX

IRISH POLITICAL SYSTEM

Politics in the Republic of Ireland is set within the framework of the country's constitution and it operates a multi-party system in which the general public are expected to exercise their civil rights through participating in election campaigns and through voting in a ballot.

There are four major political parties in the Republic, including a number of other medium and small sized parties, and a few newly registered ones, each representing a range of views. Fianna Fáil and Fine Gael are the two largest parties in Ireland, with the Labour Party usually third, fourth being Sinn Fein, followed by a number of the smaller parties. Although, historically, both Fianna Fáil and Fine Gael both share histories of rising from a split in the original Sinn Féin party in the 1922–1923 Civil War. Fine Gael from the faction of (Cumann na nGaedheal) that supported the 1921 Anglo-Irish Treaty and Fianna Fáil from the anti-Treaty faction. The Labour Party was formed in 1912, and it has usually been the third party in parliamentary strength, though it is currently the fourth largest party in parliament, as Sinn Féin in recent years, seems to have risen to prominence and surpassed the Labour Party in the 2016 general election.

Registration of a Political Party in Ireland is governed by the Electoral Acts, 1992 to 2012, and is maintained by the Houses of the Oireachtas. In order to be registered to contest national elections, a party must have either at least one member in Dáil Éireann or the European Parliament or 300 recorded members aged 18 or over. Political Parties that register only to contest elections in parts of the State, like in local elections or in elections to Údarás na Gaeltachta (Gaeltacht Authority) need to have only 100 recorded members that are aged 18 or over. In either case at least half of the recorded members must be on the register of electors.

Political Parties in Ireland

Political Parties stand as the umbrella organisation for like-minded groups of people, and elected officials play active roles in the day to day life of individuals as they hold weekly meetings with locals to hear their concerns. Individual Parties also holds annual conferences to discuss internal issues and ensure that their party views are carried forward in all areas. Prior to any elections, parties hold their conventions to a choose candidate to represent the interest of their party from those seeking representation in particular areas, including delegates to represent them at the EU Parliament in Brussels. It is not essential that a person must be linked to a ruling body in order to run for any of these elections. Candidates are drawn from parties, and as well individuals also run for elected office as Independent candidates.

Below are some of the Political Parties in Ireland

Fine Gael is a Liberal-Conservative and Christian Democratic Political Party in Ireland. It was founded in 1933 by an Irish nationalist political activist, General Eoin O'Duffy. The party is currently the governing party and is the senior partner in a minority coalition with **Fianna Fáil** and several Independent politicians.

Fianna Fáil was founded on the 23rd of March in 1926 by Éamon de Valera, a former leader of Sinn Féin. The party was last in government from 1997 to 2011. Fianna Fáil is currently the largest Opposition party in both Houses of the Oireachtas (Parliament).

The Labour Party was founded in 1912 in Clonmel, County Tipperary, by James Connolly, James Larkin and William O'Brien as the political wing of the Irish Trade Union Congress, and is a democratic socialist party. Since its formation, the party has served as a partner in coalition governments on several occasions.

 **Sinn Féin** party was founded in 1905 by Arthur Griffith, who was an Irish politician and writer. He served as President of Dáil Éireann from January to August in 1922 and was chairman of the Irish delegation at the negotiations in London that produced the Anglo-Irish Treaty of 1921. Sinn Féin is a major party in both Northern Ireland and the Republic of Ireland.

 Solidarity-People Before Profit is an electoral alliance in Ireland formed by members of two socialist political parties: Solidarity and the People Before Profit (PBP). Solidarity was known as the "Anti-Austerity Alliance" (AAA) until 2017. The alliance was formed in 2015 and replaced AAA and PBP in Ireland's official register of political parties. However, each entity retains its separate organisation and identity.

Independent Alliance is an Irish political grouping formed in March 2015 by independent politicians. It is not a typical Political Party, and has stated that it will not impose any whip on elected members, except where the group has agreed to support a government on confidence motions. Some of their members are part of the minority government with Fine Gael and other non-aligned Independent Ministers.

Green Party is a green political party that operates in both the Republic of Ireland and in Northern Ireland.

It was founded as the Ecology Party of Ireland in 1981 by Dublin teacher Christopher Fettes. The party became the Green Alliance in 1983; it adopted its current English name in 1987, while the Irish name was kept unchanged.

The Social Democrats Party was established in July 2015 by three independent TDs. The party has a co-leadership arrangement in place between its three founding members namely - Róisín Shortall, a former Labour Party TD and former Minister of State for Primary Care, former Minister for Health James Reilly and Catherine Murphy who was successively a member of the Workers' Party **Social Democrats** is a political party in Ireland.

Aontú is the new addition having only formally launched in January 2019, it is an all-Ireland political party that was and operates in both the Republic of Ireland and Northern Ireland. The party was founded by Peadar Tóibín, a TD who resigned from Sinn Féin on 15 November 2018 after opposing the party whip on the Health (Regulation of Termination of Pregnancy) Act 2018 due to his anti-abortion views.

Election and Voting System

Ireland uses a voting system called Proportional Representation with a Single Transferable Vote (PR-STV). This is a system which allows electorates to choose their most preferred candidates and still be able to vote for other candidates at the same time if they wished.

This system puts ultimate power in the hands of Electorates to freely decide up to the moment of polling who or which party to give their votes. Normally, voters will be handed a ballot with the names, and political parties of all candidates running for election in their local area and they can rank them according to their preference by ticking the boxes opposite the name of their first choice and, if wish they can do same for the second choice and so on or as the case may be. For example, if there are numbers 1-5 on the card representing candidates, and if voters ticked all the names, it means that they have technically voted for all candidates in that area, with the only difference being who got their number 1 vote. However, electorates are not under any legal obligation to vote all candidates - they have the option to give their number 1 vote to their best choice and the most deserved candidate only without placing a tick on the rest.

Eligibility to Vote

Irelands political structure allows for non-nationals to engage in local elections and can exercise their voting rights as well as stand as a candidate to be voted for in any Local Elections. They have the same rights as every Irish Citizen to vote in local elections in the country, and as well stand as a candidate and be voted for if they have attained the age of 18 years and over. Residents who are citizens of any EU State may also vote in European Parliament elections as with the local election.

To be allowed to vote, a person must be included on the Electoral Register to be able to vote or stand in the elections. However, eligibility to vote in General Elections is decided by the Status of citizenship. British citizens who live in Ireland have equal rights like all Irish citizens and can vote in all elections in the Republic of Ireland apart from presidential elections and referendum.

The rights of Irish citizens living outside Ireland to vote are heavily restricted, only members of the Armed Forces and Diplomatic staff and their spouses/partners abroad may vote in Dáil (Lower House) elections. Special voting arrangements can be made to allow those who are unable to cast their vote at the polling station due to a physical illness or disability exercise their voting rights through other means like posting.

See Table Ilustration

Resident Citizens	Local Elections	European Elections	Dail Elections	Presidential Elections	Referendums
Irish Citizens	✓	✓	✓	✓	✓
Irish citizens in Nothern Ireland	✗	✓	✗	✗	✗
British Citizens	✓	✓	✓	✗	✗
EU Citizens	✓	✓	✗	✗	✗
Non-EU- Citizens	✓	✗	✗	✗	✗

The Taoiseach announced in 2017, that a referendum would be held to amend the Constitution to allow expatriate Irish citizens to vote in presidential elections.

Early voting

This is a process that allows voters in certain circumstances to vote prior to the scheduled election day. For instance, Irish Military personnel serving at home or abroad and their spouse can vote by postal ballot, their votes are then delivered by a commercial courier service, and military courier is used for ballots cast by Irish troops in Lebanon and Syria. Voters living on islands off the West coast in Galway, Mayo, and Donegal also given prioty to vote at least two or three days before polling day. Sealed ballot boxes are usual delivered to the mainland by helicopter and by boat.

LOCAL GOVERNMENT AREAS & COUNCILS

In Ireland, each local government area has a council known as the County Council, they were created under British rule back in 1899 and has continued to exist, but there has been significant changes to the long-standing structure and a new one came into effect since 2014 under the provisions of the Local Government Reform Act 2014.

Town authorities were replaced by a system of 95 municipal districts, integrating town and county governance, and certain local authorities were also merged. There are in total 26 County Councils in Ireland and they are responsible for the local government in 24 geographical counties including the County Dublin which has under it, 3 County Councils such as South Dublin County Council, Dun Laoghaire-Rathdown County Council and Fingal County Council. Each council in Ireland has a Mayor or Lord Mayor, and Chief Executive, who is in effect the manager of the local authority or council. Currently, there are 31 Councils in Ireland, consisting of the followings:

- 26 County Councils
- 3 City Councils
- 2 City and County councils

Councillors or elected representatives are voted for in local elections by members of the local community – as they are the people's representatives at a local level. There are set numbers of Councillors elected to each local authority depending on the population of the local authority area. Presently, there are 949 councillors, who are elected in local government elections. Local authorities have the responsibilities to provide public services and facilities such as housing, planning, roads, environmental protection, fire services, and maintaining the electoral register. Councils also play important roles in supporting economic development and enterprise at local levels.

SECTION SEVEN

COUNTIES & PROVINCES

Ireland is divided into four geographical regions known as Provinces. There are 26 Counties within the Provinces, the 26 Counties were originally from what it used to be 32 Counties of Ireland altogether. But Six Counties were carved out for Britain as part of an agreement in order to restore peace between the two countries a long time ago. Those six Counties are therefore part of the United Kingdom and known as Northern Ireland otherwise referred as to as 'the north' by both the British people and the Irish people in Ireland. Although, three of the six Counties located in Ulster and belong to the UK are well within the Republic of Ireland. This part of the island is the only land border between Britain and the Republic of Ireland. Northern Ireland is currently entangled in the main topic of the Brexit negotiations between the United Kingdom and European Union because of the 'Backstop.'

The Four Provinces of Ireland: -

1. Leinster	2. Munster	3. Ulster	4. Connaught
Ulster	Antrim, Cavan, Armagh, Down, Derry Fermanagh, Tyron, Donegal, Monaghan.		
Munster	Cork, Kerry, Clare, Tipperary, Limerick Waterford.		
Connaught	Galway, Mayo, Roscommon, Sligo, Leitrim.		
Leinster	Dublin,Kilkenny, Meath, Carlow, Laois, Westmeath, Louth, Kildare, Offaly, Longford, Wicklow, Wexford		

General Overview:

According to history, a total of five Provinces existed in Ireland a long time ago, that was before the Norman invasion in 1169. The five Provinces had existed as a Unitedly Semi- Kingdoms in their own rights, each ruled by a King from the great Irish dynastic families at the time. The four Counties which are listed above (Leinster, Ulster, Munster Connaught), including a historical fifth Province that we no longer hear about in today's Ireland. It was referred simply as "the Middle" or, *an mhí* in Irish, and used to be around the area where County Meath is now located. Historically, County Meath which is a part of Leinster as we know it used to be the ancient seat of the High Kings, hence it is still often referred to as the Royal County. The Fifth Province ceased to exist due to the introduction "The Pale" which at the time was the part of Ireland that were directly under the control of the English Government. The area under Ireland's rulership became weaker at a time and consequently the Middle" between the Counties Meath and Westmeath were allowed to gradually merge into one, becoming what it is today. But the exact boundaries of the Provinces of Ireland during the Tudor period were said to have also changed several times, usually as a result of the creation of new counties.

Examples below:

- County Clare upon its creation in 1569 was transferred from Munster to Connacht. It was only restored to Munster after 1660.
- County Longford upon its creation in 1583 was transferred from Leinster to Connacht also.
- County Cavan was created in 1584 and transferred from Connacht to Ulster.
- County Louth, which had long been part of 'The Pale' was transferred from Ulster to Leinster.

The following pages give a brief introduction to the Counties that make up each of the Four Provinces as we know them now, followed by short description and vital statistics to show their unique charms and attractions, and how they all share common grounds of the ancient history and beautiful landscapes and the vast green countryside that earned Ireland the 'Emerald Isle' nickname.

LEINSTER PROVINCE

OVERVIEW OF LEINSTER PROVINCE

Leinster province is Ireland's largest Province - with a landscape as diverse as its 12 Counties. It is also the most populated of the four provinces on the island, with over 1.8 million people and close to half the population of the Republic of Ireland.

The Province was heavily colonized over the centuries. It is also home to Ireland's Capital City of Dublin, which was originally founded by the Vikings and still holds many physical examples of Medieval, Norman, Georgian and Neolithic architectures that are seen in places within the County.

❖ BELOW ARE THE 12 COUNTIES THAT MAKE UP LEINSTER PROVINCE	
LEINSTER	**Counties:** Dublin – Kilkenny – Meath – Carlow – Laois- Westmeath – Louth – Kildare – Offaly - Wicklow – Wexford - Longford.

COUNTY DUBLIN

O'Connell Bridge, Dublin

County Dublin is the most populated City in Ireland. The County is divided into three areas known as Fingal, Dun Laoghaire/ Rathdown and South Dublin. It very diverse and multicultural, with residents coming from all over the world. County Dublin is the ethnic melting pot of Ireland, made possible to a large extent by the booming "Celtic Tiger" economy of the 1990s that brought great prosperity to the County and the country at large. The Celtic Tiger years have gone but County Dublin remains the cultural and business hub of the nation and still bubbling in that glorious aftermath. Many large foreign companies have their operational bases around Dublin more than in any other areas of the country, being the largest County in the country.

Major Towns in County Dublin Include:			
Donnybrook	Balbriggan	Lucan	Skerries
Blanchardstown	Tallaght	Dublin City	Clondalkin

COUNTY KILDARE

County Kildare Coat of Arms

County Kildare is in the Midlands province of Leinster, and measures in length of about 42 miles from north to south and it is 26 miles in breadth from east to west. The area is 654.1 square miles (1,694.2 sq km). The name Kildare is derived from the Irish 'Cill Dara' meaning Church of the Oak Tree. It was named after a small Church built by St. Brigid under a large oak tree at the end of the fifth Century. Kildare County is a thriving community, believed to be the richest in Ireland outside of Dublin. It is synonymous with horse-racing and horse breeding, with three race courses such as - Punchestown, Naas, and the Curragh, all famous for the Irish Derby. County Kildare is also renowned for its world class Golf Courses and for being the Irish Army's largest military base containing its Command Headquarters and as well its training centre, located at the Curragh. Another popular point is the prestigious K Club, which is a venue for the European Open.

Major Towns in County Kildare Include:			
Maynooth	Celbridge	Leixlip	Athy
Lullymore	Kilcock,	Milltown	Nass,

COUNTY KILKENNY

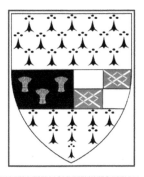

County Kilkenny Coat of Arms

Kilkenny County is located in the Southeast of Ireland in the Province of Leinster. The County's Capital is Kilkenny Town. It is said to be the Capital City of Ireland from 1641 until the Cromwell led Conquest of Ireland in 1649. Kilkenny town was granted City status in 1609. The Irish name for County Kilkenny is *Contae Cill Chainnigh*, literally referring to the "Church of Kenneth" known now as Saint Canice's Cathedral, founded by St Canice in the 6th Century. Both the County and the Capital town are fondly referred to as the "Marble City" and "Marble County" respectively because of its distinctive black marble is found in the area. The population of Kilkenny currently stand around 95,419 according to the 2016 census.

A vibrant community for modern culture and ancient history, Kilkenny has a medieval feel with well-maintained old buildings and Medieval Monastic ruins, including the 12th-century Kells Priory, an Augustinian complex surrounded by fortified walls, which is a Kilkenny Castle built in 1195 by Norman occupiers in the extensive grounds, and the 9th-century St. Canice's Cathedral. Kilkenny County is a tourist destination with lots more to offer visitors any day.

Major Towns in County Kilkenny Include:		
Thomastown	Dungarvan	Callan
Graiguenamanagh	Castlecomer	Kells

COUNTY LAOIS

County Laois is located in the South of the Irish Midlands region of Leinster. The County's Capital is called Portlaoise (pronounced Portlisha). The size of County Laois is measured at 1,719 square kilometres. According to the 2016 census, there are 844,732 people currently living in County Laois.

County Laois Coat of Arms

According To history, the first people in Laois were bands of hunters and gatherers who passed through the County about 8,500 years ago. They hunted in the forests that covered Laois and fished in its rivers, gathering nuts and berries to supplement their diets. Next came Ireland's first farmers. These people of the Neolithic period (4000 to 2500 BC) cleared forests and planted crops. Starting around 2500 BC, the people produced weapons, tools and golden objects.

Laois has a number of attractions and interesting sights and visitors to the County can actually see a stone circle for instance, and as well the remains of their Hill Forts, a Bronze Age stone standing and Ring left behind around the County at the Monamonry Clopook and Monelly.near Borris-in-Ossory and Skirk, respectively.

Laois was officially known as "Queen's County" in honour of Queen Mary ("Bloody Mary") between 1556 and 1922. The County hosts one of Ireland's most popular annual arts and music festivals, the Electric Picnic at Stradbally, and loads more.

Major towns in County Laois:			
Abbeyleix	Newtown,	Mountmellick	Portalington
Rathdowney	Stradbally	Mountrath	Coolrain

COUNTY MEATH

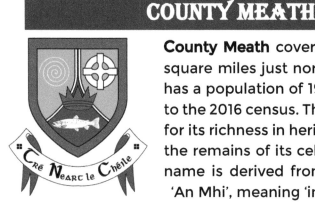

County Meath Coat of Arms

County Meath covers an area of 905 square miles just north of Dublin and has a population of 195,044 according to the 2016 census. The County known for its richness in heritage, history and the remains of its celebrated past. Its name is derived from the Irish word 'An Mhi', meaning 'in the middle' and is one of two Counties to have an Official Gaeltacht outside the West of Ireland. Meath is also known as the Royal County, and home to the ancient seat of the High Kings at Tara and the renowned Boyne Valley. It is the 14th-largest Counties out of whole 32 Counties in Ireland, and the ninth-largest in terms of population. It is the second-largest of Leinster's twelve Counties in size, and the third-largest in terms of population. The County town is Navan, where the County Hall is located.

The beautifully popular Early Christian Book of Kells that is on permanent display at Trinity College in Dublin originated from the town of Kells in the County. Also, the magnificent Norman Castle at Trim, the former County town and once home to one of the oldest religious settlements in Ireland, still stands there. **County Meath** is home to the only Official Strand Races in all of Europe, which is held on the Laytown Beach every year. It is also home to one of three World Designated Heritage Sites in Ireland. Meath has some of the most important archaeological sites yet uncovered, i.e. the landscape within Brú na Bóinne that is dominated by the three well-known large passage tombs, Knowth, Newgrange and Dowth, built some 5,000 years ago in Late Stone Age are believed to be 500 years older than the Pyramids of Egypt). Meath is also home to one of Ireland's most popular and busiest visitor attractions is the family-oriented Tayto Park.

Major towns in Meath County:			
Gormanstown	Bettystown	Duleek	Slane
Athboy	Dunshaugling	Trim	Navan

COUNTY LOUTH

County Louth Coat of Arms

County Louth is the smallest County in the Leinster region and also Ireland's overall smallest County, hence the nickname 'Wee County.' Its size covers an area of just about 318 square miles, with Dundalk as County town. The 'Wee County' however plays roles that are as important as with the other Counties in the rest of the country, especially in terms of historic and tourism potentials as well as political life in rural Ireland. Named after the village of Louth, the county has a population of **128,884 (census 2016)**. Dundalk and Drogheda are the two biggest towns in county Louth, amongst a number of other smaller towns and villages. County Louth has a rich Medieval past and contains some historic sites including the Monastic Mellifont Abbey, the Stones of Proleek Dolmen, the striking High Crosses and Round Tower at Monasterboice, including the ancient site of the Battle of the Boyne. Louth is also home to two League of Ireland's football clubs – **Drogheda United** and **Dundalk FC**.

It is also one of only a few places around the whole world where you can view a human head placed in a glass-case in St Peter's Church on the West Street in Drogheda – and it is home to the *'Head'* **of a well-known Irish son, Oliver Plunkett**, who was executed by British Forces for promoting Catholicism. A couple of years after St. Oliver's execution, the Relic of the Head was brought to Rome and remained in

Rome for about 40 years before it was brought from there to Armagh, and eventually to Drogheda where it has rested in Saint Peter's Church since 1921. St Oliver Plunkett was deemed the country's Patron Saint for peace and reconciliation. The County also plays host to many multinational companies like Xerox, which have their Software manufacturing (Xerox Technology Park) there. Same goes with a few more companies like foods and beverage production Heinz Custom Foods, Coca-Cola, among others.

Major towns in County Louth:			
Carlingford	Drogheda	Ardee	Clogherhead
	Dunleer	Knockbridge	

COUNTY LONGFORD

County Longford Coat of Arms

County Longford derived its name from the Irish 'Longford Ui Fearraill'. It was once the ancestral home of the O'Farrell Clan and historically known as 'Annaly' or 'Anghaile'. The County is a peaceful region and mainly low-lying renowned for its angling, boating and outdoor activities. It is measured at 403 square miles of clear lakes, cruising waterways and ancient boglands in the heart of the Lakelands and Inland Waterways, making it a perfect place for water sports. Known to have some of Ireland's oldest and best-preserved peatlands. The Corlea Trackway dating back to the year 148 BC the (Iron Age), was discovered in the bogs and is now on permanent display at the Exhibition Centre in Corlea, South of the County, that is also steeped in ancient Irish mythology and is associated with many mythological tales from the past. One such widely identified legend by the locals is 'The Wooing of Étain' (an Irish Tale of Love, Loss, and Jealousy). Longford has several impressive archaeological sites and boasts a wealth of artistic, dramatic, literary and musical tradition. County Longford boasts of a superb annual calendar of festivals and events highlighting rich Irish culture and traditional music. The population of County Longford was counted to be 40,810 in the census of 2016.

Major towns in County Longford include:			
Lanesborough	Edgeworthstown	Cloondare	Abbeylara
Ballymahon	Killashee	Ardagh	Ballinalee

♣ ♣ ♣

COUNTY OFFALY

County Offaly Coat of Arms

County Offaly is named after the ancient Kingdom of Uí Failghe and was formerly known as the King's County. The population of Offaly is recorded to be around 78,003 according to the 2016 census. Tullamore is the County Town and the largest town in Offaly.

The County ranks as the 30th largest Counties in Ireland. Offaly borders seven other Counties such as Galway, Roscommon, Tipperary, Laois, Westmeath, Kildare and Meath. It is rich in heritage and culture with Monuments and historic buildings of note contained in County, some of which are the Martello Tower in Bangahar, the Napoleonic

Fortifications at Lusmagh, Shannon bridge and Cloghan Castle and Birr Castle. The 24th highest peak in Ireland is in Offaly. The Slieve Bloom Mountains is also located in the Southern part of the County and it measures 527 metres (1,729 feet). The highest point is Arderin (Irish: Ard Éireann, meaning "Ireland's Height") in the Slieve Blooms Mountains. It also contains Stillbrook Hill and Wolftrap Mountains which are the county's second and third highest peaks. Croghan Hill rises from the Bog of Allen and is again located in northern Offaly.

Famous about the County, is the story of William Parsons, the 3rd Earl of Rosse and Astronomer who served as one of the Irish peers in the House of Lords. He was said to be obsessed with the idea of constructing a truly large telescope that he decided to build the world's largest telescope in his own backyard; the aptly named "Leviathan" - from the 1840s, it has been restored in recent years and is one of Ireland's most important technical monuments in the county.

Major towns in County Offaly Include:		
Moneygall	Tullamore	Ballynagar
Edenderry	Dunkerrin	Ferbane

County Offaly is most associated recently, as the home of former Irish Prime Minister (Taoiseach) Brian Cowen and for being the ancestral homeland of Barack Obama. The Barack Obama's Irish roots were discovered in Moneygall town in the County.

COUNTY WESTMEATH

County Westmeath Coat of Arms

County Westmeath is originally part of the Historic Kingdom of Meath. After the Norman invasion of Ireland, Westmeath formed the basis for the Anglo-Norman Lordship of Meath as granted by the King Henry II of England to Hugh de Lacy in 1172. In 1241, following the failure of De Lacy's male heirs, the Lordship was instead split between two great-granddaughters. One part, a Central Eastern portion was awarded to Maud (de Geneville) as the liberty of Trim, and the other part, comprising North-Eastern and Western portions were given to Maud's sister Margery (de Verdun), and in 1297 it became the Royal County of Meath. The liberty and Royal Counties were merged together in 1461. While the East of the County was in the English Pale, the West was Gaelicised in the fourteenth Century and was outside the control of the sheriff of Meath. However, the County of Westmeath was officially established in 1543. It derives its name from the Irish 'an Lar Mhi', meaning West of Meath. The county was centrally involved in the 1641 rebellion and active during the Williamite Wars that claimed most of the lands belonging to the Irish and the Normans.

Westmeath is blessed with lush pastoral land, wooded vales, lakes and rich culture. The County's Capital is Mullingar and the population of County Westmeath is just over 88,000 according to the census of 2016. Westmeath also stands as the 20th largest of Ireland's 32 Counties by area and the 22nd largest in terms of population. It is the sixth largest of Leinster's twelve Counties in size and eighth largest in terms of population. The largest town in the County is Athlone, followed by the County town of Mullingar.

Westmeath is sometimes referred to as "The Lake County", due to the abundance of lakes, streams and other waterways in the county and as a result, tourism in Westmeath is generally based on its many water amenities. It also has an extensive beef and dairy trade and other consumer products, including many historic attractions and impressive features such as the astounding and pleasant ruins of the fabled 'Seven Wonders of Fore'. The County is home of talented singer, Niall Horan of 'One Direction' fame.

Major towns in County Westmeath			
Ballymore,	Mullingar	Ballymore	Athlone
	Rosemount	Drumcree	

COUNTY WEXFORD

County Wexford (*Loch Garman in Irish is* often described as the 'Model County' because of the high number of "Model Farms" found around the County. Located in the South-East corner of Ireland over 909 square miles of unspoiled countryside, it is often described as the 'secret island'.

County Wexford Coat of Arms

Wexford derives its name from the Vikings 'Weissfjord' meaning sea-washed town. The Population of Wexford is 149,605 (2016), it is the 13th largest of Ireland's thirty-two Counties in terms of area and 14th largest in terms of population. It is the largest of Leinster's twelve Counties in size, and fourth largest in terms of population. Wexford is bounded by the sea on two sides—on the South by the Atlantic Ocean and on the East by St. George's Channel and the Irish Sea. The River Barrow forms its Western boundary.

In GAA circles, players from Wexford are known as "Yellowbellies," a reference to the colour scheme of their GAA team kit.

County Wexford was one of the earliest areas of Ireland to be Christianised in the early 5th century. Later, from 819 onwards, the Vikings plundered many Christian sites in the County. It became a Viking settlement near the end of the

9th century. It was also the most important area in which the Irish Rebellion of 1798 was fought, during which over 13,000 British soldiers launched an attack on Vinegar Hill outside Enniscorthy.

In recent years, County Wexford is most associated with being a place that holds the family history of John Fredrick Kennedy (JFK) and of Irish-American journeys. The Kennedy Homestead near New Ross is an inspired link connecting America and Ireland. Much of the County's remarkable history of early Celtic, Viking and Norman remains have been preserved and transformed into premier tourist attractions.

In 1963 John F. Kennedy, then President of the United States, visited the county and his ancestral home at Dunganstown.

Major towns in County Wexford:		
Enniscorthy	Bunclody	Killmore
New Ross	Gorey	Ballyduff

There is also the *DUNBRODY FAMINE SHIP EXPERIENCE* which is one such place that keeps retelling of the history and the story of poor and desperate Irish emigrants who left during the famine to seek better lives in America. While they died in droves from starvation and sea related illnesses, many in their thousands equally survived the horrendous hardships; eventually becoming a league of the brave men that helped to build America.

COUNTY CARLOW

County Carlow Coat of Arms

County Carlow (Irish: *Contae Cheatharlach*) is a part of the South-East Region in the province of Leinster. It is named after the town of Carlow and lies on the River Barrow to the South-East of Dublin.

Carlow was originally part of the Norman Palantine-County of Leinster; it became a separate County around 1306, at which time it was much larger than it is now, and extending to and including the coastal area around Arklow. These areas were given over to County Wicklow during 1606-07. Presently, it is the second smallest County in Leinster, measuring around 896 kilometres square, and has a population of 56,875 at the count of the last census in 2016. The town of Carlow was an important Norman stronghold and was walled in 1361 to protect it from the neighbouring Gaelic chieftains, who were eventually captured it in 1405. The County joined the Catholic Confederacy in 1641, which was defeated by Cromwell's Forces in 1650.

A centre of agriculture, but the first outbreak of the dreaded potato blight was reported in County Carlow in September 1845 and the Great Hunger wiped out half of the population of the county. The Great Famine of 1845-1847 badly affected the County as ten thousand people died of starvation and the population decreased to 34,476 in 1921. Carlow is predominately Roman Catholic. In 1891, the percentage of Roman Catholic was 88.3%.

Carlow Town is regarded by many as one of the prehistoric monuments in Ireland. One fine example is the Monolith forming the roof of the burial chamber popularly known as Browne's Hill Dolmen in the East of Carlow, estimated to weigh around 100 tons.

There are also the remains of Carlow Castle near the river Barrow. The Castle was said to have been constructed to guard the vital river crossing and also to serve as the capital of the Lordship of Ireland from 1361 until 1374.

John Tyndall - the 19th century Scientist who was the first to explain why the sky is blue, and more contemporary Saoirse Ronan - the Oscar nominated and Golden Globe awarded actress are both from County Carlow.

Major towns in County Carlow include:			
Clonmore	Clonegal	Hacketstown	Borris
Ardattin	Nurney		Tullow

COUNTY WICKLOW

County Wicklow (Contae Chill Mhantáin in Irish), is the last of the traditional 32 counties to be formed in late 1606. It is part of the Mid-East Region in the Province of **Leinster**.

County Wicklow Coat of Arms

Wicklow is named after the town of Wicklow itself, which is derived from the Vikings name *Víkingaló*, meaning "Vikings' Meadow". Wicklow is also commonly referred as *the Garden of Ireland*. It is the 17th-largest of Ireland's 32 Counties by area, being thirty-three miles in length by twenty miles in breadth, and 16th-largest by population. It is the fourth largest of Leinster's twelve counties by size and the fifth-largest in terms of population. The current population of County Wicklow stands at 142,332 according to the 2016 census.

Wicklow is bounded in the East by the Irish Sea and is a County of Rolling hills, mountains, lakes forests and gorgeous gardens and is known to be the most mountainous County in Ireland. It is also considered one of Ireland's most beautiful place, as it is blessed with an abundance of formal gardens and restored Stately homes. The Wicklow Mountains form the largest continuous upland area in Ireland, and they occupy the whole centre of the County and stretches outside its borders into Counties Dublin, Wexford and Carlow. Where the mountains extend into County Dublin they are commonly known locally as Dublin Mountains. The Wicklow Mountains and their foothills occupy almost the entire area of the county; with Lugnaquilla as the highest peak at 925 metres (3,035 feet).

The Wicklow National Park is one of the most-visited areas in Ireland, located on more than 20,000 hectares of rugged countryside.

The Glendalough Monastic Site, is one of the most important early Christian sights in a set beautiful wooded valley beside two usually tranquil lakes - Glendalough literally means Valley of the Two Lakes.

Major towns in County Wicklow:			
Blessington	Killbride	Avoca	Greystones
Bray	Ashford	Arklow	Clara

MUNSTER PROVINCE

An Overview of Munster Province

Munster Province is situated in the South of Ireland. It covers a total area of 24,675 km^2 (9,527 square miles) and has a population of 1,280,020. It is made up of Six Counties with the most populated being Cork County. During the Early Middle Ages, most of Munster was part of the Kingdom of Munster (one of the "fifths"), and it was ruled by a "King of over-kings" (the one who holds a position of seniority over a group of other kings.) Prior to this, the area was ruled by the Overlords from the early 7th Century onwards, and by the 9th Century, the Gaels had been joined with the Norse Vikings who had founded towns such as Cork, Waterford and Limerick, while 10th Century saw the rise of the Dalcassian clan, who had earlier annexed Thomond Kingdom on the northside of the River Shannon to Munster. Their leaders were the ancestors of the O'Brien Dynasty that produced the most noted High King of Ireland, Brian Boru, and several others whose descendants were also High Kings. Brian Boru first became King of Munster, and then went on to conquer Leinster before he eventually became King of Ireland. He was known mostly as the Irish king who ended the domination of the High Kingship of Ireland by the Uí Néill. By 1118, Munster had fractured into the Kingdom of Thomond under the O'Briens, the Kingdom of Desmond under the MacCarthy Dynasty (Eóganachta), and the short-lived Kingdom of Ormond under the O'Kennedys (another Dalcassian sept). The three crowns of the flag of Munster represent these three late Kingdoms. By the mid-19th Century, much of the area was hit hard in the Great Famine. The Province also was affected by events in the Irish War of Independence in the early 20th Century, and there was a brief 'Munster Republic' during the Irish Civil War.

St. Patrick was said to have spent seven years founding churches and ordaining priests in the region during the fifth Century, although a fifth Century Bishop named Ailbe was the Patron Saint of Munster. The Irish leaders Michael Collins and earlier Daniel O'Connell also came from families of the old Gaelic Munster gentry. Munster is a tourist destination for visitors to explore, with site attractions from the rolling hills of County Clare to beautiful Coastline of West Cork, Ring of Kerry and the Dingle Peninsula and many ancient Castles and Monasteries. Both Counties Cork and Kerry are two among Ireland's largest Counties and they are on the West Coast of Munster, and both have their own names that they like to go by. In Cork they consider themselves the "People's Republic of Cork" and "The Kingdom of Kerry" which has won the GAA All-Ireland Senior Football Championship many more times than any other team. It's lush green scenery and stunning coastline is coveted by visitors. The lunar Burren and Cliffs of Moher are in County Clare and several ancient castles populate the counties of Limerick, Tipperary and Waterford.

The Munster Province is also the home to Irish sports like hurling, rugby and Gaelic football (GAA). The province is very well noted for its traditions in Irish folk music.

BELOW ARE THE 6 COUNTIES IN MUNSTER PROVINCE	
MUNSTER	Cork– Clare – Tipperary – Kerry- Limerick - Waterford

♣ ♣ ♣

COUNTY CORK

County Cork Coat of Arms

County Cork is located in the Province of Munster, bordering Kerry to the West, Limerick to the North, Tipperary to the North-East and Waterford to the East. It is the largest County in Ireland by land and the largest of Munster's six Counties by population and area. At the last census in 2016, the population of the entire Cork County was 542,196 making it the third most populous County in Ireland.

The County's capital is Cork City, it is the second largest city in Ireland, with a population of 125,622 inhabitants (2016 census). Cork is referred locally to as "The Rebel County" a nickname earned around the 15th Century, however from the 20th Century, the name has been more commonly attributed to the prominent role that Cork played in the Irish War of Independence(1919-1921) when it was the scene of considerable fighting. In addition, it was an anti-treaty stronghold during the Irish Civil War (1922-23). Much of what is now known as County Cork was once part of the Kingdom of *Deas Mumhan* (South Munster), anglicised as "Desmond" and ruled by the McCarthy Clan. But after the Norman invasion in the 12th Century, the McCarthy clan were pushed Westward into what is now West Cork and County Kerry. Both the Northern and Eastern portions of Cork City was given an English Royal Charter in 1318, and for many Centuries it was an outpost for Old English culture due to the Hiberno-Norman FitzGerald Dynasty, taken it and it became the Earls of Desmond. But the Fitzgerald Desmond Dynasty was destroyed in the Desmond Rebellions between of 1569-1573 and 1579-83. The fighting devastated much of the County and in the aftermath, and much of Cork was colonised by English settlers in the Plantation of Munster.

Now, County Cork is well known for the home to the 15th-Century Blarney Castle, and the Blarney Stone with which Legend has it that 'Kissing the Stone bestows the kisser with a special gift of fluency.

Notable Corkonians include Michael Collins (Irish Revolutionary leader), and **former** Taoiseach *Jack Lynch.*

Major towns in County Cork include:	
Mitchelstown,	Carrigaline
Skibbereen	Bandon
Clonakilty	Kinsale
Youghal	Macroom

COUNTY CLARE

County Clare Coat of Arms

County Clare is a Maritime County in the Province of Munster, bounded on the West by the Atlantic on the North-West by Galway Bay on the East and South by the River Shannon.

The present County formed from a very early period, a native territory of Thomond, signifying "North Munster". The area was divided into Baronies, each occupied by their ruling families, such as the O'Loughlins, O'Garbhs, O'Briens, O'Connors, O'Deas, McMahons and McNamaras were the main clans. Together, these families are generally referred to as the Dalcassian families, from DalgCais, a name for the Eastern half of the County. But the Danish Vikings raided this County on many occasions during the 9th and 10th Centuries. They were finally defeated at the beginning of the 11th Century by the most famous of the O'Briens, which was Brian Boru, who also led the army that defeated the Danes of Dublin at Clontarf in 1014.

County Clare covers an area of 1,262 square miles of a rich and unique landscape in the west of Ireland. It is the home to the 'Burren', an ancient limestone plain of over 100 square miles of archaeological and historical standing. The nickname for the County is known as the *Banner County*, for which various origins have been suggested: like the banners captured by Clare's Dragoons at the Battle of Ramillies; or the banner of "Catholic Emancipation" raised by Daniel O'Connell's victory in an 1828 by-election for the County that led to Parliament passing the Roman Catholic Relief Act 1829.

The Capital of County Clare is Ennis, it has a population of 118,627 (2016 census). Clare boasts of historical sites and visitor attractions such as the 'The 'Burren', a unique karst region, which contains rare flowers and fauna. At the Western edge of 'The Burren', facing the Atlantic Ocean are the Cliffs of Moher, and the famous 'Bunratty Castle' which is a large 15th-Century Tower House located in the centre of Bunratty village in County Clare.

Major towns in County Clare:	
Clonlara	Bunratty
Broadford	Shannon Town
Ennis	Kilrush

COUNTY KERRY

County Kerry Coat of Arms

County Kerry is in the Peninsular South-West region of Ireland and is known for its pockets of Irish-language speakers and striking region.

The County is the fifth-largest of the 32 counties of Ireland by area and the 15th-largest by population. It is the second-largest of Munster's six Counties by area, and the fourth-largest by population. Kerry is measured to be 4,807 in Kilometres squares in size.

The common nickname for Kerry is 'the Kingdom.' It is bordered by only two other Counties such as County Limerick to the East and County Cork to the South-East. Kerry County has a total population of 147,554 according to the 2016 Census, most of whom live in or near the urban centres. The capital of County Kerry is Tralee (famed for the 'Roses' contest), which once every year, brings hundreds of young women of Irish descent from all over the world to congregate in the County town of Kerry to battle it out for the title of the 'Rose of Tralee'. The annual Rose of Tralee festival celebrates the national consciousness of the Irish through young Irish Diaspora females including some at home in a very entertaining way. The event is usually nationally televised to millions of Irish people both at home and abroad.

Other important activities in the county that visitors can look forward to enjoying includes – horse riding, fishing, water- sports, hill walking, sea angling, folk music, etc.

Major towns in County Kerry:	
Cahersiveen	Ballybunion
Listowel	Killorglin
Castleisland	Killarney

♣ ♣ ♣

COUNTY LIMERICK

County Clare Coat of Arms

County Limerick borders four other Counties; Kerry to the West, Clare to the North, Tipperary to the East and Cork to the South. It is the fifth largest of Munster's six Counties in size and the second largest by population. It has an overall population of 195,175 according to 2016 census.

Limerick City is the County town and Ireland's third largest city. It serves as a regional centre for the greater Mid-West Region. The town is commonly referred to as 'Ireland's Sporting Capital' because it has a strong sporting history with a great love for rugby games, hurling, Gaelic football, soccer and horseracing. The River Shannon flows through the city of Limerick into the Atlantic Ocean at the north of the county and below the city, the waterway is known as the Shannon Estuary.

The City of Limerick is home to the 13th-Century King John's Castle, that is found on an island in the river. Also nearby is the Hunt Museum which displays a vast collection of art and antiquities in the Old Customs House. Limerick has also a varied landscape of the Ballyhoura and Galtee Mountains in the Southeast, and the rich fertile plains of the Centre and North of the County that is known as the Golden Vale. As well, archaeological sites like the Grange Stone Circle dots the Countryside around Lough Gur, in the Ballyhoura Mountains. County Limerick provides some of Ireland's most Scenic Countryside and the charming villages of Adare and Croom. Golf, greyhound racing, fishing and water sports on the River Shannon is readily available. Limerick was designated the first ever National City of Culture in 2014.

Major towns in County Limerick include:			
Galbally	Adare	Rathkeale	Abbeykeale
Kilmallock	Rasheen,		Newcastle West

COUNTY TIPPERARY

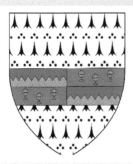

Tipperary is a landlocked Rural County that is home to mountains, rivers, lakes and farmlands in Ireland's Province of Munster. The County town of Tipperary is Clonmel, located in the Southside of the County and is a gateway for exploring the region.

County Tipperary Coat of Arms

County Tipperary was established in the early thirteenth Century shortly after the Norman invasion of Ireland. In 1838, the County was divided by Government into two administrative areas (North Tipperary and South Tipperary). At that time, the County town of Clonmel was where the Grand-Jury held its twice-yearly Judicial proceedings at the Southern limit of the County; it was said that the roads leading North were very poor, they made the journey inconvenient for Jurors resident in the area, so a petition to move the County town to a more Central location was proposed, however, this was opposed by the MP for Clonmel, so instead the County was split into two Ridings (north and south). The Grand Jury of the South Riding continued to meet in Clonmel, while that of the North Riding met in Nenagh. In 1898, the Local Government (Ireland) Act 1898 established County Councils to replace the Grand Jury for civil functions, and the Ridings became separate "Administrative Counties" with separate County Councils. Their names were changed from "Tipperary North/South Riding" to "North/South Tipperary" by the Local

Government Act 2001, which re-designated all "Administrative Counties" to be known simply as "Counties". The Local Government Reform Act 2014 has combined the two Counties and restored a single County of Tipperary as it is presently.

The population of the entire County was 160,441 at the 2016 census. County Tipperary has a strong sporting history and is home to the Gaelic Games of Hurling, Gaelic Football, Camogie and Handball. The primary Historical site in the County is the 'Rock of Cashel' an imposing Cathedral, and the Round Tower encompassing some 2000 years of history.

Major towns in County Tipperary			
Carrick-on-Suir	Cashel	Nenagh	Clonmel
Templemore	Cahir	Rosecrea	Thurles

COUNTY WATERFORD

County Waterford is situated in the South-Eastern region of Ireland, in the Province of Munster. The County itself is named after the city of Waterford which is the County's Capital town.

Waterford region was inhabited by a tribe of native Gaelic people called the Déise, pronounced "day-sha" (Irish: An Déise) who conquered the area sometime between the 4th and 8th centuries after being driven out of the region that is known today as Southern County Meath and Northern County Kildare. The overall size of the County Waterford measures at 1,857 km2 (or 717 square miles), and the population was 114,000 in the last census in 2016.

Vikings arrived in County Waterford sometime in the mid-800s and settled there. The region was likely the largest recorded Viking settlement of Scandinavia to be found anywhere in Western Europe at that time. The Vikings said to have founded Waterford City in 941, and the name Waterford comes from the Old Nose Vedrarfjord. The county is nicknamed the Crystal County due to the fine handcrafted Irish Crystal Glass works by world renown House of Waterford Crystal, located in Waterford city. The County is steeped in history, heritage and culture. It has two Mountain Ranges, the Knockmealdown Mountains and the Comeragh

Mountains. The Highest Point is Knockmealdown, at 794m. Waterford also has many rivers, including Ireland's third and fourth longest rivers, the River Suir (184 km) and the Munster Blackwater (168 km). There are many beaches along Waterford's volcanic coastlines with splendid views of the Hook Peninsula, Dunmore East, Tramore and Dungarvan towns. A large stretch of this coastline, known as the Copper Coast is a designated UNESCO Geopark, a place of great geological importance.

Waterford is also home to Reginald's Tower, one of the most prominent and the oldest Civic Structures in Ireland.

Major towns in County Waterford include:			
Dungarven	Cappoquin	Lismore	Kilure
Tramore	Dunmore	Ardmore	Dunhill

CONNACHT PROVINCE

An Overview of Connaught Province

Connacht or Connaught (either of the two spellings are correct), **is one of the Provinces of Ireland, covering the West of Ireland and largely made up of Counties on Ireland's Western Coast. Encompassing only five Counties, it is the smallest of the four Provinces.**

The name "Connacht" is derived from the Mythological Conn of the Hundred Battles. Many parts of Connacht's Gaeltacht (Irish speaking areas) retain their strong Gaelic traditions, with native Irish language spoken throughout the Province. Connacht relies mainly on tourism and agriculture – it is also noted for its breath-taking natural landscapes and stunning scenery, including Connemara, Achill Island, and Sligo's world-renowned surfing coast. A vast majority of the entire population in Connaught live around County Galway, a very cosmopolitan city within the Province.

THE 5 COUNTIES IN CONNAUGHT PROVINCE	
CONNAUGHT	Galway – Leitrim – Mayo- Sligo Roscommon

COUNTY GALWAY

County Galway Coat of Arms

County Galway is in the middle of West of Ireland, and part of the Province of Connacht. The County is named after the City of Galway. It has a total population of 258,552 according to the 2016 census. The first inhabitants in the Galway area were thought to arrive over 7000 years ago. There are several Irish-speaking areas in the West of the County. The city also bears the nickname "City of the Tribes" (Irish: Cathair na dTreabh).

The County Galway originally comprised several Kingdoms and territories which predate the formation of the whole County. The kingdoms included Aidhne, Uí Maine, Maigh Seóla, Conmhaícne-Mara, Soghain and Máenmaige.

The County became an Official entity around 1569 AD and it includes a number of inhabited islands such as the Oileáin Árann (Aran Islands) and Inis Bó Fine (Inishbofin).

County Galway is home to the largest Gaeltacht Irish-speaking region in Ireland. Nearly 20% of the population of County Galway live in the Gaeltacht (Gaelic-speaking districts over 48,907 people living within this region), which extends from Galway City through Connemara.

Irish-speaking areas areas of County Galway consists of the following;- parts of Galway City Gaeltacht, Gaeltacht Cois

Fharraige, Conamara Theas, Aran Islands and Duiche Sheoigheach. The Aran Islands are also part of the Galway Gaeltacht. There is also a strong Irish-language media presence in this area which boasts a dedicated Radio Station 'Raidió na Gaeltachta and the Foinse Newspaper' in Carraroe, that is in addition to the nations National TV channel TG4 in Baile na hAbhann.

County Galway is partly home to a number of Ireland's largest lakes including Lough Corrib (the largest lake in the Republic of Ireland), Lough Derg and Lough Mask.

Galway City is also home to Ireland's only Irish-language theatre, Taibhdhearc na Gaillimhe, and best known for the world renown yearly Galway Races.

Major towns in County Galway include:			
Ballynasloe	Aughrim	Hollygrove	Tuam
Headford	Moycullen	Oranmore	Cashel

♣ ♣ ♣

COUNTY LEITRIM

County Leitrim Coat of Arms

Leitrim is the 26th largest of the 32 counties by area and the smallest by population on the island and also the smallest of Connacht's five Counties in both size and population. County Leitrim is part of the Border Region and it is bordering the Counties; County Donegal to the North, County Fermanagh to the Northeast, Cavan to the East, Longford to the South, Roscommon to the Southwest and Sligo to the West. Fermanagh is in Northern Ireland while all the other neighbouring Counties are within the Republic.

County Leitrim or '**Contae *Liatroim'*** in Irish, is named after the village of Leitrim. In 1925, Leitrim village comprised only 30 houses with 5 of that being licensed to sell alcohol. Strategically situated, Liatroim was an important ford of the River Shannon connecting Ulster and Connacht. It is thought that the Battle of Áth an Chip between Normans and Connacht probably occurred on Drumhierney townland beside Battle-bridge in 1270.

Founded in the early modern period, Leitrim County Council is the local authority for the county, it has a population of 31,972 according to the 2016 census. Leitrim has a hilly and mountainous landscape and the shortest length of the coastline of any County in Ireland that touches the sea, and only 2.5 miles (4.0 km) long at the coastline in Tullaghan. The Shannon is linked to the Erne via the Shannon-Erne Waterway.

There are many places to choose from such as the Glencar Waterfall at Glencar Lough, the (ruined) Franciscan Friary of Creevelea, near the village of Dromahair. It may be the finest ancient monument in County Leitrim.

Major towns in County Leitrim include:			
Aghamore	Drumshanbo	Mohill	Rooski
Carrigallen	Jamestown	Fenagh	Kinlough

COUNTY MAYO

County Mayo Coat of Arms

County Mayo is part of the Province of Connacht on the West Coast of Ireland. The Irish name for Mayo is Maigh Eo, which means 'plain of yew-trees'. The County got the name from the Diocese of that name which evolved from a 7th Century Monastery that was established by Saint Colmán and some English Monks on 'the plain of yews'. Mayo became a Diocese in the 12th century, but it was amalgamated with Tuam about 500 years later.

The size of County Mayo is about 5,398 Kilometers square, and a population of 110,713 according to the 1991 census. The County Town is Castlebar.

Mayo's extensive coastline is wild and broken, with many inlets from Killala Bay in the North to Killary Harbour in the Southwest. Westport and Ballina are Port towns, with numerous islands and inland lakes. Stretching East and North from Lough (Lake) Carrowmore that is situated in the parishes of Belmullet, Kiltane and Kilcommon Erris, is the largest expanse of bog in Ireland, 200 square miles (520 square km) in area. The Principal Rivers in Mayo are the Moy and the Errif. The low peaks of Nephin (2,646 feet [807 metres]) and Croagh Patrick (2,510 feet [765 metres] dominates the landscape, and Mweelrea (2,688 feet [819 metres]), to the North of Killary Harbour, is the highest mountain in Connaught Province.

The County's attractions include delightful holiday resorts, excellent angling or fishing_waters, exciting walking and mountain climbing trails, a good choice of golf courses, opportunities for many other types of activity-holidays, as well as some of the most interesting archaeological and historical sites in Ireland. It is the County of Croagh Patrick and Ballintubber Abbey and the Marian Shrine of Knock.

Major towns in County Mayo include			
Ballinrobe	Crossmolina	Ballina	Westport
Claremorris	Swinford	Knock	Ballina

♣ ♣ ♣

COUNTY ROSCOMMON

County Roscommon Coat of Arms

Roscommon (in Irish *Ros Comáin*) is the only totally landlocked County in the Province of Connacht. The County is sat on a small size of land of about 2,463 square kilometres. It has a population according to census 2016. Roscommon Town is the County Town of this rural County with a history that dates back a few thousand years. The Medieval village of Tulsk, County Roscommon was said to be the seat of Queen Maebh (Maeve), the Kings of Connacht, and later the High Kings of Ireland. Modern day Roscommon had its name around the 5th Century, by Coman mac Faelchon, a well-known Saint who was said to have founded a Monastery there in the woods around the Roscommon area, and the Monastery became "Coman's Wood" (or in Irish "*Ros Comáin*).

In ancient times, around (1585) the Structure of Connaught was under the Rulership by a number of Lords and Chieftains of the Province who were given tenures in their territories under English law. North Western County Roscommon was known then as MacDermott Country, and part of the South was under O'Kelly occupation. This part of Ireland retained its Irish tradition longer than in other areas. Left by Oliver Cromwell to Irish proprietors after the English Conquest in the 17th Century, even as it was affected by the Penal Laws and other social changes that were imposed upon Ireland.

County Roscommon was a major stronghold and market town that continued to thrive until the Great Famine when about a third of the population was wiped off and left the area devastated for a long period, until the "Celtic Tiger" years brought in a new revival of activities and substantial developments to the area as we see it now.

Places of interest include the award-winning Famine Museum dedicated to telling the story of the great Irish Famine. The Dr Hyde Park, home of the Roscommon Gaelic football team in Roscommon, named after first President of Ireland, Douglas Hyde.

Famous People with Roscommon roots includes Irish Taoiseach Albert Reynolds, Ex-President Mary McAleese, Percy French, actress Maureen O'Sullivan, actor Chris O'Dowd.

Major towns in County Roscommon include			
Strokestown	Athleague	Arigna	Boyle
Ballintober	Frenchpark	Ballaghadereen	Lecarrow

COUNTY SLIGO

County Sligo Coat of Arms

County Sligo is also located in the Border Region in the Province of Connaucht. Sligo town is the largest town in the County and also the administrative capital. The population of Sligo is around 65,535 in 2016 census, around 19% more than just twenty years ago, making it the 3rd most populated County in the Province of Connacht, and the 22nd largest of Ireland's 32 Counties in terms of area.

The County borders with County Mayo to the West, County Roscommon to the South and Southeast and County Leitrim to the Northeast. Sligo County was officially formed in 1585 but did not come into effect until the chaos of the 'Nine Years' War ended in 1603 at the time of the Elizabethan Conquest.

Sligo enjoys different nicknames though, a renowned one is "Yeats County" (mainly after the Poet, William Butler Yeats) or "the Land of Heart's Desire" (after a Yeats poem). The Poet and Nobel Laureate William Butler Yeats (1865-1939) spent much of his childhood in Northern Sligo. The County's landscapes, particularly the Isle of Innisfree in Lough Gill are said to the inspiration for much of his poetry.

The name Sligo which is an English version of the Irish name *Sligeach*, meaning "abounding in shells." It refers to the abundance of shellfish found in the estuary, and from the extensive shell middens along the shores of Sligo bay. The name initially referred only to the river in that area, it was then was applied to the town and eventually the County, created by the English Viceroy Henry Sidney.

Yeats is buried in North County Sligo, "Under Ben Bulben", in Drumcliff. Other notable personalities associated with Sligo includes: – Revolutionary Irish Nationalist - Constance Markievicz, film director - Neil Jordan, and members of the Pop band – Westlife.

Major towns in County Sligo include:			
Tubbercurry	Monastraden	Strandhill	Bellagy
Ballymote	Collooney	Coolaney	Kilglass

♣ ♣ ♣

ULSTER PROVINCE

An Overview of Ulster Province

Ulster Province is known as "*Cúige Uladh*" in Irish, literally means "the Fifth of the Uladh" Ulster Province consists of nine Counties altogether, out of which six of them - Counties Antrim, Armagh, Derry (Londonderry), Down, Fermanagh and Tyrone belong in the Northern Ireland, while the remaining three Counties - Cavan, Donegal, and Monaghan are in the Republic of Ireland.

As the Ulster as a Province falls under the Jurisdiction of two the different Countries (Republic of Ireland and United Kingdom), it is consequentially divided into two distinct fractions. All the six Counties that form part of Northern Ireland in Ulster belongs in the United Kingdom politically, whereas the part of the region containing the above mentioned three Counties remains in the Republic. However, all the six counties in Northern Ireland are regarded as being part and parcel of the island of Ireland and sometimes counted in addition with the 26 counties in the Republic to make up the 32 Counties of the island of Ireland as a whole.

All of Northern Ireland as part of parcel of Britain ; it uses the British Pound sterling as their currency and the United Kingdom's international dialling code (+44).

NORTHERN IRELAND

Northern Ireland is well within the Ulster region of the island of Ireland, but it is part of the United Kingdom, along with England, Scotland and Wales.

Northern Ireland region was for decades the center of Sectarian tension and violence due to the subject of the dispute of whether it should remain part of the United Kingdom or return to Ireland. Some people in Northern Ireland, mainly Protestant Unionist community believe it should remain in the United Kingdom and others believes it should leave the UK and re-join the Republic of Ireland.

In the early 1990s and for several years, negotiations took place between its political parties, the British and Irish toward a reconciliation. The 'Trouble' as it was called, Northern Ireland was regarded as one of the most dangerous places in Europe as it was deeply troubled. But the "Good Friday Peace Agreement was signed, all of the Ulster region in recent years has been safe for visitors on both sides of the border. Away from the historic troubles, Northern Ireland is known for its fascinating places to visit, which include Norman Castles, Glacial valleys and Mountains, Celtic and Christian Monuments, and Coastal links Golf courses.

The capital of Northern Ireland is Belfast. It is the largest city in all of Ulster and which suffered most of the violence during the time of the 'Trouble.' Belfast has a population of 279,237) and is the main commercial centre of Northern Ireland. The City is home of the world's historic and most famous ship: the Titanic.

Movie Star Liam Neeson, TV Show Host Eamonn Holmes, Rock Star Van Morrison, Super-Star Soccer Player George Best, who died in 2005, are just a few of notable people born in Belfast.

BELOW ARE THE 9 COUNTIES IN ULSTER PROVINCE	
ULSTER	Cavan - Antrim – Donegal – Fermanagh- Down - Londonderry – Tyrone – Monaghan - Armagh

♣

COUNTY CAVAN

County Cavan Coat of Arms

County Cavan is one of the nine Counties in the ancient Province of Ulster, and one of the three Counties that fall within the Republic of Ireland. The Irish name of the County is *Contae an Chabháin*, and can be translated as "Hollow". County Cavan borders six different Counties; Leitrim to the West, Fermanagh and Monaghan to the North, County Meath to the Southeast, County Longford to the Southwest and County Westmeath to the South. Cavan is the 19th largest of the 32 Counties in area and the 25th largest by population, which is 76,092 according to the 2016 census. The County town is Cavan Town.

> Historically, the area of Cavan was part of 11th Century Kingdom of Bréifne, a small Kingdom that was ruled by the Gaelic, Brefney O'Reilly family in East Bréifne.

Cavan was said to have been under the Western Province of Connacht at first before it was transferred to Ulster in 1584 when Bréifne was shirred. It is from then that the County became known as County Cavan, and it is also for this reason that the County is sometimes referred to as the Breffni County.

The County covers an area of some 730 square miles of beautiful lakes, and play host to two of Ireland's great waterways – the River Shannon and the River Erne, and the source of many rivers. The number of lakes found in this County are believed to be well over 350 – this is also why people fondly call it 'The Lakeland County.' Lough Sheelin is the County's largest lake measuring at 18.8 km^2 (7.3 sq mi). It is situated in the South of the County and forms a three-way border on its waters between Counties Meath, Westmeath and Cavan. There are also wildlife protected lakes such as Lough Gowna and Lough Ramor, in the South and East of the County. Cavan has more to offer aside from charming lakes which clearly provides opportunities for anglers, boating, and sailing enthusiasts, as the County town and surroundings offer other things, from golf, horse riding and shopping from a bustling commercial centre, to archaeological heritage sites and much more to explore.

Major towns in County Cavan include:			
Blacklion	Drumcarban	Glangevlin	Lakefield
Kingscourt	Coothill	Coolaney	Redhill

♣ ♣ ♣

COUNTY DONEGAL

County Donegal Coat of Arms

County Donegal is also one of nine Counties of the Ulster Province and one of three Counties counted among the twenty-six in the Republic of Ireland. The Irish name for County Donegal is *Contae Dhúnna nGall*, translated literally as "Castle of the Strangers." County Donegal is the Northernmost County of the overall thirty-two Counties even though it is part of the South. It ranked the fourth-largest Irish County by area, covering an area of 1,877 square miles (4,861 square kilometres). The County is the most mountainous in Ulster consisting Chiefly of two ranges of low mountains; the Derryveagh Mountains in the North and the Blue Stack Mountains in the South, with Mount Errigal at 749 metres (2,457 ft) as the Highest Peak.

Lifford is the county town of County Donegal, although Letterkenny is by far the largest and more popular town in the County. The County according to the 2016 census, it has a population of 158,755 people.

From the 1470s until the very early 17th Century, Donegal used to be the 'Capital' of Tyrconnell (Irish: Tír Chonaill), a Gaelic Kingdom controlled by the O'Donnell Dynasty of the Northern Uí Néill. (known in English as the O'Neill Clan) of modern day County Tyrone. They were one of Ireland's richest and most powerful native ruling families from the early 13th Century through to the start of the 17th Century. But during the Great Famine of the late 1840s in Ireland, County Donegal was said to be one of the worst affected parts of Ulster, and caused vast numbers of its people to emigrate throughout the period. The Partition of Ireland in the early 1920s also had a massive direct impact on County Donegal both economically and administratively as it was cut off from Derry, which had acted for Centuries as the County's main commercial hub and financial centre. However, due to the partition, Derry together with West Tyrone was henceforward in a new, different jurisdiction officially of Northern Ireland.

The modern County Donegal was shired by order of the English Crown in 1585. The English authorities at Dublin Castle formed the new county by amalgamating the old Kingdom of Tír Chonaill with the old Lordship of Inishowen. However, the Dublin authorities were unable to establish control over Tír Chonaill and Inishowen due to the Battle of Kinsale in 1602, full control over the new County Donegall was only achieved after the Flight of the Earls in September 1607. It was one of the counties that were 'planted' during the Plantation of Ulster from around 1610 onwards.

County Donegal is culturally one of the richest areas in Ireland as it is one of the last remaining strongholds of the Irish language. The County has a higher percentage of Irish speaking households in its Gaeltacht area than in all Gaeltacht areas across Ireland.

Donegal is exposed to the Atlantic Ocean with a stunning coastline of golden beaches, dramatic cliffs and windswept peninsulas and some of Ireland's most fascinating ancient sites including the Round fort of An Grianan Aileach and the Stones of Kilcooney Dolmen, majestic mountains, and clear lakes.

St. Patrick's Church, also known as the 'Church of the Four Masters' in Donegal Town is a famous landmark that was built in the early 1930s and is dedicated to Saint Patrick.

Major towns in County Donegal include:			
Ardagh	Buncrana	Ballyshannon	Letterkenny
Greencastle	Millford	Malin	Glen

♣ ♣ ♣

COUNTY MONAGHAN

Coat of Arms of Co. Monaghan

County Monaghan is part of the Border Region Counties of Ulster and one of the three which are in the Republic of Ireland. Monaghan was one of three Ulster Counties to join the Irish Free State rather than Northern Ireland. The County is bounded by counties Louth, Armagh, Tyrone, Fermanagh, Cavan and Meath. The Irish name for County Monaghan is *Contae Mhuineacháin*, which would translate as "the County of "small hills". It is the fifth smallest of the Republic's 26 Counties in area and fourth smallest by population. It also happens to be the smallest of Ulster's nine counties both in size and in terms of population, which stands at just 61,000 (61,386) as counted in the 2016 census. The County has been in existence since around 1585 when the Mac Mathghamhna rulers of Airgíalla agreed to join the Kingdom of Ireland following the 20th-Century Irish War of Independence and the signing of the Anglo-Irish Treaty.

In 1585, the English Lord Deputy of Ireland, visited the area and met the Irish Chieftains and requested that Ulster be divided into Counties and land in the Kingdom of Airgíalla be apportioned to each of the Chiefs. A commission was established to accomplish this, and County Monaghan came into being. The County was subdivided into five Baronies which was left under the control of the McKenna Chieftains.

After the defeat of the Rebellion of Hugh O'Neill, and the Ulster Chieftains in 1603. The County, however, was not planted like the other Counties of Ulster were, the lands were instead left in the hands of the native Chieftains.

The County was named after the town of Monaghan, which is the Capital and County town. It also has a nickname, "the Drumlin County," a fitting description of the landscape of drumlins and small hills.

County Monaghan is endowed with lush rolling hills and Lakelands in the beautiful Countryside, coupled with excellent waterways which provide superb angling for the enthusiast as well as a World Class 18-hole golf courses with excellent Country Club facilities. It was home to one of Ireland's best-loved Poets of all time, **Patrick Kavanagh**. He was from the small farming town of Mucker, Inniskeen Parish in County Monaghan.

Major towns in County Monaghan includes			
Ballybay	Castleblaney	Emyvale	Glasslough
Clones	Carricmacross	Smithborough	Inniskeen

COUNTY DOWN

County Down Coat of Arms

County Down, (*Contae an Dúin,* in Irish - meaning *the Fort*) one of the counties of Ulster, is located in Northern Ireland. The county forms an area of 2,448 km² (945 square miles) and has an estimated population is approximately about 531,665. It is bordered by County Antrim to the north, County Armagh to the West and the sea to the South and East Downpatrick is the county town of County Down, named one of the most ancient towns on the island of Ireland, with archaeological evidence of Neolithic and Bronze Age settlements. Down contains both the southernmost point of Northern Ireland (Cranfield Point) and the easternmost point of Ireland (Burr Point).

The county holds strong ties to the early history of Saint Patrick. Saint Patrick was said to have landed first on the Coast of Wicklow, and from there he travelled northwards as far as Strangford Lough where he landed at the mouth of the River Slaney near Saul in County Down. There he met a local chieftain, whom he converted to Christianity and who gave him a barn that he used as his first church. Saint Patrick spent many years travelling around Ireland, converting the people to Christianity, consecrating Bishops and founding churches as he went along. Many years later, nearing the end of his life, he was said to return to Saul where he spent his last moments. He is believed to be buried in Downpatrick in the year 461 on the grounds of Down Cathedral. Although, the actual burial place of Saint Patrick remains controversial as some people have doubt about this piece of information.

There is so much more for the visitor to enjoy in County Down, from the Mourne Mountains in the South to the hundreds mile coastline in the north of glorious beaches and natural harbours, to the peace and serenity of Rostrevor Forest Walk and even more.

Major towns in County Down includes			
Banbridge	Newtownards	Castlereagh	Downpatrick
Holywood	Newsatle	Portaferry	Bangor

♣ ♣ ♣

COUNTY TYRONE

County Tyrone Coat of Arms

County Tyrone is a County in the heart of Northern Ireland in the Province of Ulster and the eighth largest by area on the island of Ireland. It is also the largest County by area in Northern Ireland and tenth largest by population on the entire island of Ireland.

County Tyrone derives its name and general geographic location from Tyrone (Tir Eoghain) a Gaelic Kingdom under the O'Neill Dynasty which existed until the 17th Century. History has it that, it was the traditional stronghold of the various O'Neill clans and families, the strongest of the Gaelic Irish families in Ulster, surviving into the Seventeenth Century.

The ancient principality of Tír Eoghain, the inheritance of the O'Neills, included the whole of the present Counties of Tyrone and Londonderry, and the four Baronies of West Inishowen, East Inishowen, Raphoe North and Raphoe South in County Donegal. The County is adjoined to the Southwest shore of Lough Neagh, it covers an area of 3,155 km² (1,218 sq. mi) and has a population of about 177,986.

The county town is Omagh. Tyrone has a rich historic culture, and fine examples of evidence of human settlements in Tyrone dating back 6,000 years are that of the well-known

Neolithic remains of the Beaghmore Stone Circles near Cookstown. Tyrone has an abundance of spectacular Scenery from the Wild Sperrin Mountains in the North, sweeping down to the rich pastoral lowlands of the South and Crystal-Clear waterways including the Rivers Mourne, Derg, and Owenreagh. The Ulster History Park near Omagh has recreated an excellent presentation of life in Ireland over the past 10,000 years.

The County holds the story of Thomas Mellon, a famous emigrant, born in Cappagh in County Tyrone. He left for the United States of America with his farmer parents as a young boy and grew up to become a very successful as Lawyer and Judge, then a Tycoon in USA Banking industry.

The original family house they used to live in County Tyrone now forms the centrepiece of the Ulster American Folk Park Museum near the County town of Omagh in County Tyrone. Visitors to the County can also enjoy the wonderful outdoors and natural landscape with an array of activities across the County. *The population of County Tyrone is just over 150,000.*

Major towns in County Tyrone include:			
Strabane	Dungannon	Cookstown	Clogher
Omagh	Aughnacloy	Coalisland	

COUNTY ARMAGH

County Armagh Coat of Arms

County Armagh is named after its County town of Armagh, it is one of the 6 Counties that make up Northern Ireland and adjoined to the Southern shore of Lough Neagh. The county covers an area of 1,326 km² and has a population of about 174,792. County Armagh is known as the "Orchard County" because of its many apple orchards in the area. The County is historically the ecclesiastical centre of Ireland for some 1,500 years. The name 'Armagh' is derived from the Irish word 'Ard Mhacha' meaning "height" and Macha, referring to the legendary Queen Mhacha, who was said to have built Fort Navan (Emain Macha).

Ancient Armagh was the territory of the Ulaid before the Fourth Century AD. It was ruled by the Red Branch, whose capital was Emain Macha (or Navan Fort) near Armagh. The site, and subsequently the city, was named after the goddess Macha. The Red Branch play an important role in the Ulster Cycle, as well as the Cattle Raid of Cooley. However, they were eventually driven out of the area by the Three Collas, who invaded in the 4th Century and held power until the 12th Century. The Clan Colla ruled the area known as Airghialla or Oriel for these 800 years. Once the ancient seat of Kings, Navan, to the west of Armagh town, was the earliest capital of Ulster. It is a site of unparalleled importance, which reflects over 7,500 years of evolution.

Visitors to the 'Orchard County' can enjoy a wide range of activities all year round, including its annual celebration of Apple Blossom Festival in May. The occasional game of road bowls played in rural Armagh and County Cork is also popular among locals.

The Irish King, Brian Boru, is also buried in Armagh Cathedral.

Major towns in County Armagh includes				
Portadown	Craigavon	Keady	Lurgan	Newry

♣ ♣ ♣

COUNTY DERRY

County Derry Coat of Arms

County Derry is officially known as Londonderry, and its one of the six Counties of Northern Ireland. Prior to the partitioning of Ireland, it was one of the Counties of the Kingdom of Ireland from 1613 onward and then of the United Kingdom after the Acts of Union in 1800. The County covers an area of 2,074 km² (801 sq. mi) and has a population of around 247,132 (2016). The largest town is Derry City and the County town is Coleraine. Derry is an old walled city which lies on the west bank of the River Foyle, spanned by two road bridges and one footbridge. The city now covers both banks (Cityside on the west and Waterside on the east).

The county is the second-largest city in Northern Ireland and the fourth-largest on the island of Ireland. The name Derry is derived from the Irish 'Doire' meaning oak grove. (*Contae Dhoire* is the Irish name; *Coontie Lunnonderrie* is its name in Ulster Scots). The name of the county has been a point of political dispute, with Unionists advocating the use of Londonderry, and nationalists advocating the use of Derry. Despite the official name being the longer, the city is more often called as Derry.

British authorities prefer to use the name "Londonderry", while in the Republic of Ireland, both the city and County are almost always referred to as Derry only. The County was founded in 1613 as part of the Plantation of Ulster by King

James I of England. Twelve London Guilds were contracted to develop it and also to rebuild the settlement of Derry, and in recognition of their work, King James I, named the new city and County after the London companies by adding the prefix "London" to "Derry". Until then, the County itself was formerly known as **County Coleraine.**

County Derry or Londonderry as the case may be, is home to a number of important buildings and landscapes, including the well-preserved 17th-Century City Walls of Derry, which is classified as one of the best examples of a 'European Walled City.'

A tragic part of Derry's history is that of the events on Bloody Sunday. On 30th of January 1972, British soldiers opened fire on civilians during a peaceful protest march, killing several people and wounding a number of others in the process.

Major towns in County Derry include:			
Coleraine	Limavady	Portstewart	Magherafelt

COUNTY ANTRIM

County Antrim Coat of Arms

In ancient times, Antrim was inhabited by Celtic people called the Darini. In the early Middle Ages, Southern County Antrim was part of the Kingdom of Ulidia who pre-Gaelic Celts were and probably related to the Picts of Britain. Between the 8th and 11th Centuries Antrim was exposed to the inroads of the Vikings. In the late 12th Century, Antrim became part of the Earldom of Ulster, conquered by Anglo-Norman invaders. A revival of Gaelic power followed the campaign of Edward Bruce in 1315, leaving Carrickfergus as the only significant English stronghold. In 1588 the Antrim coast was the scene of one of the 24 wrecks of the Spanish Armada in Ireland. Then during the Tudor era in the 16th Century, many adventurers from Britain attempted to Colonise the region and many of the Scots settled in Antrim around this time. However, the modern County Antrim as we know it, is situated in the North Eastern corner of Ireland, and as one of the six Counties of Northern Ireland in Ulster Province, with a population of about 618,000. The County town of Antrim is Antrim. It is one of Northern Ireland's most desirable and picturesque destinations and home to several important historical buildings and monuments. The Causeway Coast and the

Glens of Antrim are both beautiful and unique and offer stunning coastlines, particularly the coastal valleys of the Glens of Antrim around Ballycastle. The Giant's Causeway in the County is a unique landscape and recognised UNESCO World Heritage Site.

County Antrim is the ancestral home of the 26th President of the United States, Theodore Roosevelt.

Major towns in County Antrim include:			
Newtownabbey	Ballymena	Ballyclare	Larne
Carrickfergus	Greenisland	Portrush	Lisburn

COUNTY FERMANAGH

County Fermanagh (Irish: Fir Manach or Fear Manach)

County Clare Coat of Arms

meaning "men of Manach") is one of the thirty-two Counties of Ireland and also part of the Six Counties of Northern Ireland in Ulster, with a population of 61,805 as of 2011.

The County Fermanagh borders several Counties such as Tyrone—to the Northeast, County Monaghan to the Southeast, County Cavan to the Southwest, County Leitrim to the West and County Donegal to the Northwest. The County town is Enniskillen, situated in the middle of the County and it is the largest settlement in Fermanagh. The entire County of Fermanagh is mainly rural, as it is located largely in the basin of the River Erne and dominated by two connected lakes: Upper and Lower Lough Erne, including water that spans an area of 1,851 km² (715 Sq. miles). In ancient past, Fermanagh was a stronghold of the Maguire clan–Donn Carrach Maguire who was the first of the Chiefs of the Maguire Dynasty. However, on the confiscation of lands relating to Hugh Maguire, Fermanagh became divided in a similar manner to the other 5 Counties among Scottish and English undertakers and native Irish. It was made into a County by the Statute of Elizabeth I, but it was not until the time of the Plantation of Ulster that it was finally brought under Civil Government. The area's abundant water facilitated early settlement, and late stone-age hunter-gatherers were said to have lived on fish, fruits and nuts and small animals. Later settlers, about 6,000 years ago brought farming skills, clearing forests and rearing animals. They erected stone tombs – passage graves and dolmens. Fermanagh has many examples of the remains of these, that can still be seen including many superb artefacts which are still standing. One such example is a 12th Century Round Tower on Devenish Island which still remains intact along with a small church and a ruined Augustinian Abbey even though, Viking raiders were reported to have penetrated and unleashed counter attacks on monasteries along the area surrounding Devenish Lough Erne during the ninth Century, and occasionally returning over the next Century.

Many opportunities and tourist attractions exist throughout the County, including many prospects for the outdoor enthusiasts, going from horse riding to cycling routes and more.

The playwright Samuel Beckett (1906-89), remembered for his plays of the Absurd, such as Waiting for Godot and Endgame, was said to have attended Portora Royal School in Enniskillen in the early 1920s. Other famous people include world-renowned Poets Oscar Wilde. Both were born in Enniskillen.

Major towns in County Fermanagh include:			
Enniskillen	Irvinestown	Lisnaskea	Roselea

SECTION EIGHT

BUSINESS & ECONOMY

Economy:

IFSC BUILDING, DUBLIN

Historically, the Irish economy has been based on agriculture and was almost totally dependent on farming which provided the country with food and income for thousands of years. Although, dependence on agriculture remains in Ireland and farming is still very vital but Ireland now has a mixed economy. A good percentage of the workforce is still engaged in subsistence farming mostly in the rural areas, producing food and other agricultural products for both domestic uses and for exports purposes. However, since the early 1990s the Irish economy transformed from being predominantly agricultural to a modern knowledge-based one which is heavily reliant on Foreign Direct Investments and services such as trade, finance and the technology industries have generated substantial national income for the country.

Ireland experienced unprecedented economic growth during this period which led to a major economic boom that came to be known as the Celtic Tiger, transforming the Island into the thirtieth richest country in the world and as a result, the Celtic Tiger period attracted many foreign investors and foreign companies to Ireland, and which dominated the economy and at best helped to support it alongside home investments. However, the boom period was not meant to last forever; Ireland was severely hit by the global economic downturn which caused the pace of growth to slow down during in 2007, leading to the burst of the property bubble in 2008 and the economic boom eventually came to a halt because much of the growth was without real capital to back it. Ireland gradually and officially entered a recession, which eventually saw the Irish economy badly crashed.

With the recession everything changed; the buoyant Irish economy suddenly turned from one of the most prosperous countries in Europe into one that was fighting for survival and struggling to find its feet. Unfortunately, it resulted in the closure of so many businesses and subsequent loss of jobs nationwide. The impact of the recession was felt by everybody around the country in one way or the other. Only very few were able to hold on to their jobs and many more were willing to work at meagre jobs just to make ends meet if they were lucky enough. Those who were found to have high college and University degrees couldn't find decent jobs anywhere anymore and unemployment rate sky-rocked. The Irish populace lost total confidence in the economy amidst an air of pandemonium, forcing thousands of the Irish youth to leave the country to look for other means of earning a living in neighbouring countries as a result. It was reported then that emigration from Ireland between 2008 and 2013 come to around 120,100, around 2.6% of the total population according to the Census of Ireland 2011, made up mostly of young people aged between 15 and 24.

The Irish government needed to take a drastic action in order to halt the downward spiral of the economy and subsequently stop Irish youth from leaving the country in droves and so it accepted €85 billion program of assistance from the European Union, International Monetary Fund (IMF) and bilateral loans from the United Kingdom, Sweden and Denmark in order to balance up the country's accounts. A four-year National Recovery Plan was put in place, which involved budget cuts and reduction in public spending generally, During the period, people were asked to tighten their belts while the government tried all it could, a condition majority of Irish people felt it was too harsh; it included the sale of government assets as well but in the long run, Ireland was able to resolve its financial crises.

Ireland officially exited from recession in 2010 and exited its EU-IMF bailout programme in December of 2013. Since then the Irish economy has picked up and has been going on a steady recovery. Now there seem to be an even stronger presence of multinational corporations in the country than ever before, and the past few years, the economy has resuscitated Foreign Direct Investment, and Home Investment, which were the driving force of the boom era and has been instrumental to the continued growth of the economy presently. Most of the multinational companies behind Ireland's boom economy are mostly world-renowned industries who choose to have their European Headquarters in the country and as a result, providing a wealth of opportunities to so many people as they in turn, make a substantial contribution to the Irish Economy towards its continued growth.

Ireland is an open economy and ranks high as economically free economy in the world. According to the 2019 Index of Economic Freedom, Ireland's Economy is ranked at the 6th position. It stated in addition that it ranked 2nd among 44 countries in the European region, and its overall score is well above the regional and worldwide averages. Although there is political uncertainty in the country due to Britain's plan to leave the EU, Ireland's economic future remains firm, competitive, and secure. Unemployment rates are currently down to 6 percent and more people are reportedly at work in the country.

Source: https://atlas.media.mit.edu/en/profile/country/irl/

There are so many Multinational Foreign Direct Investment Corporations in Ireland operating in fields such as Finance, ICT, Pharmaceuticals, Social Media, etc.

Multinational Corporations in Ireland include the followings:

❖ GSK	❖ IBM	❖ Boston Scientific
❖ ebay	❖ Facebook	
❖ Apple	❖ Microsoft	❖ Intel Ireland
❖ Pfizer	❖ Dell Ireland	❖ Cocoa-Cola
	❖ Google	❖ Huawei

Main Trading Partners: *The United Kingdom is the most important trading partner within the EU, whereas that might change after Brexit. However, outside the EU, the United States is Ireland's topmost export destinations.*

Below is a list of other trading partners with Ireland

United States United Kingdom Belgium Luxembourg
Switzerland Germany Netherlands France China Spain Japan
Australia Mexico Poland, & more.

Main Import Products to Ireland:

Ireland is currently ranked as 37th largest importer in the world. Below are some products imported by Ireland.

1. Aircraft, spacecraft
2. Pharmaceuticals
3. Machinery including computers
4. Mineral fuels including oil
5. Electrical machinery/equipment
6. Chemicals
7. Vehicles
8. Petroleum products,
9. Plastics
10. Optical, technical, medical apparatus
11. Perfumes & cosmetics
12. Textiles and clothing, etc.

Main Export:

Ireland is the 29th largest export economy in the world and the 13th most complex economy according to the Economic Complexity Index (ECI).

- Pharmaceuticals & medical devices
- Chemicals, & more
- Food & Dairy Products
- Data Processing Machinery
- Agriculture Beverages
- Tourism
- Planes & Aircrafts, etc

NATURAL RESOURCES:

The primary natural resources of the Republic of Ireland includes the following:-

Gypsum	Natural gas	Lead	Limestone
Dolomite	Petroleum	Silver	Peat
Copper	Barite	Mining	Zinc, etc

DOING BUSINESS IN IRELAND

Ireland may be a small country, but its impact could be felt around the world as it continues to attract a huge amount of foreign direct investment, and the government of Ireland encourages such foreign investors to come and invest in the country, particularly if it has prospects of creating employment opportunities for Irish people.

The Irish economy had emerged from one of the harshest financial crises not so long and is clearly seen to be scaling new heights recently, it has gained the admiration of other countries especially as the business climate has been steadied, and government is stable. There have also been a few other reasons including the fact that the country has proved to be one of the most welcoming destinations for international business and foreign direct investment, and as well a great place for small and medium scale domestic businesses to start and grow. Ireland is also business and investor-friendly country, in addition to the fact that it offers various measures and incentives through its tax schemes to encourage the interested investor, depending on the nature and size of the proposed investment. The Irish economy is one of the fastest growing in the Eurozone, and as a Member State of the European Union and part of the EU Single Market, Ireland's indigenous companies enjoy the benefits of having no restrictions to access the other EU Member States and the internal EU market estimated of half a Billion people. These benefits generally extend to its home-based foreign corporations too, which makes doing business in the country more interesting for investors.

Although, Post-Brexit Ireland may bring its challenges economically and otherwise, but it also presents slightly more advantage for Ireland over the rest of other European countries, being the only native English-speaking member left in the Eurozone by then. This in addition to its open market policy and its transparent, common law-based legal system will make doing business in Ireland more appealing as it is than in most other EU countries.

Some of the fastest growing industries in the country are:

- Finance
- Education
- Food & Beverages
- Business Services
- Pharmaceuticals
- Technology
- Tourism
- Environmental goods, etc.

As a fast-growing economy, Ireland offers a combination of a highly skilled, educated workforce, and multicultural human capacity that readily support and accelerate the growth of any business ventures.

SME Prospects

In terms of SMEs, there are opportunities for new start-ups and expansions taking place around the country that are generating good profits for the owners of small businesses. In some instances, there are banks that are ready to financially assist the entrepreneurs to help set up and grow their small business.

Opportunities to set up a small and medium business in Ireland exists in various sectors, such as textiles, footwear, fashion and beauty products, childcare & education sector, including franchised retail outlets for telecommunications products, or the fast-foods industry are just some very popular options that are making profits in the domestic market and which offer investment opportunities for new investors that are doing business in Ireland.

• Taxation:

Anyone who operates a business anywhere in the Republic of Ireland is expected to pay tax. But Ireland has a competitive tax structure which makes the country the ideal location for foreign investment. Because of low cost of corporate tax the country has managed to attract many global giants to the country by offering generous incentives such as low corporation tax schemes in return of their investments in the country, which make doing business in the country very attractive and they are happily locating their businesses and European headquarters to Ireland and have continued to create new employment opportunities.

The activities of these multinational companies have in no doubt resulted in Ireland's vibrant and diverse workforce, which have made the country one of the largest exporters of pharmaceutical goods, medicals and software-related goods and services in the world. The Irish economy has indeed bounced back from the downturn that not long ago prompted many people, particularly young millennials to leave Ireland, and has continued to attract a significant level of foreign investments.

Revenue might be sought in order to be certain about settling any tax liabilities or to obtain tax advantages in Ireland.

Incorporating a Business & Legal Requirements

It is a legal requirement that all business enterprises in the country must be registered with the Companies Registration

Office (CRO), therefore it is essential that a foreign investor wishing to set up a business operation in the Republic of Ireland should take all steps necessary to obtain local incorporation of the Irish branch of their company or subsidiary.

Registration of a business name is an essential requirement if any individual, partnership or corporate entity wishes to trade under a different name other than their own name(s). A private limited company (LTD) can be run by a Sole Director as long as they are resident of a European Economic Area country (EEA) however, only legal residents of the Republic of Ireland can register as Sole Traders or Partnerships in Ireland. Non-EU nationals are required to have a Stamp 4 and letter of business permission from the Department of Justice to register a business name in the country.

Types of limited companies you can set up in Ireland

- ❖ Company Limited by Shares (LTD)
- ❖ Designated Activity Company
- ❖ Company Limited by Guarantee
- ❖ Public Limited Company
- ❖ Unlimited Company
- ❖ Limited Liability Partnership
- ❖ Societas Europaea Company

Non-Residents may wish to register a Branch of their existing company in Ireland. Irish Residents can register their business as a Sole Trader/ Partnership as an alternative to a limited company.
Source: www.CRO.IE/CORE

It highly recommended getting clearance about the business you are about to engage in either through the nearest Irish embassy where staff may be able to give advice and information on specific topics.

Business Hours: The average working week for people in Ireland is usually 30 or 40 hours, in most cases, this could fluctuate considerably depending on work commitments and what is in the contract of employment between employer and employee. Weekends are usually work-free except for people who work in a certain profession and must follow duties. On the contrary, there are some people who are workaholics who like to work at the weekend to earn extra cash.

The standard office day begins at 10.00am in the morning until 5.00pm in the evening, with a little over an hour for lunch-break taken between 1.00pm and 2.15pm. Many offices, including government departments, are closed between these times. But these do not apply to the Gardaí (Police), Defence Forces, trainee doctors, etc, including certain category of employees who control their own working hours and rest periods. There are separate regulations governing the working hours of young people under the age of 18, which are ideally regulated by the Protection of Young Persons (Employment) Act 1996. Employers are also required to compensate their employees for weekend and night working. For example, they are entitled to receive higher wages more than their normal daily wage.

JOB OPPORTUNITIES IN IRELAND

The overall population of Ireland particularly in rural areas is largely drawn to the metropolitan cities because of more job prospects, and since the recovery from the recession which caused many firms to cut back on recruitment jobs in the first place, opportunities have increased significantly now with the growing population. The Irish government has also taken active initiatives to bring about a positive change in the jobs market. Career options have been on the increase and different international companies set up in Ireland are providing more jobs prospects to the Irish job market within different kinds of categories that are available in the country.

According to reports, the Irish economy grew three times faster than any other European country in 2017. That is very positive given that Ireland's unemployment rate was up to around 17% when the economy was at the height of the worst financial crisis during the recession. Currently, it has come down to 6% and is below the EU (7.3 %) and Eurozone (8.6 %) overall average. This means that Ireland employment rate is at its highest level going by the figures since 2008, and it is now estimated that for every 10 jobs lost in the recession, at last 7 have been replaced. Having said that, people who are seeking employment in jobs that requires qualifications in Ireland, it is advisable for them to be better prepared before arriving in the country because some Degrees from outside the Eurozone and other Western countries might be subjected to further scrutiny in order to establish the fact that your credentials meet certain levels in the educational framework of qualifications in Ireland, and to be sure that they are formally recognised and fit for the applied positions. Ideally, one must be legally resident in the country in order to work, and so another important point would be to ensure that you have the right visas or work permit before applying for a job here.

Being fluent in English and in a second language is an added advantage, especially to work with Multinational companies in Ireland. Generally, employers are most likely to select suitable candidates who possess the right skills and have good a level of written and spoken English.

Job opportunities are available in various fields. The list below is only an example:

- Human resources
- Education sector
- Management based
- Information Technology (IT)
- Telecommunications
- The Financial sector
- Construction
- Automobile industries
- Manufacturing
- Entertainment
- Hospitality. etc.

BANKING SECTOR

An Overview:

The banking industry in Ireland is very important for the stability and the development of the Irish economy. The Central Bank of Ireland (CBI) is responsible for overseeing the banking functions and financial regulations, authorisation and supervision in the country. Domestically, they have an obligation to ensure financial stability and consumer protection for all banks and other firms providing financial services in the country, but at the same time also incorporated the European Union's (EU) directives that provide general regulations of the banking system to other EU countries on a similar scale. When the property bubble burst occurred in 2008, it left Irish banks technically bankrupt as the sector encountered various financial problems and which led to a very costly bailout of the economy by the European Union and the International Monetary Fund (IMF). The Irish government injected over €60 billion bailout funds to save the sector. Ultimately, the banks regained their financial power and its eventual stability and operating conditions have continued to improve.

Below are Some Popular Banks in Ireland

- **Allied Irish Banks (AIB)**
- **Bank of America Merrill Lynch International**
- **Bank of Ireland**
- **KBC Bank Ireland**
- **Permanent TSB**
- **Ulster Bank Ireland**
- **Bank of Montreal Ireland**
- **Barclays Bank Ireland**
- **Citibank Ireland**
- **EBS**
- **Hewlett-Packard International Bank**
- **Intesa Sanpaolo Bank Ireland**
- **JP Morgan Bank (Ireland)**
- **UniCredit Bank Ireland**

- **Wells Fargo Bank International, etc.**

GENERAL NOTES : It is easy to open a bank account in Ireland provided you can show proof of a permanent address and some forms of utility bills and other personal identification proofs. The Banks in the Republic of Ireland operates Monday-Friday, from 9:30 am - 5:30 pm. Recently, some bank branches have started to open on Saturdays.

There are many ATM machines (Automated Teller Machine) in all cities across the country. Most banks will normally have an ATM outside the bank, this makes withdrawing money quicker than going to stand in a queue inside. With the ATMs, you can use your foreign bank cards or credit card to draw out cash, and this service is available to use 24 hours a day in most cases but there is usually a daily cash withdrawal limit of €600 from an ATM. Bigger amounts may only be cashed from the cashiers inside a bank including Bureau de Change services.

Currency of Ireland

The Official Currency used in the   Republic of Ireland is the Euro – the official 'single currency' of the European Union. The Euro was adopted in Ireland in the year 1999 when it replaced the old currency that was used in Ireland. It was known as the Irish Pound or

Punt in Irish. The Punt was Ireland's currency until 1st January 2002 when the Euro came into full circulation.

The Euro currency denominations are in seven different banknotes (five euro note (€5) which is the lowest value euro banknote; others are in €10, €20, €50, €100, €200, and €500 as the highest volume note). There are eight Coins including cents (C) in denominations of 1cent, 2cents, 5cents, 10cents, 20cents, 50cents, €1 and €2 coins. They are issued by the National Central Banks of the Euro-System or the European Central Bank. The official Euro sign (€) used for the Euro is a Capital Letter C with a double strikethrough making it look similar to letter E, while the cent symbol is a simple letter C. The Euro (€) sign is based on the fifth letter of the Greek alphabet epsilon (ε) and said to symbolise the cradle of European civilisation.

AGRICULTURE IN IRELAND

Source:www. sfsi.ie

AGRICULTURE in Ireland dates as far back to the Neolithic settlers known as New Stone Age people who brought the technology of farming to Ireland before the Bronze Age. Unlike the Hunter Gatherers who spent most of their time hunting the wild food, the Neolithic tribes were said to be a more settled farming community that practiced agriculture. They brought with them domesticated animals and made various farming tools which they used to cut down trees and cleared farming areas for growing their crops. The Stone Age farming history continued down the lineages up until this present day and was for long the mainstay of the Irish economy. Although, that is no longer be the case now as Ireland has since transformed into modern technology and knowledge-based mixed-economy status. Notwithstanding though, agriculture has always been the cornerstone of the Irish economy as a vital industry and is very important to Ireland, with a large percentage of the country's workforce and which provides hundreds of thousands of jobs both directly and indirectly of the total working population, particularly the rural dwellers whose major occupation is farming. The lands are proved to be incredibly fertile, coupled with a mild climate and plenty of rainfalls, most especially in the Midlands and Southern region. The farms in Ireland are very much utilized for farming and grazing; they produce billions of Euros worth of agri-foods every year for its domestic use and export for Ireland.

The sector is usually dominated by family-owned farms in Ireland, with approximate of about 139,000 of them, producing mostly dairy products, livestock, and beef which especially accounts for up to two-thirds of gross agricultural proportions of agri-food the exports. Ireland is known as the largest exporter of beef in all of Europe and placed as the fourth largest in the entire world. The agri-food sector is one of Ireland's most important indigenous manufacturing sectors. It includes approximately 600 foods and drinks firms throughout the country that export over 80% of food and seafood to more than 150 overseas countries. The sector also plays vital roles in the production of other staple foods for Ireland which is a hugely valuable part of the Irish economy, contributing a value of around €24 billion to the national economy, and provides 7.7% of national employment, according to the Department of Agriculture, Food and the Marine (DAFM) reports that the agri-food sector in Ireland

Source: Teagasc *the national Agriculture and Food Development Authority in Ireland providing integrated research, advisory and training services to the agriculture and food industry and rural communities. Website: http://www.teagasc.ie/agrifood/*

Agricultural products include the followings:

Sheep & Cattle Wheat Potatoes Barley Dairy Products Seafoods Oats Beverages Grains Poultry Cereal, etc

SECTION NINE

CULTURE & LIFESTYLE

The cultures of Ireland serve the same purposes and translate same meanings and ideals for its people, just like any groups of people anywhere in the world who wants to express their way of life thr vough a wide variations of things such as, their language, music, art, literature, folklore, sports, foods and drinks, politics, and obviously a beer, all these are an exciting mixture which combines to form a true traits of Irishness and also what makes the country so interesting.

An attempt is made in the following pages to explore as concisely as possible, the core features and other events in Irish customs and traditions, including the people, language, music, family unit, etiquette, art, cuisine, sports, care of children, etc.

THE PEOPLE

Fáilte! - Welcome!

Ireland has its own traits and cultural standards which defines them as a people. This go far deeper and beyond beer drinking and eating Irish potatoes which more than often people from elsewhere in the world associates with the Irish. In as much as that being a known part of the personality of Irish people and which they proudly like to maintain, the people of Ireland are found to be some of the most kind-hearted human beings to walk the earth.

As a country, Ireland has been known worldwide as a welcoming place and Irish people are generally known more than anything, for their warmth, good sense of humour, and gracious hospitality towards strangers, hence the popular Irish phrase 'Ireland of the Welcomes' or **'Céad Míle Fáilte'** (pronounced Kade-mila-fallsha)—meaning 'One Hundred Thousand Welcomes!' These are culturally welcoming gestures extended to foreign visitors. (Personally, I see the country as a 'house standing with open doors and full of welcoming people.') The Irish are also famous for their Patriotism to their country and tends to uphold their nationality with pride wherever they find themselves around the world. Irish people are passionate about politics, sports and always display a strong sense of commitment to being caring and compassionate to the less-privileged. Their kind nature means that they have a burning desire to build a community for the overall good of their country – an Irish trait that has evidently been extended to many settled new-Irish as well which has in turn created a sense of community that is felt by all residents.

Generally, Irish life revolves very much around people and the acts of building community ties with neighbours and promoting social harmony. This is something that most foreigners, particularly some of those from certain parts of the world find rather surprising when they arrive. Irish people do not give huge emphases on the context of societal divides based on physical wealth, or better still financial boundaries between a class of people in terms of riches and the poor, or the working class, rural workers, labourers and so on, even at the apex of society. But this does not translate to mean that Irish people don't care much about the values of their wealth – far from it. In fact, there are many internal problems that are directly linked with poverty and people who are living below the poverty line. It is there to be seen and people can feel it as they walk the streets in parts of the country. Politically, the Irish government isn't immune to constant criticisms either because of it, that is why there are constant rallies and protests taking place across the country from time to time. But the fact remains that Irish people treat life so differently and they look after their own and for good reasons too, which largely stems from their past, yet there is the general air of respect for other human beings regardless of societal standing.

Those who struggle to earn a living or cannot find jobs are not disregarded either; Irish government takes care of the vulnerable in society through the nation's welfare payment systems. In reality, there are the poorer or also the richer, but the government creates opportunities for all citizens to enjoy equal access to education, healthcare and jobs, for that reason there is a very little divide amongst the populace.

In the past, a strong class of societal distinctions existed, with clear evidence from those periods of Irish history that showed nothing more than total dysfunctions in all forms, and the struggles from one state of chaos to another accompanied with all the bloodsheds and brutalities which reigned throughout. Thankfully, those eras are gone, and Irish people have learnt from the sufferings of their past. Ireland is now a society that upholds true values for humanity and not a case of only the rich getting richer while the poor been left with absolutely nothing to live on. Another positive trait of the Irish is, if there are issues of concern which relates to national unity, they always stand in a united front to tackle such issues which may threaten their identity and belonging, which they do through various means, be it dialogues or protests, or amicably through negotiations to achieve possible outcomes in the best interest of their country.

Overall, Ireland is always going to be known as a welcoming nation - because of its people!

Communication Style

It is important to understand a few things about the Irish in terms of lifestyle especially how they communicate, because miscommunication is what leads to all levels of misunderstandings. Majority of Irish people are outgoing, and some are quite reserved but overall, they are very friendly and communication style can be quite direct to the point, but with others it is always with intuition leaving you to work out what their statement meant. So, when starting a conversation with an Irish person, it is better to commence with a smile and be polite with initial greetings. However, while these polite 'hi or how are you doing are nice gestures to begin a conversation and great on the face value, they're not to be taken literally unless they know you already and genuinely want to know about your well-being. Another thing to bear in mind, especially once Irish people become satisfied that you're not just a regular tourist, they tend to ask probing or rather sensitive questions like one's immigration status, how long you've lived in the country and a lot about 'do you like it here?' No need to be alarmed, just be civil with your replies, but at the same time, do not get carried too away by their friendliness if you become deep in conversation and decide to take the pleasantries to the next level by suddenly asking about the health of their great-grandparents and how the step-children are doing in school. This may be frowned at even with the best of intentions. To avoid this kind of miscommunication which could be misconstrued to be rude and intrusive. Unless you know a person well, stick with direct response only.

Cultural upbringing in some countries forbids their people to gaze directly at someone when communicating, not because they have something to hide, especially if the other person is older or superior in whatever ranks in society; it is simply not socially acceptable and may be interpreted as being aggressive and confrontational. This is the direct opposite in Ireland. Maintaining direct eye contact is very important when you engage in a conversation with someone regardless of a person's age and status. This is as a sign that you are respectful and that you appreciate what the other person is talking about. There are some Irish people who are extremely direct communicators and have no difficulty stating what is on their minds and would be brutally honest, depending on the type of conversation they are having, and there are others who tend to use suggestive or too many probable words to try to put across what they mean which means that during such conversations, nothing is really said on clear terms. It is important to ask questions and be clarified under certain circumstances to avoid possible disagreements subsequently.

In business circles and during professional conversations with Irish people, it is important to use 'first name' and while it is not wrong go by 'Mr /Ms or Mrs last name'. It is preferable and more common to address people by their first name. While it is almost a sin in some countries where failing to attribute such titles as Sir, Madam, Dr, Barrister, General, Colonel, Sergeant, Chief, Professor, Engineer to those who have earned it, the average Irish person is not too worried about it, unless on very rare occasion and in very specific location and within certain circles would anyone be so formal. Outside of such formal situation it is almost inappropriate to do so in a casual setting. Also, if an Irish youngster the age of your niece walked up to you and calls you by your first name, do not get angry or label such as a child as lacking respect or on who has a poor upbringing. Children in Ireland can call people older than themselves by their first names except for their mum and dad. On a general note, the Irish have friendly and affectionate names that they use to call people that some foreigners on the other hand, especially those who have no experience of the West may feel some discomfort or find it rather alarming. Such pet names like, 'my love, my dear, sweetheart, honey, dearie, sweetie-pie, darling, chicken, etc.'. Irish are famous for their good-natured humour and they show it in many ways including using pet names and should not be taken literally or personally. They also have the tendency to engage a stranger with small talks either in the streets, Cafés and on the bus or just about any public place. A sound example of this is the Irish Taxi Drivers; they are better known for engaging their passengers with tremendous amount of chit-chatting, almost as important as though it is part of a requirement for their job, but they only do so to make strangers feel more welcomed to the country, their discussion topics could be as wide and varied, from the weather, family, sports, politics and religions, to your country of origin.

Etiquettes (Dos and Don'ts)

Ireland's etiquettes are like those with the rest of other Western countries and very closely in-sync with British ways of doing things because of their shared history. However, there are some general rules of social etiquette which apply across every class, and religious barriers that new visitors in Ireland should be aware of while in the country. Although, nothing too stringent to be troubled, courtesy and the display of the most basic level of understanding of the system will help newcomers to ease into society with fewer hassles.

- It is common to be introduced by a third party when meeting someone for the first time, and formal introductions and greetings are often vocal and accompanied by a handshake or a kiss on the cheek. This is normal for both men and women. An appropriate response to an introduction is a gentle smile and "Pleased to meet you".

- Socially, greetings are important but more often people look directly at each other in public spaces, and often say "hello" or 'how are you' as a standard day to day greeting or they may not say anything at all, just smiles. If approached for verbal chat, talk about your family and ask about theirs, if this is not agreeable by the standard of your culture, you can talk about the weather or something about the local community etc. Note that direct eye contact must be maintained.

- Be aware, that the Irish wouldn't want to be bothered by

overstretched introductions such as a long list of good wishes for a counterpart's family and good health following a handshake. They certainly won't appreciate if you got carried away and brought in the extended family; they may find it rather unsettling and odd.

- Irish people are not endeared to loudness and boastful behaviours and such an attitude is considered offensive. It is normal in some cultures to speak loudly in conversations, as normal as it may be for you this is considered rude in Ireland, and it is better to adopt a soft tone of voice to avoid been mistaken for someone that is arrogant.

- Being polite is very important in Ireland. People use 'thanks, please, excuse, pardon, and sorry' quite often. For example, if a passenger gets off the bus or out of a taxi, you say 'thank you' to the driver. Same at the supermarket checkout in any retail scenario. Nothing stops a customer from expressing thanks to the person who have just served you even though you have just paid for that service.

- Queuing in public places is normal always. Everyone in Ireland is expected to wait in line for their turn, regardless of a person societal status. Someone may kindly ask an old person to stand in front of them as a show of respect for older people but jumping the queue is generally frowned upon by the public; if you do, it may leave a hundred pair of eyes staring at you as they find this kind of behaviour despicable.

- It is considered rude to stare at people unless you have the intention of speaking to them. Although it is not necessary, but it is polite to leave a tip for the waiter after a meal in the restaurant.

Last but not least, you will find that some people are very up frontal with conversions with the way they respond and also very direct with their questions. For example, and as already mentioned, 'Do you like it here?' is a question that is very famous with Irish people when they meet a foreigner, and I'm sure every non-national gets asked this particular question at some point. No need to take it personally, you can simply show them that you've got a bit of their best traits by replying in good humour.

Time Keeping:

Irish people are time conscious and place considerable value on punctuality so generally speaking, people are expected to honour appointment times. For example, if you have a doctor's or dentist's appointment or a job interview, you should arrive on time. If you are unable to keep an appointment, it is expected that you call to cancel it. This applies to other important or any professional meetings.

Same if you are supposed to meet with an acquaintance or friend for lunch for example, or if are invited to someone's house for dinner for that matter, they will expect you to be there at the specified time and not late with more than a few minutes. If for any reason that you can't be on time due to unforeseen circumstances, perhaps due to bad traffic or road accident or family emergencies, in any case, you must call to inform them that you'll be arriving late. Showing up half an hour later or worse one or two hours late without a tangible reason automatically means you do not value the other person. If somehow you are faced by unavoidable circumstances such that you may not show up at all, then you must cancel the appointment in advance or better still, never accept an invitation in the first place if you have no intention to honour it.

On a general note; When invited over to someone's house for dinner, it is normal to bring a small gift for the host if you are honouring a dinner invitation. Something nice and small like a box of chocolate, flowers, or a bottle of wine are appropriate gifts as a means to express your appreciation for the invitation. If the occasion is some sort of anniversary, a wedding or birthdays, then this can be a bit different in terms of the what to bring with you for the celebrants but choose your presents more carefully to match the occasion.

Display of Emotions: Irish people do not raise their voices, but occasionally some people may appear to be emotionally agitated and there'll be shouting or display aggressive behaviours in the streets. But on the other hand, public display of affections such as kissing or demonstrations of affection from people of the opposite sex or same gender are common and accepted in Ireland as would a mother to a child or between siblings and other family relatives or friends. Spontaneous emotional outbursts of joy at celebrations of successes, marriage proposals or the birth of a child, or promotions at work is also normal but not so common outside at random, instead people prefer to organise to have a get together with family and friends to celebrate their good news quietly. Although that cannot be said about significant Sports periods such as when a Match is being played, as there are a lot of emotions usually tension running high after the country or favourite team scores or wins. People feel overwhelming joy and pride of their team because of the victory over another country and they express this as a show of 'patriotism' which usually involves screaming, and shouting that seemingly knows no limit in private homes or in the streets and pubs. The opposite takes place occasionally if there is are different outcomes as well as times when people may as well vent their anger openly in public places as a result of certain disappointments. Open emotional displays such as crying for the loss of loved ones or from hurt is also normal.

Gender Perspective

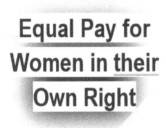

Equal Pay for Women in their Own Right

It is universally acknowledged that women are the backbone in the family because they are the ones who hold everything together. Women do the household shopping, does most of the chores in the house and practically runs everything in the house including their husband, in addition to their own work or business. While men are mostly regarded as the breadwinners who are meant to provide for their wives and children, and they tend to enjoy more leisure time with acquaintances. But while this may still be the norm in many countries, campaign for the emancipation of women over many decades have created totally new shifts in many societies and the role of women in society has changed drastically.

In Ireland, women are entitled to equal rights, equal respect, equal opportunities and equal social status as the men in all spheres of life, including the workplace and in business circles. Gender Equality still has a long way to go in Ireland as disparities still exist at various levels of society, although modern Ireland represents a sharp improvement from the chauvinist nature of their past when women had many responsibilities, they had very few rights as to how the country was run. Gone are those days when it was felt that a woman's place was at home, raising children and looking after the family. Things are different now, women come together to discuss politics and other issues that affect them. The glass ceiling that prevented women from pursuing their dreams have been shattered in many fronts - but there are reasons why women are complaining still about how society treats them differently to the men. Today's Irish women want more out of life and there are many skilled women in the workforce who are already balancing their full-time jobs with running the household. Many women now occupy top managerial positions in large business enterprises and other public offices, including political offices. Modern Irish women have so far proved to be more than a mere bench-warming spectator even in the midst of the male-dominated professional jobs such that the country has been led by two female Presidents.

In comparison to many countries on the issues of gender equality, Ireland has changed and much has also been achieved in its attempt to closing the gender gap or scaling down the barriers that exists between men and women. But there are a lot of other challenges still left to be tackled in order to meet all development goals that the world agrees with regards to gender balance. Women Empowerment campaigners have helped to create the awareness that a woman's world no longer revolves around the house and the children alone. The campaign for equality has helped to changed mindsets for women and for governments around the world and we can see equality in many areas that are being further straightened under various government ACTS in recent years, some of which can be seen reflected in the number of outdated laws with regards to women been debated. Irish citizens have voted in referendums to change and amend various policies in the constitution many times, together with new initiatives in favour of women and there seem to be a good proportion of men who are now genuinely interested in equality of women too and other gender equality issues in general. Take the home front for instance, it is no longer uncommon now to find men who happily stay at home to take care of the children and carry out household chores while their wives are in work. There are some men who also work from home and are happy to share equal responsibilities of running the home with their wives both financially and otherwise.

Having said that, the issue is one that is still dangling within Irish Society because there is still a long way to go to achieve the balance that we expect to see. No doubt that the country has made significant progress. But more action is necessary to keep improving the social benefit of women and balance the equations because women are still a very small part of decision-making in Irish society.

IN VIEW

Irish women have had to protest many times calling for a reform of the system to provide greater access of independence for women. Only from 1918, women in Ireland could vote at age 30, while men could at age 21. 100 years later, Irish women have been able to vote in various referendums laws to the Irish constitution and also able to freely vote in general elections

MARRIAGE AND DIVORCE

Marriage:

Marriage is a union based on pure love and emotional connections between two individuals. Matrimony in Ireland is important and considered holy and sacred and viewed practically as the strong pillar that is binding the fabric of Irish society as it ensures the continuation of family lines. But in general, marriages have brought families together. Traditionally, in Ireland, a handful of selected guests are usually invited, from the bride and the groom's families and friends coming together to celebrate the joining together of two individuals purportedly in love and vows in their presence to spend the rest of their lives together in holy matrimony in a ceremony that is usually more elaborate than engagement ceremonies. In the not too distant past in Ireland, when two people got married they stayed married, and people got married before they had children, it's the traditional pattern that people followed especially because marriage in Ireland was closely guarded institution and heavily influenced by the Catholic Church, therefore weddings followed religious patterns usually conducted according to the norms of the respective religious teachings. But times have moved on and marriages are now being conducted in more places other than the Church.

Civil weddings also take place in the Registry office, and Muslim weddings in mosques or for others it can be anywhere, depending; a couple can decide to get married on private grounds and in open spaces and so on. There is also more than just the customary type of marriage which usually takes place between a man and a woman. Since the marriage equality that took place in Ireland in 2015 when the country voted in a nationwide referendum to legalise same-sex marriage, and to change the Constitution to extend Civil Marriage Rights to same-sex couples, two people in love regardless of their gender are allowed to freely wed without fear of persecution. Ireland is the first country in the world to introduce marriage equality through a national referendum. It means that by law same-sex couples can legally get married to each other and allowed to adopt children if they wish.

Thirty-fourth Amendment of the Constitution of Ireland (Marriage Equality) Act 2015 permits marriage to be contracted by two persons without distinction as to their sex.

Divorce:

So much has changed in Ireland within the Marriage Institution and people's views on marriage keep changing too. Certain rules around it are no longer taken literally like before. For instance, divorce was once prohibited under law and almost not accepted in Irish society. Those who had children outside wedlock were victimised and ridiculed. Now not all children are born to married parents and divorce has become quite common and somewhat rampant in Ireland. In some instance, people are deliberately choosing to have children as lone parents without being married – like cohabiting couples starting families without being married, which in some cultures may seem very odd but is normal in Ireland. The issue of divorce itself is quite a complicated one still and not a straight forward because it has also changed from being prohibited and unacceptable as not much of that decision is left with the Catholic Church anymore. Now if a couple decides to get a divorce, they actually can do so, except that the process can be very costly and takes a long time to complete, including a mandatory four-year period of trial-separation to be observed by both husband and wife.

The prohibition on divorce in the 1937 Constitution was repealed in 1995 under the Fifteenth Amendment. Currently, the Government has agreed on a new proposal to hold a referendum that will help to reduce the waiting period before a couple's divorce can be granted.

Voting on this referendum is due to take place on 24th of May 2019.

Polygamy in Ireland

Believe it or not, polygamy was a trend in olden days Ireland, meaning that men marrying many wives and then having many children were said to be quite common practice at then, it was a practice that continued in Ireland until the end of the Middle Ages. Polygamy is very much prohibited in today's Ireland. There are people who in certain religions that allows men to take up to four wives, and others from cultures that permit a man to marry as many wives as he desires. However, such privileges do not extend to anybody once they are living within the jurisdiction of the Republic of Ireland. If a person already has more than one legally married wife from another country, such marriages are termed null, void and illegal, with the exception to the first wife only and any subsequent marriages are not valid under Irish law. On more general terms under Irish law, people are allowed only one wife or husband under a civil wedding, regardless of religion, culture and otherwise. A person cannot enter into a new marriage while still legally married to another and while a husband or wife is still alive. Any perpetrators may be subjected to a jail term of many years.

FAMILY LIFE

Like in many cultures, family is highly valued in Irish society and traditional values support those values and encourage close ties. The typical Irish family consist of two parents and their dependent children, but this has evolved over the years. It is understood that family units of 10 or more were quite common in Ireland in the past, but most of the Irish nuclear family are now smaller in size than they were before. The number of children per family has shrunk significantly compared to a few decades ago.

Irish children live with their parents until they reach the age of 18 or 19 years old when they leave home to go to college/university, get a job or travel the world—Most of the youth aspire to travel around the world before they return to settle and this has nothing to do with economic reasons, although, many others also aspire to emigrate to find happier life elsewhere, in most cases they always return home after their adventures or studies abroad because of close family ties. Extended families in the past used lived close by to support one another which is the bonds that kept them together. But some of these traditions in modern Ireland, have gradually changed due to social developments as a way of progression and evolution; it is no longer conducive for everyone to carry on living close to their families in the same neighbourhoods anymore.

Another way that has changed in Irish tradition, is the one that has to do with the women. Like in most countries, the dynamics of procreating in the family rests mostly on the shoulders of the women-folk, a difficult obligation that women were expected to fulfil. But the modern woman in Ireland is career focus and success driven more than ever before. She wants to enjoy a new level of independence and more financial and social freedom than a desire to create babies as soon as possible and continue for as long as possible. For most modern Irish women, just like her counterparts in every civilised society, this may only come as afterthoughts, and even then, she might not plan to have a dosen, many choose to have just one or two children or adopt even in order to maintain a healthy lifestyle and keep her family more close-knit.

FAMILY TYPES

There are different family types of families in modern Ireland, for example; you may find that the two adults present in a household with children may not necessarily be a married couple or the traditional husband and wife living together and bringing up their children. They might just be co-habiting. There are also a high number of single-parent households in Ireland where the children are living with just the mother or the father. In either circumstance, there could be several reasons responsible such as separation, economic, divorce, health issues and even death. But it is public knowledge that marital separation and divorce being somewhat rampant or much more common than before, by far accounts for the highest factor of single-parent families than other reasons in Ireland.

There are even more variations to the types of families in Ireland such as in the list below.

Nuclear Family: The nuclear family is the traditional type of family structure consisting of an adult male and female with one or more children (including fostered and adopted).

Lone Parent Family: Lone parent or single parent family consists of one parent (either gender) raising one or more children on their own.

Blended Family: Blended family unit is composed of a married couple and their offspring including children from previous marriages.

Extended Family: The Extended family is one that is containing the nuclear family in addition to and their close relatives such as, aunts, and uncles the children's grandparents, etc

Step-Family: Step-family consist of a couple living with each other's children from previous marriages without their own offspring.

Cohabitation: Cohabiting family is the form of a couple living together who aren't married.

Childless Family: A childless family are basically a married couple with no children.

Gay or Lesbian Family :– This family type is made up of same-sex couple living together with children that are either adopted or children born through surrogacy.

CARE FOR CHILDREN

Naturally, children born in Ireland are regarded with pride because they are a source of joy for the family. Children, as in every culture represents a family's future and the future of their community and the country, and because that, they are also often regarded as the main reason for many marriages for many.

Caring for children begins in the womb when the mother is pregnant and has to attend a maternity hospital for regular antenatal checks to monitor the development of the pregnancy and foetus under the watchful eye of healthcare experts right up until the baby is born. Support and advise for the mother then continue thereafter on how to better look after her newborn baby who requires lots of special care. Mothers are especially encouraged to breastfeed her newborn because of the health benefits to the baby and the bond it creates between mother and child. Care for babies at that stage continues until they can walk or get around on their own, but until then mothers carry their babies around in buggies and prams. While at home in the house, mothers would often leave their baby to sleep in their cot and if awake they'll be kept close in some form of a rocking chair or baby bouncer with toys to play with, allowing their mums to perform their daily chores in the house. But generally, the level of care for babies only changes as the baby grows from one stage of development to the other and mothers must adapt to every stage. The government of Ireland have made special provisions available for the care of babies not just through the hospitals and other clinical means but parents are supported through the monthly welfare payment under the Child Benefit schemes, including free Pre-school years which allows a child to attend a nursery school or creche for a specified number of periods in a week for free. Child Benefit for children continues to be paid to every child until they reache 18 years in full-time education or 16 years old if they are not in education.

IN VIEW

Working women in Ireland enjoy a compulsory maternity leave of 26 weeks, with extended 16 weeks in addition to unpaid leave beginning immediately after the end of the main maternity leave. In 2016, the Irish government also introduced for the first time 'Paternity Benefit' meaning that new fathers are also entitled to take 2 weeks' statutory paternity leave to stay at home when their babies are first born to allows them give some assistance to the women to work less when their babies need them most.

CHILD CEREMONIES IN IRELAND

Child Naming & Baptism:

Child Naming ceremonies are held to welcome a new baby into the family and therefore very special and important just as the baptism. In Ireland, Child Christening takes place more frequently as the majority of families belong to the Roman Catholic Church, Methodist Church, Presbyterian and some other Christian Faith and tends to follow the Christian tradition as did their own parents. Child Christening ceremonies are usually held in the Church and involves a naming ceremony, in other words, it is the ceremony of baptizing and formally naming the child. But not all churches practice infant baptism, for example, churches like the Baptists, Apostolic, Jehovah's Witnesses, Pentecostals and a few others have the inclination to perform simple blessings or thanksgivings as an alternative to welcoming a baby into the Christian church. A blessing usually takes place as part of the main church service, but preparations for all church related baby naming ceremonies are similar because any of the above mentioned, always requires the parents of the child, godparents and some relatives to go in front of the church to say a few words followed by a prayer by the officiating Priest or Pastor, while the rest of the church promises to help the family look after the child – a process which always ends with some form of merriments inside the church premises at the end of the service or elsewhere with more friends joining families to celebrate the gift of their baby. There are families that may or may not belong in any religious denominations by any standard and perform other forms of traditional naming ceremony to celebrate the arrival of their baby according to cultural norms and acknowledge the names given to the baby. Usually, the name of the child is chosen before the ceremony. As with such cultures, the person officiating the ceremony may dip his or her hand in a bowl of water or oil in some cases and then touch the forehead of the baby and whispers the name into the baby's ears before saying it aloud for all around to hear it. A naming day is a more informal occasion in this regard but to a great extent, it takes similar process of gathering of friends, family and well-wishers to get together to eat, drink and to celebrate the welcoming of a baby to the world. At this stage, gifts are then lavished on the newborn and the parents. This form of child ceremony is mostly common with people from Ireland's new communities who try their best to preserve the traditional values of their own native countries.

Holy Communion

The First Holy Communion is a Christian tradition during which a person first receives the Eucharist. In Irish Catholic tradition, the first holy communion ceremony is taken very seriously. It is usually performed in church when a child reaches the age of around 7-8 years old. It celebrates the first time that a child accepts the bread and wine at a Catholic Sunday Mass (known as the Eucharist). It is necessary for the child to have been Baptised (Christened) prior. The First Holy Communion celebration in Ireland is a grand-breaking

Catholic ceremony and usually a community affair in that requires all children at an appropriate age bracket in all primary schools across the country to follow the procession every year - ideally between May and June. Preparations for a child's First Communion is almost like that of a 'mini wedding' because parents spend a lot of money to ensure the child receiving the communion is presented in white flower-girls style dresses, including a veil and a little handbag and umbrella – for the girl, and boys in a full suit which comes in all kinds of quality depending on how much parents are willing to spend. Families spend the rest of the day celebrating the occasion and the child is then showered with so much and presents as they do on their birthdays.

Currently, Catholic schools in Ireland are permitted by the law to give priority to children who are baptised during the school's admission selection process and can refuse admission to some children based on religion. Although more recently, the Education Minister announced arrangements for the removal of such barriers in schools.

Confirmation

Confirmation is a rite only performed to those already baptised and have received their Holy Communion. It is to confirm the promises made on their behalf at baptism and to prove that the child is receiving the gift of the Holy Spirit and become full membership to the Christian community. The preparation is very similar to that of First Communion. A Bishop usually conducts the service at a specially organised Sunday Mass for the children receiving the Confirmation.

This is usually is followed by family celebrations and gift-giving rounds for the child.

Child Rearing and Chores

The understanding of child discipline in some countries is very different compared to Ireland. There are many countries where it is normal to expect children as young as 6 and 7 years old to start performing a share of the household duties in the house. Such type of child discipline may be frowned at in Irish society and simply not allowed because it is not a pattern that is used in Western countries. The upbringing of children remains the central focus for all parents and guardians in every family regardless of who are the birth parents, and there is a sharp contrast to what is allowed in Ireland and other countries outside Europe that should be taken seriously. Childhood in Ireland is regarded as a time of freedom and happiness – a time for play and social learning while they are still young, and parents owe it to encourage more autonomous behaviour and independence in children. Parents in Ireland are much more permissive and trusting of their offspring. Practically, everything surrounding any positive relationships between children and teenagers with their parents is basically based on trust and on encouragement – if not agreement, which can seem rather strange to parents brought up in some of those other countries which allow corporal punishment as the only way to discipline children.

Irish parents are never keen on pushing the child too much to do something that they are not good at or anything they don't want to do. Same principles apply in schools and teachers use the same methods in teaching rather than push, force and punishment, and it doesn't mean the relaxed method equals poor education standards in students. Irish students are in fact doing very well and the standards of education in Ireland is regarded as one of the best in Europe. Although, there is no guaranteed blueprint formula for better parenthood anywhere in the world, in fact, it is a continues struggle for most parents and some draw strength and experience from their own upbringing and cultural values and wants to be the best role model for their children. But they must also understand that Ireland is a different culture and therefore have different rules to how children should be treated. There are stringent rules around disciplining a child and there are dire consequences for parents who do the opposite which many foreign parents do find shocking, depending on which part of the world they're from and their own style of child upbringing. It is advisable for new settlers to adapt to the country's way of life and learn about what is allowed and vice versa because certain ways of child upbringing or discipline will only end badly. Foreign parents from a different country may be used to discipline their children in certain ways not accepted in Irish society and they may do so out of fear of losing their cultural values and own identity, and not necessarily because they are wicked. But they may end up getting in trouble with Irish Authorities and have their children taken away and put into State care.

CARE FOR THE ELDERLY

The primary responsibility of caring for someone's older relatives is that of family members under normal circumstances. But in Ireland, the State shares in that responsibility to care for the elderly because it owes a duty of care to old people in the country. Government liaise with several local agencies and through its own department of Social Protection to provide help with a range of services to support older people in Ireland, in areas of their wellbeing, income, health, personal capability and in various areas to enable them to live a happy and meaningful life as they continue to age, including an enabling environment within which they can live out their remaining life. For example, people over the age of 65 enjoy 'Senior Citizens Perks' meaning there are some entitlements to certain things like free bus pass and rail travel within the Republic, as well as free bus and train tickets if they are travelling to the North of Ireland, they do not need to pay TV license, and their fuel (gas or electricity) have been subsidised. There are few more benefits for old and retired people and a good health support system.

People in this generation are leading very busy lifestyles and can't really give up work to look after their ageing parents so, many rely on State support even for themselves to make ends meet financially, and so the most common way of caring for the older relatives at a certain age has been to send them to residential care homes when they know that the older person has become too frail and can no longer care for themselves so they chose this option for their own peace mind knowing that their aged parent or relative is well looked after in an environment where they can be in the company of other older people that they can socialise with. But those who have the means without thoughts on the invasion of privacy would take in their relatives into their homes.

IN VIEW

All People born on the island of Ireland and who have reached their 100th birthday receive a special message from the President of Ireland, wishing them a happy birthday and congratulating them for their longevity. The letter is usually accompanied by an award made by the President of Ireland. This is a scheme that is often referred to as "the Centenarian Bounty" and is open to people living in Ireland who have reached 100 years, as well as to Irish citizens born on the island of Ireland who have reached 100 years and who are living abroad.

Source: www.president.ie/en/about/centenarian-bounty

Funerals:

Irish people everywhere share in the same old traditional beliefs among Christians and some major religion that following death, a person's soul is released and judged by God before either descending to hell or hopefully ascending to Heaven to sit at the right-hand side with God. But regardless of beliefs, when someone dies, it is normally a great loss to the immediate family and friends who are left to mourn and grieve the sad loss of their departed loved one.

The family of the departed announces the passing by posting a brief message from the family. They have a wake in the church. The day of the burial, the mourners generally retires to the nearest pub or community centre and spend the rest of the day there where the deceased is celebrated and fondly remembered by only the positive legacies that they left behind and through words of kindness only. It is an important part of Irish culture to drink and toast to the dead, however, and understandably, those who have passed on too young, e.g. children and adolescents, tend to have much less elaborated funerals in which case a prayer for the innocence of their soul and a more personalised goodbye messages are left with flowers to comfort very close members of the deceased family, as it's a more ideal way to commiserate with them.

FOOD & DRINK

Food: Food plays a significant role in our lives as a people and as human beings in general. people love good foods and a well-prepared meal is part of the hospitality when visiting family friends and when marking special occasions. It will be right to say that anyone who loves to have a good meal will be impressed by traditional Irish cooking as well. Foods in Ireland are typical of Western Europe standard, with many similarities with foods that you may find in Britain most especially; a good example is 'Sunday Roast' served on a Sunday is a traditional British main meal but is the same in Ireland and also very popular in many parts of the country.

Sunday roast typically consists of roast beef, roast potatoes, gravy, Yorkshire-pudding and vegetables such as parsnips, Brussels sprouts, peas, carrots, runner beans, and broccoli, but cooking styles may sometimes vary between Irish and Britain styles. Most Irish cuisines tend to be based around popular staple such as 'Irish Potatoes' which is the national crop of Ireland and therefore form the base of many Irish diets. They are naturally the most widely eaten dishes in the country and usually accompanied by special Irish stew or soups cooked with meat, such as pork, lamb, beef and poultry. In fact, most meal types in Ireland often have some amount of potatoes with them. For example, common everyday dishes such as Colcannon, Cottage Pie, or the all-time favourite, Mashed potatoes. Fish is also very common in many dishes and usually served with good old chips, which is another favourite cuisine that has increased popularity in Ireland and sold in restaurants and in Delis across the country.

Ireland follows the traditional three meals a day, with the main meal of the day being lunch eaten around noon and dinner usually eaten in the evening consisting of a smaller meal, and deserts. However, people who work tend to eat a small meal in the middle of the day possibly sandwiches and soups on the go and in restaurants and then enjoy a well-prepared dinner in the evening at home with family.

Breakfast is an important part of the daily meal and traditional Irish Breakfast consists of fried or grilled bacon, eggs, sausages, pudding, and fried tomato served with plain toasts with butter and a variety of bread. Nowadays, busy lifestyles have led to a change in breakfast habits in many ways most familiar with city dwellers having to do with taking only a cup of tea rather than settle to eat a full breakfast and rushing out the door or skipping breakfast altogether. Like in many big cities in parts of Europe, eating habits have also changed over the years in Ireland. The younger generation of Irish people would for the most part prefer to eat out in restaurants instead of religiously following a pattern of homemade meals. Another reason may be because they have developed a different taste for the world's finer foods as there more food on offer in Ireland and widely varied to suit a variety of tastes. Many established restaurants being run and owned by foreign people and offering ethnic meals other than foods that are traditionally Irish. There are many Continental and ethnic restaurants that featuring their own culinary traditions and Irish people have a taste of different cultures through these foreign foods which have are fast becoming a part of modern cuisines of Ireland. Majority of supermarkets throughout Ireland sell a huge variety of foods to consumers including ethnic foods from Eastern Europe, Asian, etc. Pizzas have also become a main Irish staple food and are widely available and come in delicious toppings and flavours to satisfy every taste bud. Nearly every supermarket in the country would sell the pre-packaged and frozen alternative that can be bought and cooked at home, in addition to the many pizza outlets from where ready to eat pizzas can also be purchased.

Popular Foods in Ireland

1. Traditional Irish Stew
2. Potato and cabbage
3. Barmbrack
4. Dublin Coddle
5. Irish Soda Bread
6. Colcanno and champ
7. Irish Christmas Cake
8. Corned Beef with Cabbage
9. Black and white pudding

Vegetarian Option:

There is a wide variety of vegetarian options available with increased demand for Vegan or animal-friendly dishes. Vegetarians can find a lot of dishes among a range of favourites on menus at restaurants, pubs and fast-food outlets. Leading Irish supermarkets stock a wide variety of meat-free options like Tofu and Quorn products which are great options that can be easily used to prepare delicious homemade Vegetarian meals such as soups, stew, or filled tortilla wraps and more staples like noodles, dumplings, potatoes, rice, mash, etc. They also have additional alternatives such as the different varieties of mushrooms, green beans, eggplants and a mix of other vegetables to make your vegetarian meals more attractive and interesting and also be enjoyed as a side dish or as a main meal for a complete vegetarian experience. There are other eateries serving international cuisines including a wonderful variety of Vegetarian cuisines.

Salads:

A typical Irish salad may vary as much as from exotic fruits mixes, vegetable mixes, to corned beef, hardboiled eggs and baked beans blended with lettuce, carrots, cabbage, tomatoes and spring onions, turnips, spinach, peas, to even more consistent meat salads, and even fruit salads served as desserts. More consistent salads include the wild and brown rice salad, shrimp salad, coconut rice and potato salad, and as well, and seasonings such as lemon, garlic and chilli sauces are used to give a special flavour to the whole salad dish. A variety of vegetables can be found in abundance literally from all corners of the island especially in city supermarkets and farmers markets.

Vegetables & Fruits:

It is easy to find different types of fresh fruits and vegetables to buy from everywhere all year round. Although some are more commonly found in the shops than others depending, they are in season. However, there is always some delicious fruit types to indulge in whatever season; there are always some kinds in season. Generally, Irish public is encouraged to eat 'your five-a-day' which is a variety of different fruits and vegetables to get the nutrients our bodies need to stay healthy. Fruits such as bananas, apples, berries, oranges, clementine, kiwi, cherries, limes, lemons, prove to be the some of most popular fruits in the country, including some tropical and exotic fruits like mango, avocado, pineapples, and watermelons. Fruits like Papaya, coconuts, oranges, mangoes, grapefruits, are also are very common.

- **Vegetables Found in Ireland:** Potatoes, Broccoli, Cabbage, Carrot, Onion, Thyme, Celery, Leek, Swede, Tomato, Pumpkin, Lettuce, Parsley,Parsnip, Rhubarb, Cauliflower, Cucumbers, Sweet Peppers, Mushrooms, Brussels Sprouts.

Snacks: Some of Ireland mouth-watering snacks include traditional Irish Brambrack which is a type of fruit loaf baked with crystallised cherries and raisings. Irish jam doughnuts which are usually balls of dough with jam or other fillings inside, Irish Soda Bread topped with Smoked Salmon, Irish Fruit Scones with dry raisins, Cranberries and Mix in dry fruit. Irish Cream Brownies and a wide variety of cakes that are prepared in all corners of the country and most commonly made with fresh fruit. Apples, plums, strawberries, and cherries are used regularly on cakes such as Irish chocolate Cake layered with Baileys, Buttercream Frosting and many other very well-known types of Irish cakes that are used as dessert. Not forgetting to mention good old Hot Cross-Buns which is traditionally eating during Good Friday and Easter.

Healthy Snacks options can include: Yogurts, Cheese, Celery or Carrots, Popcorn, Rice Cakes, Rice Pudding, and Custard as well. etc.

Bread

Bread is a big part of the Irish diet, not just eaten for breakfast. Bread is used for sandwiches with various fillings, like cheese and thinly sliced beef, lamb or pork cooked ham, chicken, turkey, tuna, grilled rashers, etc. Bread is especially considered a main meal in children's lunch boxes and is important for a healthy diet.

Fast food Option can be anything from sandwiches, baguetes to fried wedges and chicken, in addition franchised fast-food outlets such as McDonalds, KFC, etc.

Drinking in Ireland

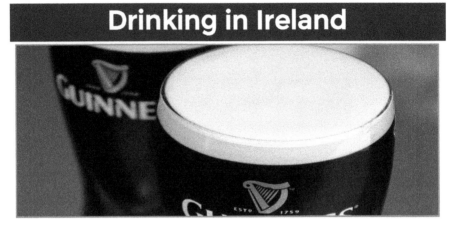

Some people have a stereotypical view about Ireland and drinks and noted as a country of heavy drinkers. A notion that is not exactly far-fetched from the truth because Irish people love their pint of Guinness which has become an important part of Irish culture. The 'black stuff' as they call it, is brewed in the country.

While there are various reasons why Ireland is famous for its drinking culture, one of the simple reasons is the fact that Ireland is a country well known around the world for producing fine beers and whiskeys. There are several Independent Irish breweries and distilleries producing and exporting international top brands of beer and whiskey including other types of Irish alcohol that are as well liked by a huge population of people around the world. But the second main thing Ireland is most associated with aside from St. Patrick, is the much-loved Guinness Stout. It is the most popular and much preferred brand because of its natural goodness and its delicately balanced taste of bitter and maltiness. Guinness Stout is mostly consumed around St.

Patrick's Day and on Arthur's Day. The world-famous brew is also very popular in the West African country of Nigeria, the people are believed to drink more Guinness than Irish people - being the first country where Guinness was brewed outside the Republic of Ireland. People from all parts of Nigeria love the 'black stuff', so much that Nigeria is ranked the world's second-largest market for Guinness, behind only the United Kingdom while Ireland is placed third.

Pub Culture: Despite popular beliefs that one cannot truly be Irish unless they are drinkers. There is even a saying that '*An Irish who doesn't drink is as rare as getting gold at the end of the rainbow.*' But not all Irish people drink alcohol. Irish Pub Culture is a tradition taken almost as church life itself for a lot of Irish people. Pub culture is what makes Ireland so popular in a kind of way. Most visitors are said to plan their itinerary around visiting different traditional Irish pubs when they come to Ireland, not just to indulge the drinks as Irish Pub culture is not always about drinking alone. The pub is seen as the centre of every community in small villages in rural Ireland and urban centres people often always to socialise. It is where the locals sit and gossip with one another about everything, from politics to the next football games and what else that is happening in the neighbourhood, and a non-alcohol drinker would normally fit into the itinerary to have a taste of that experience.

Traditional Irish pubs can be so appealing for all category of visitors because of the welcoming and relaxed atmosphere they generally provide for customers, from splendid foods as well as live music and shows—and the drinks too. Many families with children also visit the pub to spend time together and listen to traditional Irish music. While there are others who go there to attend celebrations or to hold pub quiz sessions. Pub owners in Ireland are great on their part as they do so much to draw in the crowds from their localities and beyond, with the offering of great foods, pool tables and huge screen TVs showing all the latest live sporting games, in addition to good selection of ice-cold beers and of course, the good old pint of Guinness beer which they love very much.

Until 2019, there was a law prohibiting the sales of alcohol on Good Friday, that ban has now been lifted. The legal age to buy alcohol in Ireland is 18 years

Smoking in Irish Pubs:

A smoking ban is in place in Ireland, meaning that people are not permitted to smoke in public places. Restaurants, pubs, and other such places are obliged to have designated smoking areas to accommodate smokers, so it is best to ask about the spot before lighting a cigarette in a pub in Ireland.

Pub Opening Hours

Monday through to Thursday, the pubs open from: 10.30am – 11.30pm, Fridays and Saturdays from: 10.30am – 12.30am, while on Sundays from 12.30pm – 10.00pm.

OFF-LICENCE TRADING HOURS

MONDAY – SATURDAY

10.30am – 10.00pm

Other Beverages:

Irish breweries also produce a wide variety of non-alcoholic beverages for public consumption that visitors can still enjoy without the alcohol. There is a selection of non-alcoholic Irish drinks which are very common and are made available in many varieties from malt drinks, soft drinks and an assortment of fruit juices - to lemonades and sparkling apple ciders, that can be bought from every supermarket everywhere in the country. Popular everyday beverages among the Irish include tea and coffee and it is common to see people walking around with a cup of coffee in hands throughout the day, however there are options for hot chocolate drinks and bottled water which are widely sold in every shop.

FASHION IN IRELAND

Every country has its own fashion style and Ireland being a Western country means that fashion is mainly of western style, although Trends are in some ways more relaxed than in other European cities like London for example.

To begin with, Irish clothing like the Irish kilt has a long history and can be traced back of olden times, especially the Aran Sweaters which is seen as a symbol of Gaelic identity was originally intended to keep Irish fishermen of the Aran Islands warm and dry. But the sweater has since become one of Ireland's best-known contemporary fashion wears and people are free to wear it whenever they please especially on cold days. On the other hand, Irish fashion has advanced beyond that and there are designers that are producing more sophisticated fashion trends, but Ireland do not have a distinct traditional attire to stick with that you can see people wearing up and down in the streets every day. However, Irish people can be sophisticated with what they are wearing which could be clothing that are well in vogue and trending or a blend of both old and new styles. But in all, having a good fashion sense and dressing in moderation and better presentation matter most. Ideally, everyday clothing tends to be the more casual and comfortable types that are commonly worn by both men and women throughout, like a pair of loose-fitting trousers or jeans and a loose-fitting or fitted shirt or blouse and the good old sweaters and jumpers in winter seasons.

Millennials fashion habit may be different though, as most prefer buying clothes that show their individuality and personality through their clothes rather than follow the traditional shopping patterns from season to season or from a particular store or brand.Another factor to consider about fashion in Ireland is the weather. Irish weather is a great influence and determinant on what people wear every day because of its unpredictable nature. People could be seen wearing a hooded jacket and tracksuit bottoms and others wearing just a sleeved or T-shirt at the same time depending on what they perceive the temperature to be like throughout the day or according to what the weather was like at the time of leaving home. Irish weather can change from windy to a few showers or at best, spells of sunshine all at once and that determines the temperature at a given day.

Business attires can be anything from a normal suit with a tie, and casuals can be something like a jacket or blazer in place of a suit. A more formal outfits to wear to dinner parties can just be a pair of trousers, a waistcoat, a collar shirt and a bow tie to go with and a nice pair of shoes. Quality, colour and style may vary depending on the nature of the event itself. The weather is also there to be considered, so it's a good idea to have a fine trench-coat to go over whatever that is worn inside. Although there are no set rules or expected standards to how any woman in Ireland should dress as females tend to be more versatile with taste and quality when it comes to fashion. A typical female would always dress appropriately to suit the occasion and be presentable. As Ireland becomes one of the most multicultural cities in Europe, fashion styles seen in the streets are also evolving and has become quite common to see women in Ireland wearing very glamorous fashion brands from right around the globe, in all sorts of weather attending a variety of events, more especially at cultural events, festivals or theatre performance and weddings. Another example is the Horse Racing festival known as the Galway Races, held every summer in Galway City. This is an old age festival that boast a tradition which brings out the best in women fashion. For one day only in July of every year and as part of the festival, women in Ireland adorns some of the most stylish hats and high heels in a friendly competition to find the best dressed and most attractive. The winner is usually rewarded handsomely with a cash prize.

SECTION TEN

ARTS & ENTERTAINMENT

Ireland has a rich and vibrant culture of art and entertainment that represents the varied aspects of Irish lifestyle, inspiring others around the world. One of the major aspects of Irish art is the human expression that finds their way through varied art forms that is well demonstrated not only through artwork, but through performances like dance, drama, literature, and singing. Historically, the artists of Ireland wrote and performed songs, poems and tales, painted pictures and kept accounts of history by their invaluable experiences and preserved the culture of the country. And that is still been done today by artists everywhere in Ireland.

The Irish Arts Council distributes annual grants to support the arts and artists of various forms, including individual writers, and composers etc.

Irish Literature

Literature occupies a special place in the heart of Irish people and the society at large, and for centuries it had the unique power to influence the cultural life of the Irish people and has also played a significant role in forming Irish culture and identity as well. Its riches of folklore creativity, reflecting the mixture of a lively traits in Irish cultural tradition by the writers who through the ages have used their gift of writing in virtually every known genre of literature including fiction, poetry, drama, travelogue, biography and autobiography and other non-fiction dealing with such topics as education, philosophy, medicine, law, economics politics, and history, etc, to preserve the culture of Ireland and help the rest of the world to understand more about what the country is all about. Ireland is known for producing many distinguished writers, poets and playwrights and they are valued and very much celebrated.

The following list below provides a glimpse to some of the major literary figures in Ireland including the historic four Nobel Prize literature winners, among the more contemporary big names.

Oscar Wilde, James Joyce, William Butler Yeats, George Bernard Shaw, Samuel Beckett, Seamus Heaney, Jonathan Swift, Eavan Boland, Maeve Binchy, Roddy Doyle, Colm Tóibín, Fintan O'Toole, Marian Keys, etc.

Dublin City is a big part of the UNESCO Creative Cities Network, which currently has around 180 cities. The (UCCN) was created in 2004 to promote cooperation and cities that have identified creativity as a strategic factor for sustainable urban development. Dublin was also designated the 4th UNESCO City of Literature in 2010. The City have been granted different accolades and world recognition because it is the birthplace and home of Ireland's literary greats.

The Irish Writers' Centre is an organisation that is established to provide literary activities and other related support services for both well-known and aspiring writers throughout Ireland from its base at Dublin's City Centre.

Music in Ireland

Irish Music Scene

Music is part of Irish life and Ireland has produced many international acclaimed musicians in all genres of music and singers. Ireland's history of traditional music goes back several hundred years. Traditionally, Irish folk songs are usually sung in the form that it tells a story through them, and it makes it more appealing to its listeners. In fact, it is said that 'there are folk songs for every Irish occasion from storytelling to expressing sorrowful event.' Irish traditional music is usually accompanied by several traditional musical instruments such as the fiddle, tin whistle, flute, the little round Irish drum known in Irish as the Bodhrán, etc.

 Contemporary music on the one side has produced several first-rate artists including bands and solo musicians from the different musical genres, including rock, pop, metal, electronic, punk, etc. Contemporary Irish bands such as Boyzone, U2, Westlife and Thin Lizzy, are just a few and Solo artists such as Phil Lynott, Sinéad O'Connor, Bob Geldof, Enya, Samantha Mumba, Damian Rice, Andrea Corr, are only but a few Irish artist who have contributed to the rich music scene in Ireland and have at the same time made great impact with their voice around the world.

Irish Dancing

Irish Dancing is the traditional folk dance of Ireland and it  holds deep symbolism to Irish life. Irish dancing is characterized by the fast tapping and movements of the foot and firm control of the upper body in ways that makes it to resemble American tap danceing. Irish dancing is popular in all parts of the country and among diaspora Irish around the world. The dancers wear very colourful and flamboyant costumes, usually a mini dress emblazoned with sequins and fancy footwear, worn with black tights for ladies or with ankle white socks for younger girls and accessorised with beautiful wigs, tiaras, jewellery, and so on. While the male dancers wear equally wear sequinned waistcoats, bejewelled shoes with long dark trousers, tie, and white long-sleeved shirt.

Irish dancing has rules that must be followed in order to achieve their unique and artistic expression of the body posture including the arm and foot movement and other techniques. However, different teachers and dance leaders have managed to incorporate their own imaginative techniques and procedure into their routines to in order to match their own steps and reach for maximum entertainment. The jigs and reels are derived from traditional Irish dance and also popular and enjoyed by the people of Ireland, although its origin is also associated with Scotland.

Traditional Irish dancing was made even more popular by River Dance– the most famous performance dance in Ireland and associated with the Irish Diaspora communities abroad.

The Irish Film Industry

The *Irish Film* and Television industry in Ireland is quite a successful one. The sector exists to support audio visual and the entertainment industry activities in Ireland and it's a key factor in Irish society. It plays significant role in promoting home grown talents who through their craft continue to enrich the tapestry of Irish Theatre, Screen and other visual media in the entertainment industry, to international stage as a part of its cultural exports, and as a way of selling Ireland throughout the world. Ireland's reputation is projected through the quality of films it produces and the messages they send out. The sector is overseen by Irish Film Board which is Ireland's national film agency, it manages the development and production funds for the Irish films, television dramas, documentaries and animation.

The Irish government is very much committed to see the industry continues to grow and succeed, it makes significant financial contributions to support the industry's work in providing creative filmmaking to entertain, and to encourage a worldwide audience to see Ireland as a film destination with attractive production environments, as well with a deep talent pool, including casting companies to work with foreign production companies.

Irish creative filmmaking talent has been recognised on the international stage over the years, including many Irish actors and directors have made their marks on the global film industry.

Ireland's film industry itself is estimated to be worth in excess of half a Billion in turnover annually.

Below are a few Irish actors and actresses of international repute:

- Maureen O'Hara
- Colin Farrell
- Saoirse Ronan
- Pierce Brosnan
- Charlotte Bradley
- Cillian Murphy
- Brendan Gleeson
- James Nesbit
- Liam Neeson, to name but a few

SPORTS IN IRELAND

Croke Park stadium is the headquarters of the Gaelic Athletic Association. It is one of Europe's largest stadiums.

Sports in Ireland

Ireland is a sporting nation and the people of Ireland have a great love for all sporting activities, as it is considered a big part of Irish society. Sport plays an important role in helping to promote a healthy lifestyle and in nurturing talents across the country.

Ireland is notable for playing a variety of sporting games for which attracts thousands of spectators regularly at stadiums and sports arenas, it also takes part in several major international games.

POPULAR SPORTS PLAYED IN IRELAND

Soccer:  The Republic of Ireland's National Football Team represents Ireland Men's National Team MNT (nicknamed boys in green) and Ireland Women's National Team WNT, both plays at international levels. They are governed by the Football Association of Ireland (**FAI**), it stages its home fixtures at the popular Aviva Stadium in Dublin.

Football is a much-loved sport by the Irish, but it is worth knowing that while Football/Soccer happens to be the most played team sport in Ireland, it is not the most popular sport. Ireland's national games are Hurling and Gaelic Football. Ireland has enjoyed a great number of successes in international sporting arena especially with Soccer games which often have the highest level of participation and is proven to be the most popular leisure activity for both young and old in the country, but it is still only the third most popular spectator Sport after Gaelic Football and Hurling. However, there a wide range of sporting options to offer sports enthusiasts but they don't have the same following like Hurling and Camogie which enjoys a nationwide popularity at all level.

Gaelic Football : This is classified as extreme sports that require high skills to excel. The game is played at Club and County level every year with teams from each of the 32

Counties in Ireland competing in a Championship for a place in the All Ireland Finals. It is the biggest competition of the game in the country in a bid to find a winning team deserving the honour to lift the coveted Sam Maguire Cup. The finals take place every year in September in the Ireland's famous and largest stadium—Croke Park Stadium.

Irish Hurling Game: The Hurling sports was

brought to Ireland by Ireland's Ancient Celtic culture around 2000 years ago and said to be the oldest field team sport in all of Europe. The game is similar to American Field Hockey but has more in common with the Scottish Gaelic team game known as Shinty. Still under the governance of the GAA, Hurling is an amateur sport played at county and club level and also holds a country-wide annual competition where county-based teams compete for a place in the All Ireland Finals. With the Hurling competition, teams are not restricted to home-based players from within Ireland's 32 Counties alone. Teams are invited to come from London, and New York to join in the battle in Croke Park in September each year as part of the biggest sporting events in the country, which usually has a large turnout of close to 100,000 spectators each time. The winning team is normally awarded the coveted Liam MacCarthy Cup (a trophy that was first awarded in 1923).

The Camogie: The Camogie is the women's version of Hurling, the only difference is, it has some variations in the rules compared to the men's Hurling, but it is still very much alike. But it is played only by the ladies and young girls.

Gaelic Games: Gaelic Games *is otherwise known as the GAA Games*, as it is comprised of *Gaelic football, Hurling and Camogie* including *Gaelic Handball and Rounders, all* under the Gaelic Athletics Association (GAA). *It is organised by the association to encourage Irish people living outside the shores of the Emerald Isle to do their best to carry on the touch to preserve their home tradition by hosting the Irish GAA games in their host countries.*

Rugby: The Irish Rugby Football Union is the governing body of Rugby Union in Ireland, which is played at local and international levels on an All-Ireland basis. It has produced world renowned Rugby players.

Cricket: The Irish Cricket Team is also administered on an All-Ireland basis by Cricket Union Ireland. It has smaller clubs around the country for training upcoming future Cricketers.

Netball: Netball is represented by the Ireland National Netball Team.

Golf: Golf is a very popular sport widely played in Ireland. There are over 400 Golf Clubs throughout the island, and more than 300 Courses countrywide. The country has produced several internationally successful Golfers including several top players like Pádraig Harrington, Paul McGinley and Darren Clarke achieving significant success internationally.

Horse Racing: The history of horseracing in Ireland

dates as far back as the 18th Century's, with racing taking place as early as the early 1700s. Every year in Ireland, Galway City plays host to one of the greatest horse racing events in the world, famously known as Galway Races. The event takes place in the Summer and lasts for seven long days of great entertainment, and a fashion contest to pick a best-dressed lady. Over 100,000 people attend the races every single year in County Galway.

There are more sports of international repute played in Ireland, with teams representing in Boxing, Basketball, Cycling, Sailing, Hunting, Lawn Tennis, Baseball, Greyhound Racing, Motorsport, Softball, & Handball, etc.

Sports Stars

Ireland has a long list of Sports Champions who have won Gold, Bronze and Silver Medals in all sporting activities.

The followings are just a few of Irish greats in various fields:

- Pádraig Harrington (golf)
- Brian O'Driscoll (rugby union)
- Joey Dunlop (motorcycling)
- George Best (soccer)
- Roy Keane (soccer)
- Robbie Keane (Soccer)
- Katie Taylor (Boxing)
- Connor McGregor (Boxing)
- Sean Kelly (cycling)
- Sonia O'Sullivan (athletics)
- Christy Ring (hurling and Gaelic football)
- Vincent O'Brien (horse racing)
- Paul McGrath (Soccer)

(Source: Wikipeadia.org)

Media in Ireland

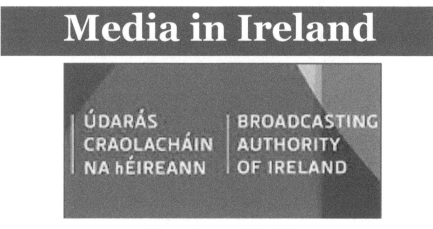

Photo: Courtesy of the BAI

The history of Media in Ireland began in 1922, and it has come a long way from the foundation state to the present and representing all media formats such as the traditional media outlets like Broadcast Media, Print Media and more recently Electronic Media, including Social Media. According to records, Ireland first made media technology history from the development of Radio to the inauguration of Television in the 1950s and 1960s and since then, the country has moved on to have a media environment that is well populated in both print and broadcast forms. But what is still lacks is a diversity of contents to fully reflect the present state of multiculturalism in the country.

Print Formats: Print media in Ireland consists of a number of dailies, evenings, Sundays, weekly national and regional national newspapers, journals and magazines. There are also occasional indigenous consumer prints and publishers that make up the print media in Ireland.

The most prominent national print newspapers in Ireland include Irish Independent, Irish Times, Irish Examiner, The Herald, Sunday Independent, Sunday World, etc. and as well as many other local and regional newspapers that dominate Irish print media.

Radio:
Raidio Teilifis Eireann (abbreviated as RTE) dominates both the Radio and Television sector in the Republic of Ireland. It is the Public Service Broadcaster with the largest Television Station in the country. Its State-run radio and television services reaches virtually all parts of the 32 counties in the Republic and beyond in some cases. RTÉ is part-funded by the licence fee collected from Irish households being the publicly-owned public service broadcaster. It operates most of the well-known television and radio stations in Ireland and provides a comprehensive service in English and Irish languages through the following channels; RTE1, RTE 2, TG 4, RTÉ News Now and a host of Radio Stations that make up the total RTE Broadcast Services.

Apart from Radio Stations owned by RTE, there are also a plethora of other stations scattered around the country, and most of these stations are local and regional Radio Stations, including a few Commercial Stations and Community Radios, each operating at their designated levels respectively.

Television Broadcast Service: The numbers of the privately-owned media are very small in Ireland given the country's population, especially in terms of television. A few privately owned stations are there and so far TV3 Group (now Virgin Media) seem to be the only clear and direct competitor of television broadcasters to the state-owned RTE. Virgin Media is a commercial TV network that operates three free-to-air Television Channels that used be known as TV3, B3 and 3e are now renamed as Virgin Media One, Two and Three since it rebranded as a subsidiary of Virgin Media Ireland and operates from its base in Dublin.

Online Media: The use of online media platform is a unique type of services on the internet for providing and enabling as an alternative source for the public to communicate and share information with family, friends and business acquaintances, or simply express their views about current affairs issues, and has become increasingly popular around the country. Additionally, virtually all of the Irish media also have an Internet presence, with special features that allow the people to air their opinions on a variety of topics. With all the above in mind, Ireland's media environment can be very well described as fair rich but there is a need for diversification.

Print media in Ireland operate freely within the confines of the law but Broadcasting (commercial and public) - is however regulated by the Broadcasting Authority of Ireland (BAI) - the Authority responsible for the licensing of radio and television services in Ireland.

SECTION ELEVEN

EDUCATION & HEALTHCARE

IRISH EDUCATION @ A GLANCE

Education is a fundamental right to every child in the Republic of Ireland and school attendance is compulsory until a child finishes Secondary school, or until they turn 18 years. Throughout Ireland, education is provided free of fees in both Public and Community schools from primary level up to University, except for private schools where parents are probably expected to pay tuition fees.

Ireland is a famous destination for study and Irish society is one that celebrates learning throughout all ages and across all disciplines from Literature to Science and from Art to Medicine, etc. There are different kinds of schools in the country, right from Childcare through to Primary and Secondary Schools, and Universities which are recognised among some of the world's bests. Ireland also provides many Vocational schools and other learning options established and available in every County in the country, which is why the literacy rate in Ireland is quite high at 89.1 per cent the average of most Western countries.

The school system in Ireland (Primary and Secondary Schools) have been under the patronage of the Catholic Religious denominations, which means that most of the schools are run within the ethos of the church, but the curriculum is set by the Department of Education and Skills. Primary schools are known as 'National Schools' (NS) for short, however, there are also a growing number of none denominational schools now springing up across Ireland called the 'Educate Together Schools' they have no religious affiliation and are available at primary level only at the moment, but offers the best alternative for non-religious parents in the country or those who do not wish to educate their child in the Catholic schools. Meanwhile, there are also private, fee-paying schools, and Gaelscoils which are schools where subjects are taught through the Irish language.

State examinations are taken nationwide in Ireland; starting with the entrance examinations taken by the 6th year pupils who have completed their primary education and going into secondary schools the following September, this is followed by the Junior Certificate exams (Junior Certs) taken by 'Third Year' students in all secondary schools. The same applies to prospective students who are looking to gain admission into Universities and Colleges, in this case they must have to have sat for, and successfully passed and gained required POINT for their subjects in the 'Leaving Cert' results. This is administered by the CAO (Central Applications Office). The CAO is the organisation responsible for overseeing undergraduate applications to colleges and universities in Ireland.

Another aspect of Irish education is that most Secondary schools offer what is called Transition Year (optional) which is observed by students in their fourth year in secondary school between the Junior and Senior cycles. This is a less formal year without exams and is usually a chance to allow students to try and complete a wider range of subjects and gain some work experience.

The School year in Ireland generally starts in early September and finishes in June, with some holidays and midterm breaks in between.

Childcare Education

There are numerous Childcare Providers available in Ireland to suit every family's needs. Types include Childminders, Play Schools, Montessori Schools, Nannies, Au pairs and Creches.

The Free Pre-School Year

There is a Free Pre-School programme in Ireland for all children of pre-school age known as the Early Childhood Care and Education Scheme (ECCE). Children who are entitled can avail of it to 2 full academic years, involving 3 paid hours a day, 5 days a week at participating pre-schools settings around the country. This has been provided by the Irish government to assist families to meet up with Childcare costs and normally administered by the Department of Children and Youth Affairs (DCYA).

Formal Education System in Ireland includes:

- Compulsory 6 years of Primary education (aged 6 up to 12)
- Three years of Junior Circle and Senior Circles respectively (total of six years of secondary education) aged 12 up to 17-18)
- Four years of University or in College education, finally directing toward a bachelor's degree in their choice of subjects.

School days begin as follows:

- 9am -1.30pm. Junior and Snr infants in primary school
- 9am – 2.30pm. First class to 6th class in primary school
- Secondary school is usually from 9am to 4pm with possible half days once weekly in some schools.

Irish Language in Irish schools

The Irish language is a compulsory subject in primary and secondary schools in Ireland and particularly required for Leaving Certificate. However, some students qualify for an exemption under certain circumstances. For instance, if a student is experiencing learning difficulties such as dyslexia or in the case that a student has not resided in the country in their early years, up to their first 11 years of age.

Third Level Education System

Third level education is offered in Universities, Colleges of education and Institutes of Technology around the country. There are plenty of opportunities for anybody who is interested in furthering their education in Ireland at these levels, with options to undertake both taught and research-based Masters and PhD courses. Any one of the options are available to study and be completed on a part-time or full-time basis. Third-level qualifications in Ireland are categorised as Levels 6-10 in the National Framework of Qualifications (NFQ).

See the pie chart sample below:

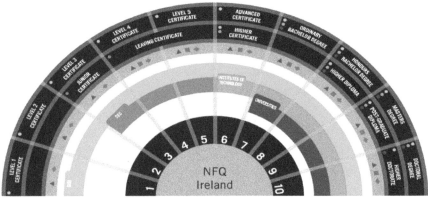

- **Advanced Certificate (NFQ Level 6)**

- **Ordinary Bachelor Degree (NFQ Level 7)**
- **Honours Bachelor Degree (NFQ Level 8)**
- **Masters Degree (NFQ Level 9)**
- **Doctoral Degree (NFQ Level 10)**

Source: http://www.nfq-qqi.com/index.html

Vocational Education:

Vocational schools or career colleges as some refer to them are mostly responsible for educating those who may have found themselves out of mainstream education from time to time for reasons best known to them. Vocational education is established to help anyone in this category to acquire life-skills and prepare them for an expanding market in medium and low-skilled jobs, including self-employment.

HEALTHCARE DELIVERY SYSTEM IN IRELAND

Ireland has one of the most developed healthcare systems in the world and healthcare professionals who are highly trained. Healthcare service in Ireland is provided by the State and available to everyone. Every resident is entitled to receive free healthcare through the public healthcare system, managed by the Health Service Executive (HSE), but some people are required to pay a subsidised fee for prescriptions and certain medical services depending on certain conditions based on their income, diagnosis, and age. Most residents have issued registered Medical Card which they can use to avail of free healthcare services at their General Practitioner (GP), Dentists, the hospitals and also in the pharmacies. Some people only have GP Visit Card which only allows for free GP visits but not all the benefits of having a Medical Card. But those who do not qualify for a Medical Card at all are those who have an income that crosses the threshold permitted and therefore not entitled to free public medical services and must pay the costs for each time they visit (GP) or need prescribed drugs. They must also pay costs for when they stay in the hospitals, including some other medical services, although the rates may be subsidised in some cases.

There are also a great number of private medical centres available in the country. These on the other hand, could be consulting clinics, hospitals and private maternity centres which cater to those who can afford them. This level of healthcare provides specialised services to patients referred from the primary healthcare level through out-patient and in-patient services of hospitals and GPs for general medical, surgical, paediatric patients etc. The Minister for Health has full responsibility for setting overall health service policy in the country for both public and private.

Emergency care is provided to patients who present to a hospital emergency department. Visitors to emergency departments in non-emergency situations who are not referred by their GP may incur a fee. Meanwhile, people who are from one of the 28 EU countries, or from Iceland, Lichtenstein, Norway and Switzerland, who have a European Health Insurance Card (EHIC), which covers them for most Medical Care are also entitled to free medical treatment in all hospitals in Ireland under the Health Service Executive.

 There are plenty of pharmacies in Ireland, and they are a good first stop for travellers seeking medical advice or a local referral. Most towns have one or two pharmacies and urban areas have more in an area. The pharmacies generally operate from 9 am to 6 pm Monday to Saturday, but many pharmacies in urban areas open late and on weekends are open on Sundays too.

SECTION TWELVE

EMIGRATION & IMMIGRATION

EMIGRATION

Ireland has a long history of emigration - dating back to the 1600s when young unemployed Irish sought their fortune overseas and boarded ships heading for places like Boston, New York and Philadelphia in America. During the 1700s around 250,000 Irish people have emigrated annually, and the rate continued at that level for some years. Most of the people at that time were said to emigrated from the North of Ireland and they were those either agreed to or were prepared to work as servants without pay for many years in return of free passage. But much of the history of Ireland has been about the story of emigration, from then right up to the Great Famine—one of the largest migration-waves the world has ever witnessed. It was a terrible migration period were Irish people left their country in en-mass to start a new life in another country. The most recent wave was during the recession when the country's economy was teetering on the brink of collapse and Irish people once again felt the need to emigrate to other countries to look for a better life. Since then, over 30,000 people have emigrated from Ireland.

THE GREAT FAMINE

The Great Irish Famine, also called the Irish Potato Famine - occurred in Ireland in 1845-49. Often described as the darkest period of in Irish history, the Famine was a period of mass starvation, disease, and emigration in Ireland.

The 18th Century was also the period Ireland Catholics were under Penal laws which denied them of their basic rights, including owning/leasing land, etc. And as a result, were exploited by the British who used their crops for profit. The potato crop was relatively easy to grow in the Irish soil, and it was the only food crop left for the Irish people in that by the early 1840s more than half the Irish population had come to depend almost exclusively on it as their most only staple food. Unfortunately, in 1845, a type of dreaded disease accidentally arrived Ireland, referred simply as 'Late Blight.' It was an airborne fungus type of disease that occurs in the most important vegetable crops—Potato and Tomato, it attacked the plants and they rot within two weeks once infected.

The blight disease was said to thrive in moist weather, which was the case with Ireland in that year; it had unusual humid weather in that year, it infected much of the crop and they all rotted in the fields. That was followed by more-devastating harvests the following years from 1846-49. Each year's potato crop was almost completely ruined by the disease, meaning there were no harvests in those years, causing the famine to happen. About one million people reportedly died from starvation and from other famine-related diseases. Around two million Irish emigrated and many more died onboard rickety boats at sea; the country's population plummeted drastically and it continued to decline for decades, that by the time Ireland achieved independence in 1921, the country's population had dropped to almost half of what it used to be in the early 1840s from around 8 million to just above 4 million because of overseas emigration and lower birth rates.

The period 1847 was recorded as the year that saw the greatest emigrations in Ireland to overseas countries such as the United States, Canada and Australia. Irish Emigrants flooded Great Britain but at the time Ireland and UK was one country and therefore they were not recorded as emigrants.

By the 21st century, an estimated 80 million people worldwide claimed some Irish descent; which includes more than 35 million Americans alone who claim Irish as their primary ethnicity including a large proportion of the population of Britain having some connection to Ireland.

Immigration

Historically, the number of Irish people leaving the country was always huge due to economic reasons than the number of foreigners moving to Ireland, but most recently, Ireland has gone from emigration to a country which has become a top choice destination for immigrants who move to Ireland to settle. The Celtic Tiger period helped in many ways to change the history of Ireland; while many newcomers perceive the country as a 'House Standing Tall with Open Doors' to welcome people who decided to relocate to live in the country. This was in addition to some Irish people from the Diaspora who also moved back to live in their motherland. During the entire Celtic period in each year, Ireland witnessed thousands of foreigners moved to Ireland to start a new life. Ireland's immigrant population rose up and at that point, more than 535,000 of non-indigenous Irish nationals recorded living in the country. They had all come from around 200 different countries to settle down in Ireland. But each of these people has their own story, their history, traditions, even fashion that they display on their bodies throughout the country that helps tell of their backgrounds and their original stories, unique to them. They all have contributed to the country's population growth and as well make the country the place it is today as they have all brought something different which now influences Irish cultural life. They also have a duty to keep their own distinct cultural beliefs and traditions alive through the practice of their various religion, food, fashion, songs, festivals and other traditional celebrations and to pass on their most cherished values to their own young ones to take to the next generation of a united future of Ireland. If not for anything else; they all have one thing in common with Irish emigrants - a similar goal or ambition to create a better life for themselves and their families in their host country.

The story of Saint Patrick teaches us all about the impact that migrants can make in a country. Saint Patrick was an immigrant to the country - a Romano-Briton who had been enslaved by Irish raiders, before escaping and turning to religion. But he became the most famous and most celebrated immigrant in the history of Ireland because he brought Christianity to the country, it's an excellent example of how migrants can make a big difference in Irish life today. After all, it takes many countries nowadays, to really make a successful nation.

SECTION THIRTEEN

TOURISM IN IRELAND

Welcome to the Enchanted Land of Beauty!

*T*he overall history of Ireland is founded upon it's religious and cultural values and in all represents Ireland's identity as a cultural society and one which is reflected through its tourism industry. Many people only ever know about Ireland and associate it with its tales of tiny leprechauns with hidden pots of gold at the end of a rainbow, or at best, about Saint Patrick driving away snakes from the island. The Emerald Isle is endowed with an abundance of ancient customs and heritage that boasts of some of the world's most enchanting locations and beautiful landscapes and there is so much more to explore, and things to do and see in Ireland.

Generally, Ireland's tourism has been a thriving sector, it is of great importance to the Irish government as it plays a major and important role in the marketing of 'BRAND IRELAND' to the wider world. keeps attracting millions of visitors to the country every year and as a result helps drive growth in the economy, earning a good GNP and employing hundreds of thousands of people across Ireland. The country's principal tourist destination is Dublin City, it has the most visitor attractions in the country, but the Counties also offer fantastic range of attractions for its millions of tourists.

According to reports by Tourism Ireland—the leading organisation responsible for promoting the island of Ireland overseas as a leading holiday destination, 'a staggering 11.2 million overseas visitors came to Ireland in 2018, an increase of 6% from 2017.'

The Emerald Isle is well known for its frequent indulgence in celebrations and cultural events, which on its own is another system for keeping the country steady on the world's tourism map. Visitors come from all corners of the world to visit Ireland by choice and savour all that Ireland tourism has to offer - which is everything that is been said about its history, people and culture; and as often described, a place of incomparable beauty, with velvet blue skies and rolling green hills, and full of fantastic and amazing beauties that are split and scattered in all parts of the country. A place to discover and gain knowledge and at the same time uncover hidden histories about Villains and Heroes from Centuries— and above all, a place to enjoy different adventures.

Festivals in Ireland

Ireland is full of ceremonies and festivals that seem to take place almost endlessly. Anyone who is visiting the country can easily notice them from fairs of some kind to traditional art shows or some forms of cultural celebrations happening somewhere throughout the country. These celebrations are part and parcel of the people's lifestyle and tourists are usually welcome to participate in an event of their choice when they visit Ireland. Also, because there are such a mix of nationalities in the country, many of the celebrations are held by each community groups who have brought their very own cultural events and festivals that showcases their identity in the capital and in other parts of the country, serving as a unifying factor for them and the people of Ireland. Today, many people find themselves enjoying Africa Day or India Day celebrations or 'Ireland's Festival of Nations' founded by the writer of this very book; it's an annual multicultural festival that celebrates all foreign cultures together in the same venue.

Below are only a few selected festivals that take place in Ireland every year. Each festival has its own style of ceremonies and meanings:

ST PATRICK'S FESTIVAL:

St Patrick's Day festival is the most important festival in the Republic of Ireland, celebrated annually on 17th of March every year, marking the death of Saint Patrick who was the foremost Patron Saint of Ireland.

Saint Patrick's Day was made an official Christian 'Feast Day' in the early 17th century and observed by the Catholic Church and a few other churches.

Saint Patrick was born in Britain during the late 4th Century, he was kidnapped at the age of 16 and taken to Ireland as a slave. But he escaped returning later about 432 to convert the Irish to Christianity. He had established monasteries, churches, even schools before died on March 17, 461. There is the myth that he drove snakes out of Ireland and that he also used the Shamrock leaf to explain the Trinity to the people as he converted them Christianity. Today, the Shamrock is most associated with the festival and one of the State's mostly recognised Symbols. Ireland came to celebrate the day to commemorate Saint Patrick and the arrival of Christianity in Ireland, but the religious occasion has since become a secular celebration that is more about the heritage and cultures of the Irish in general.

People travel from all over the world to visit Ireland on the 17th of March every year, and it is a great day for Irish descendants everywhere to show their pride of place in the world. All Irish consulate abroad make it as a point of duty to mark the day with the people of the countries where they are based, while the government of Ireland sees it as an opportunity to market Irish tourism abroad. Irish Ministers and other government officials usually travel to various countries for that purpose, including the Taoiseach (Prime Minister) who visits the United States of America to meet with Irish communities over there and eventually holds bilateral talks with the US President, during which a bowl of Shamrock is presented as a symbol of the deep connection between the countries.

The celebrations generally involve public parades with displays of flamboyant pageantry, elaborate floats, and marching bands taking place across the country in Ireland and on the streets of major cities around the world. The parades, said to have been held first in 1724 in Boston, United States by a group Irish immigrants, to honour their homeland and create an ethnic community there in Boston St. Patrick's Day is now a cultural day that everyone enjoys celebrating everything green and Irish not only at home but in faraway countries by the Irish diaspora communities around the world.

Other Festivals

ROSE OF TRALEE

The Rose of Tralee Festival is an international event established since 1959 that sees women of Irish descent from all over the world travel to Ireland to take part in the competition for a chance to be crowned Rose of Tralee. The festival is usually televised on RTE national TV Station over three days.

IRELAND'S FESTIVAL OF NATIONS

Ireland's Festival of Nations (IFON) is a new addition to the elaborate numbers of festivals held in Ireland each year. Founded by the writer of this very book that you're reading, it is the only ethnic festival in Ireland that showcases all foreign cultures at a venue. It has been termed "Ireland's alternative to Britain's "Notting Hill Carnival" by the media and it is steadily growing.

BLOOMSDAY FESTIVAL:

Bloomsday celebrates Leopold Bloom, the central character in James Joyce's novel Ulysses, for which the day is named after. Ulysses follows the life and thoughts of Leopold Bloom and a host of other characters - real and fictional and the festival tries to mimic and bring to life. **Bloomsday Festival** celebrations come in many different forms - it often includes dressing up as characters from the book and in clothes that would have been the style of that era. It is produced and programmed by the James Joyce Centre in Dublin.

FLAVOURS OF FINGAL

The Flavours of Fingal a mix of foods and farming attractions, such as best of local Irish food, crafts and trade stands etc. The festival takes place within the historic walled garden of Newbridge House and Farm, Newbridge Demense in Donabate, County Dublin.

FLEADH CHEOIL NA hÉIREANN:

Fleadh Cheoil na hÉireann is a traditional Irish music festival, running for over 60 years across Ireland.

ELECTRIC PICNIC

Electric Picnic is an annual arts-and-music festival which has been staged since 2004 in Stradbally, County Laois

GALWAY INTERNATIONAL ARTS FESTIVAL

Galway International Arts Festival is a major cultural event which produces one of Europe's leading international arts festivals.

EARAGAIL ARTS FESTIVAL

Earagail Arts Festival is a bilingual (Irish and English language), multidisciplinary arts festival which takes place in the month of July in County Donegal.

Major Tourist Attractions in Ireland:

Ireland has so many top attractions located in all corners of the country with places to go and things to do, from Museums to national parks, beaches, monumental sites, and other attractions that are easily accessible to everyone and tourists alike. Places like the Capital, Dublin City and other larger towns probably have a more modern type of places to visit but smaller towns around the country also boast of some of the most spectacular sceneries in the country.

The following is a list of some major attraction sites the Emerald Isle has to offer.

- National Museum of Ireland
- Fota Wild Park
- Mizen Head Light House
- The Ring of Kerry
- Kinsale and Charles Fort
- Kylemore Abbey
- Croagh Patrick

- Blarney Castle
- Kildare Village
- The Aran Islands
- Achill Island
- Dunmoe Castle
- Hill of Tara
- Trim Castle
- Bray Seaside
- The Connemara National Park

Top Sightseeing in the Capital - Dublin City

The Spire
Temple Bar
Dublin Castle
Mansion House
Merrion Square

Dublin's City Hall
Famine Museum
The Phoenix Park
The Epic Museum
Áras an Uachtaráin

Guinness Storehouse
Chester Beatty Library
Government Buildings
Mount Joy Sq. Park
Christ Church Cathedral

National Botanic Gardens
National Library of Ireland
Book of Kells (Trinity College)

Best Time To Visit

There is no specific 'best time', every season offers great opportunities to enjoy a visit in the Emerald Isle. The period around St. Patrick's Festival in March is very popular with tourists because all counties in the country is usually in a great festive spirit.

Summertime is generally considered the best time, although the weather can still be a determining factor even in Summer. The week between Christmas and New Year's Day is a busy time as well and certain things are expensive, for example, hotel room rates can become slightly higher and a room can sometimes become difficult to find even, same as airline tickets during high periods. In terms of travel expenses, there are low-cost flights readily available from the country's popular budget airline Ryanair and the national carrier, Aer Lingus.

Irish weather and temperatures change daily, and it varies between Summer and Winter seasons so, it is best to check at time of departures to be sure of current conditions. If there are no severe weather warnings in place such as a yellow or red-alerts, there will be no reasons for visitors not to enjoy their stay.

Where To Stay

There are good hotels in all parts of the country which equals the standards in other Western countries. All major towns in Ireland including the Capital, have on offer a mix selection of accommodation available to tourists, with amenities ranging from Car hire to laundry service, or Bureau de Change for easy currency conversions if you are not from an EU country. But there are also Three-Stars level hotels scattered around the capital and other places, they're usually more affordable with superb Customer Service. Bed & Breakfast also offer quality services.

There are also hostels which offer basic accommodation at a reasonable cost. In other instances, some Universities do sometimes offer rooms to accommodate regular visitors during summer months. Generally, hotels in Ireland are usually over-booked and advance booking is highly recommended. Further information can be obtained from the Ireland Tourism website at www.Ireland.com

Things to do In Ireland

There is almost always plenty of places to see and things to do regardless of when you visit Ireland. The Emerald Isle is a wonderful destination packed with so much to inspire the curious adventurer with the many places to visit and things to do. **Followings are some examples:**

Getting Married in Ireland

Say 'I do' In the Emerald Isle & enjoy an Irish wedding experience.

Getting married anywhere in the Republic of Ireland is possible and there are many spectacular venues a couple can choose from in the country at which to exchange vows or hold a wedding reception, depending in which city. Ireland is a popular destination for weddings & honeymooners.

Many famous couples like the Beckhams, the O'Driscolls, Paul McCartney & Heather Mills have all had their weddings in Ireland and there is nothing stopping you too, from having your dream wedding in the Republic of Ireland. There are excellent Wedding Planners and Consultants in all Irish towns who can help with all aspects of planning a successful wedding and putting in place everything necessary to get married on behalf of a couple in Ireland, unless in the event that a couple decides to take a 'do it yourself' approach by trying to deal with everything themselves. It is good try to save money where possible but planning a wedding from abroad is hard work and it is worth considering about engaging a Wedding Specialist rather than carry all the responsibilities and risk a nervous breakdown in the process.

Most Wedding Specialists have packages which include everything, from arranging for the Bridesmaids, Entertainment, Photographers, Limo, Flowers and Venue for the reception, and applying and obtaining a date for your marriage from a Registry Office or a church, and booking a local Clergyperson in advance to perform the ceremony, depends on the type of wedding and the couple's backgrounds or preference for where the solemnisation process can take place. Wedding Planners are more familiar with the process and how to get things done quickly and make a wedding look splendid and interesting. However, advance planning is highly advisable in case paperwork and documentation are required for the registry office. In the case of paper works, they'll need to be supplied in their original copy or Notarised copies and must be in English unless they're in Irish. If paperwork is not in English or Irish, these may also need to have a notarised translated copy of all documents and be sure to bring along the original copies on your wedding trip, particularly Birth Certificate. But whichever is the type of wedding, be it traditional, white wedding and any other types, a couple is guaranteed to have a fabulous day getting married in the Emerald Isle that is the

Republic of Ireland. Please seek more clarification from the Irish Embassy closest to you about the current procedure and up to date requirements of a non-citizen before you set about traveling to Ireland for your wedding. If the decision to get married in Ireland is anything other than two people who are genuinely in-love wishing to tie-the-knot in a foreign country, and is for immigration purpose, then the appropriate authorities must be notified to ensure the correct procedures allowed in this jurisdiction are complied correctly.

Go Shopping!

THE IRISH LOVE TO SHOP–SO SHOULD YOU!

Ireland may be a small country but it is full of shopping opportunities for tourists to experience the shopping traditions in one of the leading stores around the country and Indulge in some local heritage brands. Homegrown and internationally recognised memorabilia of different cultural luxury brands, from fashion, books, and other branded goods are waiting to be uncovered.

Ireland boasts of a good number of Shopping Malls, e.g the Jervis Centre in Upper Abbey Street is a busy and bustling Shopping Centre in Dublin, opened in 1996. Dublin City Centre area comprises of many retail stores of various brand names. Take Temple Bar for example, It's a very popular shopping area, almost like 'Ireland's International Market for Tourists' because of the dynamic shops displaying intricate cultural items ranging from candles, to Chinese calligraphy, rare books, to fashion of different shades, including jewelleries, cosmetics, food, stationery, medicine, and basically anything under the sun, all at different price levels. There is also Grafton Street, which is another Shopping area that is so popular and located right in the middle of the City Centre—it's a 'haven' for foreign visitors, with its attractive and high-end shops and fine eateries. The lively street is also a prime location for professional buskers and other street performers who daily throng the area to show off their various impressive talents to shoppers and bystanders.

There are many large Supermarket chains in Ireland, including foreign name such as Lidl, Tesco, Aldi, Marks & Spencer, etc. Irish owned superstores are Dunnes Stores, Super Value and a few others. Superstores are usually well stocked with various items from, Foods, Household items, Stationeries, Clothing, Bakery, and Deli for all the hot meals – some even have Cafés or restaurants on site to cater for hungry shoppers who can take a break from their shopping and actually sit down to eat some foods before continuing. Shopping hours vary but most of the superstores are open from early in the morning until late. But, some of them open late on Sundays as well and during certain Bank Holidays and close early also. Ssmaller shops like the Corner-shops, tend to stay open for longer hours, depending on where they are located. These sell essential items to locals, but these can be either more expensive or cheaper depending on what you're buying.

Farmers Markets are quite popular in Ireland. In hindsight, they are mostly known to be catering for the locals mostly and offer fresh fruits and vegetables which have been brought in directly from the farms by local producers. Other products that can be seen on display at a farmer's market in addition to the usual fresh crops, seafoods, cheese, tender meats, can range from freshly cooked meals that are ready to be tasted, to handmade stuff for sale.

The followings are some ideas of simple everyday things to add to Highlights of your visit to Ireland.

- **Go Hiking Surfing, Kayaking, Walking**
- **Play Golf, Go Partying/Dancing/Clubbing**
- **Attend Church Service**
- **Wine & Dine in a Fine Restaurant**
- **Go Sightseeing on a Tour Bus**
- **Go Horse Riding, Hill Walking**
- **Go to the Cinema, Café,**
- **Visit the Library, Nightclub**
- **Socialise with locals in the Pub and enjoy a pint Guinness, etc.**

KEEPING IN TOUCH IN IRELAND

Communicating Home While Away in Ireland:

With good coverage of mobile phone networks throughout the country, tourists are guaranteed to stay connected with loved ones back home. Roaming agreements exist with some of the major mobile phone companies so international call rates per minute are cheap, Mobile phone activities such as Data, Voice calls and SMS does not incur extra roaming charges to another EU country. It means that charges would remain the same as they are at home for travellers visiting from within the EU. Irish (SIM) connection for any network can be purchased in shops anywhere in the country at a very cheap rate. To dial outside from the Republic, you must first dial the number 00 followed by the International Code of the intended country and phone digit numbers.

Transport System in Ireland

Source: www.Luas.ie

Ireland's Public Transport system is very efficient and affordable; it operates in and around most metropolitan cities but more in Dublin. The roads are of European standard and of good quality and do not pose an unnecessary danger to drivers unless if areas of a secondary road become impassable due to repairs and other conditions.

Mode of Driving: It is worth mentioning that all Irish vehicles are right-hand drive, and the **driver's** side is on the **right** hand **drive** of the car; it simply means that drivers in Ireland, maintain the left side of the road and they seat on the right side in the cars because the cars have right-hand steering wheel. This may seem awkward for people coming from countries that drives on the right side of the road and are used to driving right-hand steering vehicles. Drivers who are new to driving in Ireland and who come from a country which use the opposite driving method must learn to reverse their mindset when they get behind wheels in Ireland to avoid ramming into other drivers.

Such drivers must also be extra careful about traffic lights and pedestrian crossing, including cyclists. More importantly, they must pay attention to the new Luas/tram tracks if driving in the capital.

For visitors who want to see Ireland, a tour bus is the best way to go especially if in a group and scheduled to visit many places or traveling to the countryside. You may also want to do so by car in which case, your best bet would be to hire a private car that is Chauffeur-driven, this may be more expensive. Marked taxis are readily available in major cities especially in Dublin. Taxi drivers operating in Ireland are thoroughly checked and registered and are highly regulated with the Irish Taxi Regulators under the transport department. On the other hand, if you fancy driving yourself, there are many private rental companies that offer private cars and other types of vehicles, depending on your option. But if you are not familiar with Irish roads, it is advisable you keep off the latter option as it might not be safe even with the help of GPS and Satnav. It is much safer to be in the hands of a competent and experienced driver who are more knowledgeable about the road systems and strict driving rules in Ireland.

Fares:
Fares are pretty much straightforward; they are set on standard fee depending on the destination and drivers are given the exact cash amount. There is a prepaid travel card option such as the Leap Card, which is an easier alternative if travelling by bus. Meanwhile, taxi fares go by the metre where a fare is automatically calculated and printed out according to the distance travelled. Most drivers accept cash only while some may have a credit-card payment device that allows them to accept card payments inside the car.

Tips:
Passengers are not under any obligation or by law to give tips to any drivers. You can give tips out of your own your volition if you so wish, perhaps to a cab driver. Train, Tram and bus drivers do not require tips and would not accept it either.

Travel by Rail:
It is common knowledge that train journeys are generally quicker than buses, and cheaper in fares. In Ireland, Larnród Éireann, known as Irish Rail in English, is the operator of the national railway network and oversees the Irish Railways Services, which runs on main routes daily from the two main stations in Dublin, Heuston station and Connolly station, linking to the rest of the country's cities and towns, including Belfast. Trains tickets can be paid for and obtained at any train stations and from designated deports. Cash transactions are not allowed on the train.

The Luas: The Luas is a new tram service in Dublin which run through the city centre and connects other parts of Dublin. Although the new tram lines do not link the airport yet, its two operating lines (Red & Green Lines) link suburban areas of Tallaght, Saggart, Sandyford, and a few more places, stopping at major points across the city.

Dublin has a steadily improving public transport network including the DART, Luas, Dublin Bus, and Dublin-Bikes which is a self-service bike rental system made available throughout the city centre.

SECTION FOURTEEN

TRAVEL INFORMATION & ADVICE

GETTING TO IRELAND

Getting to Ireland is easy, with several airlines serving the country from all over the world. There are a few gateway cities to which one can get to Ireland either by air or by sea and in some cases by road which is only possible from Northern Ireland in the United Kingdom, and by Sea ferries at Dublin Ports, Cork, and Rosslare from neighbouring countries like France and Spain or some towns in Britain such as Holyhead, and Liverpool.

FLY TO IRELAND

Ireland's National Carrier, Aer Lingus flies directly to New York. For more information, check out (www.aerlingus.ie)

The Republic of Ireland has four International Airports (Dublin Airport, Cork Airport, Knock Airport and Shannon Airport), all serving many European and intercontinental routes with scheduled and chartered flights.

Dublin International Airport (DUB) is the main International Airport in Ireland with two terminals open 24 hours daily. The popular Terminal 1 is reserved for domestic flights such as Aer Lingus which is the national carrier and long-haul flights such as American Airlines, etc. while Terminal 2 is reserved for landing other foreign flights all year round, including Irish low-cost airline Ryanair.

The airport is located on the North-side of Dublin is the busiest airport in Ireland. It is the main gateway into Ireland because it's in the Capital City (about 6 miles from the city centre), but it is not the only entry point into the country. Flights to Ireland from Britain and other European countries are quite straightforward and are available from all main city airports across Europe. Meanwhile, the London and Dublin route is the second busiest international air route in all of Europe, with Ireland's National Airline Aer Lingus, and Ireland's budget operator Ryanair among a few others plying routes to and from Ireland and many cities across the United Kingdom. Other international airlines also operate flights from worldwide destinations to Ireland daily. The distance from London to Ireland is about 464.494 Miles and flight time from **London** to Ireland is approximately 1 hour and 20 minutes, and from **New York** which is about 7 hours and 30 minutes. There are, however, no direct flights from certain parts of the world to Ireland and traveling from one of such destination requires a connecting flight.

Some of the biggest airlines flying to Ireland

British Airways (BA), Air France, KLM, Lufthansa, Turkish Airlines, Qatar Airways, Ethiopian Airlines, Etihad Airways, Emirate flights, Iberia flights, among a host of other flights.

Sail to Ireland

Photo:**commons.wikimedia.org**

Ferry travel is the second travel option available to passengers going to the Republic of Ireland, With Ireland and the UK so close to each other, sometimes it takes only 2 to 3.5 hours of sail time from the United Kingdom (UK) to Ireland and vice versa, depending on the efficiency of the vessel. The regular ferry service provides the best travel alternative for both foreigners and Irish people using Dublin/Holyhead route which is very popular among British travellers who chose to sail to Ireland. The Sail & Rail option makes it even more satisfying to travel between the UK & Ireland as it is affordable for returning passengers to Britain because the tickets extends beyond merely crossing the Irish sea, it covers passengers' train journey from Holly Head for instance via train services that are operated by Virgin, ScotRail and Arriva Trains to main destinations point in London. However, ferry companies in general operate busy schedules around Ireland, France, Holland, Scandinavia, the Baltic, Northern Ireland and the UK, catering not only for passengers, but also vehicles and cargo units on a daily basis, with daily departures of up to 4 sails or more, depending on weather conditions.

(Always check for more information with Dublin Port websites.)

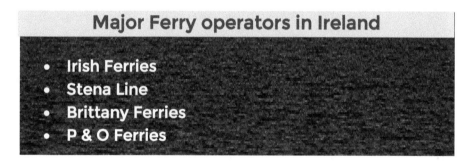

Major Ferry operators in Ireland

- Irish Ferries
- Stena Line
- Brittany Ferries
- P & O Ferries

Go to Ireland on Land

The only land route into the Republic of Ireland is in Northern Ireland. There are regular trains between Belfast and Dublin and it takes around two hours between the two parts of the

Island. Making the journey by car is straightforward and hassle-free. There are several major roads linking Nothern Ireland and the Republic.

Travel Documents

Visas and Passport

All foreigners planning to travel to the Republic of Ireland require valid travelling documents, e.g. a valid passport and a visa before arriving in the State, whether by air, sea or land, except people from certain countries who do not require a visa to land in Ireland, for example, citizens of other member states of the *European Union* (EU), however they are advised to check what form of identification might be required with the individual airline, tour operator or travel agent before leaving their home destination. Usually, a photographic ID such as a passport or driving licence is required.

An Irish visa is a certificate placed on your passport or travel document to indicate that you are authorised to land in the country subject to any other conditions being fulfilled. This means that you may still be subject to immigration control at the point of entry even if you have a visa. You may also need to register with the immigration authorities.

Expiring Passport: Foreign nationals travelling to Ireland are required to show a passport valid for at least six months beyond the date of departure unless stated otherwise. If you have an international travelling passport that is nearing its expiring date, you are advised to renew it before approaching the Irish Embassy for a Visa.

Application requirements: Letter of invitation from a reputable company in Ireland or individual is required, this should be written and addressed to Visa Section of the Irish Embassy in your country—normally showing proof of sustaining self while in the country. These should be included in your application pack in addition to other visa requirements. Application for a visa by minors must always be accompanied with a full Birth Certificate plus a photocopy of same showing names of parents, letter of consent from the parents and photocopies of parents' passports.

In most cases, the process can be completed online. For more information about forms required and other conditions, including visa fees, contact the nearest Irish Embassy/Consulate to check updated visa requirements.

Irish Nationals Applying for a New Passport: Irish citizens are eligible to apply for and receive Irish passport either at home or abroad provided you have Irish nationality. Any person born in Northern Ireland is automatically eligible to apply for an Irish passport, and anyone born in England, Scotland or Wales who has an Irish parentage can also apply for Irish citizenship and passport. If you are in another country other than Ireland, you are required to apply for a new passport from the Irish Embassy in that country. Proof of citizenship (e.g. copy of an original birth certificate or naturalization certificate) two colour passport photos and valid photo ID may be required. Irish passports naturally belong to the Irish Government, therefore it can be cancelled or withdrawn under certain circumstances, e.g. if you are a wanted person, or you are suspected of a serious crime and an arrest warrant has been issued or a court order restricts you from travelling, etc.

Visa Types:

Tourist/Business:

Tourist and Business visas are usually giving as Single-entry for 3 months. A Short Stay tourist visa allows people to travel to Ireland for up to 90 days, this goes also for business and for work which lasts 14 days or less, while international students who wish to study in Ireland can apply for a period depending on their course of studies and certain conditions. All short stay visas are classified 'C' and allow for up to 90 days but does not allow for any kind of work or use of any publicly funded services.

A separate application must be made to immigration for permission to work, if not they will not be able to work in Ireland. It is also important to have a job offer before looking for a visa to travel to Ireland for work. Providing false or misleading information or documents in a visa application may result in a refusal and in some circumstances, applicants may be banned for up to 5 years from further applying for an Irish visa. For information, always check with appropriate departments and necessary websites such as http://www.inis.gov.ie.

Multiple Visa:

A multiple entry visa permits allows a person to travel to Ireland during the dates shown on their visa for short trips only, depending on the type of visa required and conditions associated with it.

For anyone planning on staying in Ireland of more than 3 months either for study or work or joining a family member who already resides in the country, it is advisable to apply for a single entry, long stay or 'D' classified visa.

Transit Visas:

Transit passengers continuing their journey by the same or first connecting flights must hold a valid and relevant visa for the final country of destination or return documentation and may not have to leave the airport, except for nationals of EU member States who do not require a transit visa and certain countries currently under the Visa Waiver Programme. A valid visa for the country of destination must be in your passport before approaching the Irish embassy for a transit visa for the purpose of passing through an Irish port in order to travel to another country.

Re-Entry Visa:

The mandatory Re-Entry Visa referred as the permission stamp placed in passports at the Garda Station or at INIS Burgh Quay – has now been abolished. Usually, people who live in Ireland and are awaiting their Irish Residence Permit or those ordinarily resident in the country based on certain Stamps had to apply to have this visa type stamped in their passport for urgent travel purposes before leaving the country, without it they may be refused entry back into the country. The official INIS website recently show a notice about the 'Abolition of adult re-entry visas.' Meaning there will no more requirement for a re-entry visa to leave and return to Ireland from 13 May 2019.

Schengen Visa:

The Schengen Area is an area without internal borders, within which citizens of many non-EU nationals, business people and tourists can freely move around without being subjected to further border checks within the EU. The Schengen States have rules to ensure the security of those living or travelling within the area. It should be of note however, that the Republic of Ireland and the United Kingdom are outside the Schenghen area and NOT all EU countries are automatically part of the Schenghen area. For example, Bulgaria, Cyprus and Romania are EU members but not yet fully-fledged members of the Shenghen area.

There are currently 26 European countries that are part of Schengen, of which 22 are EU member states.

See following table:

EU Countries in Schengen Area

Denmark	Spain	Slovakia	Czech Republic
France	Sweden	Portugal	Estonia
Belgium	Slovenia	Poland	Luxembourg
Norway	Italy	Austria	Netherlands
Malta	Greece	Hungary	Lithuania
Finland	Latvia	Switzerland	Liechtenstein
	Iceland		Germany

For the most current and up to date entry/exit requirements, visit the Irish Embassy in your country of residence to obtain more information.

The European Union (EU)

The European Union (EU) is an economic and political union of 28 countries that operates an internal (or single) market which allows free movement of goods, capital, services and people between member states. Meaning that citizens from any of the European Union in Europe are free to move within these countries without the need for a visa. Every EU citizen has a right to reside in another member state for a period up to three months without any conditions or formalities other than the requirement to hold a valid identity card or passport.

(See below list of the 28 Member States of the European Union)

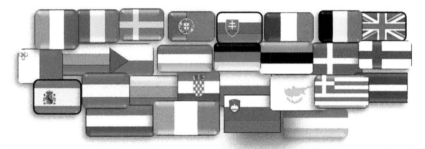

Lithuania - Sweden - Portugal - Estonia – Germany - Spain – Austria - Slovakia - Czech Republic - United Kingdom - Romania - Italy - Poland Belgium - France - Bulgaria - Denmark - Latvia - Slovenia - Cyprus Finland - Ireland - Hungary - Greece - Malta - Croatia - Netherlands - Luxembourg

Brexit:

On the 23rd of June 2016, citizens of the United Kingdom (UK) voted to leave the European Union (EU). Then on 29th of March 2017, the UK formally notified the European Council of its intention to leave the EU by triggering of Article 50 of the Lisbon Treaty. As at when that happens, the Union of 27 Member States will continue to forge ahead without the UK. But in the

meantime, and as at the time of publication of this book, the United Kingdom remains a full member of the EU and rights and obligations continue to fully apply in and to the UK while negotiations are ongoing.

Money:

It is very important to know in advance how much money is available to you on your visit, so you can spend wisely and according to your budget. On the other hand, visitors may bring unlimited amounts of foreign currency, provided a declaration of such is made to Customs at the port of entry. Bureau de Change depots are usually available at major International Terminals on arrival to the Republic to exchange your money for Euro currency. You may also use your bank cards at ATMs in cities around the country.

Health Matters:

Health risks in Ireland are minimal but it is advisable to take some health measures before arriving in the country, in case vaccinations and medications against certain vaccine-preventable diseases are required, especially if travelling from areas outside of Western Europe. Get clearance from a doctor, preferably one provider that specialises in Travel Medicines and who can determine what is needed depending on factors such as health and immunization history of the visitor, and planned activities. It is also advisable to obtain travel insurance to cover any potential overseas medical costs that cover all planned activities while in Ireland and ensure such travel insurance has medical cover. Members of EU countries including Iceland, Lichtenstein, Norway and Switzerland, can use a European Health Insurance Card (EHIC), this covers most of their medical care while in the Republic.

Customs & Duty-Free

People travelling to Ireland from outside the European Union (EU), the Canary Islands, the Channel Islands or Gibraltar can bring in goods within duty-free allowance without paying Customs Duty, Excise Duty and Value-Added Tax (VAT). Exceeded allowances may incur Customs Duty, Excise Duty and VAT at the airport or port of arrival. Some goods are prohibited, while others are subject to conditions.

See flowing page for regulations: -

Customs Regulations in Ireland
Ireland Duty Free:

Visitors over the age of 18 years may bring the following goods without incurring customs duty.

200 cigarettes, 100 cigarillos, 50 cigars, or 250g of tobacco.

- 1 litre of spirits (whiskey, gin, vodka, etc)

- Up to 4 litres of wine

- 16 litres of beer

Customs Duty, Excise Duty and Value-Added Tax (VAT), where applicable, are charged on goods that are more than the duty-free allowances. (up to €430)

Note: *If you are travelling to Ireland from another Member State of the European Union (EU), you can bring in an unlimited amount of most goods. However, the amounts of alcohol and tobacco products are limited, and some goods prohibited, while others are subject to conditions.*

Source: Revenue website.

Prohibited Imports:

A limited range of goods are prohibited or restricted at import and export. The following are the main categories of goods affected:

- Illegal or dangerous drugs
- Domestic Cats or Dogs
- Indecent or obscene goods
- Certain foodstuffs, mainly meat, milk, fish etc
- Products of endangered species
- Protected items of international heritage
- Medicines
- Firearms, weapons, fireworks or explosives
- Live or dead animals, fish, birds or plants.
    Source: (Ireland customs website.)

SAFETY IN IRELAND

*E*very society has its fair share and every country now experience some form security issues, right from petty crimes like pick-pocketing & burglary to assaults & robberies and more dangerous criminal activities which may include gun & knife and acts of terrorism, including hate crimes, etc. These are issues of concern worldwide and Ireland is no exception. Unfortunately, we live in a world where threats to people's live and properties have become the norm and no country is totally free of some forms of these crimes. However, in comparison to some countries, Ireland is relatively safe to do business in, study, live in and spend holidays. Millions of tourists visit Ireland every year and more than 90% of them leave with best and positive impressions.

There are no known danger spots in Ireland where strangers are more susceptible to attacks than other residents that tourists ought to be especially wary of. Anyone planning a trip to Ireland or those new to how things work in the country should apply caution when exploring unfamiliar places and when out exploring the towns, or if on daily excursions especially with regards to personal belongings. Ireland is a country many people find to be charming, but it is better to err on the side of caution and not indulge in activities capable of putting anyone in a vulnerable position.

Emergency Numbers in Ireland - 112 or 999.
In an emergency, contact - Garda Síochána (Police), Ambulance, Fire and the Irish Coast Guard - by dialling 112 or 999.

SECTION FIFTEEN

TRIVIAS

(Test your Knowledge)

What are the colours of the Irish Flag?
Orange White Green
White Green Orange
Green White Orange
Green White Red

What is the name of Ireland's first female President?
Mary Harney
Mary McAleese
Mary O'Rourke
Mary Robinson

What year did Easter Rising take place in Ireland
1916
1919
1922
1961

Which of Ireland's 4 Province has the fewest Counties?

Ulster
Connacht
Munster
Leinster

What is the longest river in Ireland?

The Liffey
The Shannon
The Suir
The Barrow

What is the name of the national airline of Ireland?

Ryanair
British Airline
Aer Lingus
Air Ireland

Which Irish County is the ancestral home of the 26th President of America, Theodore Roosevelt?

County Donegal
County Dublin
County Antrim
County Cork

Which is of these is the oldest University in Ireland?

Dublin City University (DCU)
National College of Ireland (NCI)
University of Dublin (Trinity College)
University College, Cork (UCC)

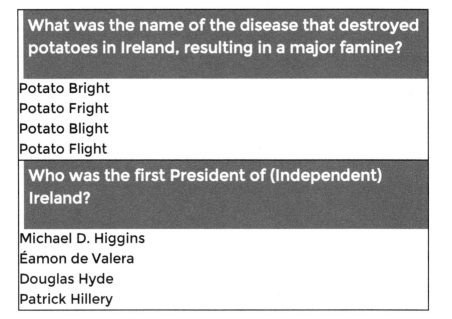

What was the name of the disease that destroyed potatoes in Ireland, resulting in a major famine?

Potato Bright
Potato Fright
Potato Blight
Potato Flight

Who was the first President of (Independent) Ireland?

Michael D. Higgins
Éamon de Valera
Douglas Hyde
Patrick Hillery

CREDITS

All mappings and most photos in this publication are generated from Wikipedia, the free encyclopaedia and from various other sources, including some materials which maybe entitled to copyright, and every effort has been made to trace copyright holders to some photographic items, and we apologise in advance for any unintentional omissions. We would be pleased to insert the appropriate acknowledgement in any subsequent edition of this publication.

Reference & Bibliography

I personally found the following websites to be very useful resource during my research for this book and I'm grateful to those organisations & individuals for setting them up on the internet.

https://en.wikipedia.org/wiki/Government_of_Ireland_Act_1920
https://www.nationalgallery.ie/marriage-strongbow-and-aoife-characters
https://president.ie/en/the-president/michael-d-higgins
https://countryeconomy.com/gdp/ireland
http://www.irishhistorylinks.net/Irish_History_Timeline.html
https://www.yourirish.com/history/medieval/king-henry-ii-invades-ireland
http://www.gomapper.com/travel/list-of-countries-near/ireland.html
http://www.cso.ie/en/studentscorner/statisticalfactsaboutyourcounty/
https://en.wikipedia.org/wiki/List_of_mountains_in_Ireland
http://www.ireland.com/en-us/about-ireland/discover-ireland/ireland-counties-and-provinces/
http://www.irishcentral.com/roots/the-four-provinces-87247367-237687791.html
http://www.irishstatutebook.ie/eli/1997/act/20/enacted/en/html
http://www.citizensinformation.ie/en/employment/employment_rights_and_conditions/hours_of_work/working_week.html
http://www.dochara.com/the-irish/facts/people-society/
http://www.mapsofworld.com/ireland/stock-exchange-ireland.html
https://en.wikipedia.org/wiki/Irish_Sign_Language
https://countryeconomy.com/countries/ireland

https://en.wikipedia.org/wiki/Republic_of_Ireland–United_Kingdom_border
https://en.wikipedia.org/wiki/Climate_of_Ireland
http://www.botanicgardens.ie/herb/census/flora.htm
https://en.wikipedia.org/wiki/Rivers_of_Ireland
http://www.lookaroundireland.com/ireland-travel-guide/rivers-of-ireland/
https://www.britannica.com/place/River-Shannon
https://en.wikipedia.org/wiki/Irish_Confederate_Wars
https://en.wikipedia.org/wiki/Vikings
http://www.ipcc.ch/
http://www.ireland.com/en-us/about-ireland/discover-ireland/mountain-beauty/
http://www.rootsweb.ancestry.com/~irlkik/ihm/mapmtn.htm
http://www.military.ie/info-centre/what-we-do/
https://www.irish-genealogy-toolkit.com/flag-of-Ireland.html
https://www.oireachtas.ie/?tab=seanad
http://www.mapsofworld.com/ireland/stock-exchange-ireland.html
http://www.independent.ie/lifestyle/the-six-top-growth-industries-in-ireland-today-26561305.html
http://www.economywatch.com/world_economy/ireland/industry-sector-industries.html
https://tradingeconomics.com/ireland/foreign-exchange-reserves
http://atlas.media.mit.edu/en/profile/country/irl/
http://www.worldstopexports.com/irelands-top-10-exports/4350
http://www.teagasc.ie/agrifood/
https://www.cso.ie/en/index.html
http://www.agriculture.gov.ie/agri-foodindustry/
http://www.vote.ie/index.php/why-vote/it's-your-right!
http://www.worldstopexports.com/irelands-top-10-exports
http://ec.europa.eu/ireland/key-eu-policy-areas/agriculture/index_en.htm
https://www.heraldry-wiki.com/heraldrywiki/index.php?title=Waterford_(county)
https://en.wikipedia.org/wiki/History_of_Ireland#/media/File:Ei-map.svg
https://www.tripsavvy.com/counties-in-the-province-of-leinster-1541839
https://www.heraldry-wiki.com/heraldrywiki/index.php?title=Londonderry_(county)
https://www.heraldry-wiki.com/heraldrywiki/index.php?title=Londonderry_(county)
https://www.irishpost.com/news/all-32-irish-county-coat-of-arms-and-where-they-come-from-115697

Lightning Source UK Ltd.
Milton Keynes UK
UKHW021006090619

344062UK00008B/61/P